20TH CENTURY AMERICAN SHORT STORIES

AN ANTHOLOGY

Jean A. McConochie
Pace University

Heinle & Heinle Publishers
I(T)P An International Thomson Publishing Company

Pacific Grove • Albany • Bonn • Boston • Cincinnati • Detroit • London • Madrid • Melbourne • Mexico City
New York • Paris • San Francisco • Tokyo • Toronto • Washington

Heinle & Heinle Publishers
20 Park Plaza
Boston, MA 02116 U.S.A.

International Thomson
    Publishing
Berkshire House 168–173
High Holborn
London WC1V7AA
England

Thomas Nelson Australia
102 Dodds Street
South Melbourne, 3205
Victoria, Australia

Nelson Canada
1120 Birchmont Road
Scarborough, Ontario
Canada M1K5G4

International Thomson
    Publishing Gmbh
Königwinterer Strasse 418
53227 Bonn
Germany

International Thomson
    Publishing Asia
Block 221 Henderson Road
    #08–03
Henderson Industrial Park
Singapore 0315

International Thomson
    Publishing—Japan
Hirakawacho Kyowa
    Building, 3F
2-2-1 Hirakawacho-cho
Chiyoda-ku, 102 Tokyo
Japan

The publication of *Twentieth Century American Short Stories,* An Anthology was directed by the members of the Newbury House Publishing Team at Heinle & Heinle:

Erik Gundersen, Editorial Director
John F. McHugh, Market Development Director
Kristin Thalheimer, Production Services
    Coordinator
Elizabeth Holthaus, Director of Production and Team
    Leader
Amy Lawler, Managing Developmental Editor

Also participating in the publication of this program:

Publisher: Stanley J. Galek
Project Manager: Margaret Cleveland
Assistant Editor: Karen P. Hazar
Associate Production Editor: Maryellen Eschmann
Manufacturing Coordinator: Mary Beth Hennebury
Interior Designer: Winston • Ford Design
Compositor: Pre-Press Company, Inc.
Cover and interior photos: Jon Nickson
Cover Designer: Kim Wedlake

Library of Congress Cataloging–in–Publication Data

An anthology of twentieth century American short stories/[compiled
    by] Jean A. McConochie.
        p. cm.
    ISBN 0–8384–6146–8
    1. English language—Textbooks for foreign speakers. 2. United
States—Social life and customs—20th century—Fiction. 3. Short
stories, American. 4. Readers. I. McConochie, Jean A.
PE1128.A56 1994
813' .010805—dc20   94–43027
                                                            CIP

Copyright © 1995 by Heinle & Heinle Publishers

Heinle & Heinle Publishers is a division of International Thomson Publishing, Inc.

Manufactured in the United States of America.

ISBN 0-8384-6146-8

10 9 8 7 6 5 4 3 2 1

For my mother,
Marian Brenckle McConochie,
who introduced me to the enchantment of literature

Contents

Contents

Contents

Contents

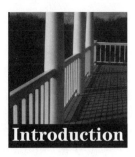

Introduction

A growing number of teachers are looking for collections of great stories unencumbered by lengthy activities, discussion questions, and assignments. They prefer to draw on their creativity so that their students are exposed to and learn to appreciate literature in a way that works in their own classrooms and that is in line with the academic goals of their institution. *20th Century American Short Stories: An Anthology* allows them to do just that. It consists of twenty-four excellent short stories, each accompanied by an **Introduction,** which consists of important biographical information for each author, and a glossary, entitled **Unusual Words or Meanings.** It contains no pre- or post-reading activities. With this streamlined organization, teachers can draw on other relevant materials as they see fit, while students have in their possession an outstanding collection of modern American short fiction that they will enjoy while in the classroom, and will keep with them long after their classroom experience is over.

How the Stories Have Been Chosen

While the choices necessarily reflect the editor's tastes, the selections are intended to suggest the cultural and ethnic diversity of twentieth-century American fiction. Some of the stories in this book are humorous; others are serious. Some are set in large cities—New York, Chicago, Los Angeles; others take place in suburban or rural areas of New England, the South, the Midwest, or the West. Together, the stories explore universal questions of relations within families and between the sexes, changing customs and traditions, and conflicts of culture that aren't always recognized by those involved. All are superb tales that can be read again and again with increasing pleasure.

All of the stories are relatively short, ranging in length from approximately five hundred to approximately six thousand words.

The first twelve are appropriate in content and vocabulary for high-intermediate and the second twelve, for advanced students of English as a second or foreign language. The stories are also suitable for high school or college students whose first language is English, though they would probably find the "Uncommon Words or Meanings" section unnecessary.

The selections are from all but the first two decades of the twentieth century; over half have been published after mid-century. All of the twenty-four stories represent an American point of view, though two stories are set outside the United States, two are by British authors who place their stories in an American context, and five of the twenty-four authors spoke another language before they learned English. While many of the stories have been translated into other languages, all of them were originally written in English.

How the Anthology is Organized

The **Introduction** to each story presents the author in the context of his or her time and previews the story. Where appropriate, it also includes suggestions for further reading.

Unusual Words or Meanings provides brief explanations of words that can't easily be found in a dictionary: cultural references (such as brand and place names), idioms, slang, words in languages other than English, and words used in a meaning other than the most common (here defined as the first meaning listed in the *Oxford Advanced Learner's Dictionary*, Third Edition). Words are defined only as they are used in the story and are presented in the order in which they appear in the story. Nouns are glossed in their singular form, preceded by *a* or *an* if the noun is countable, and time-oriented verbs are glossed in their *to* (infinitive) form.

Each **story** is presented as the author wrote it: nothing has been simplified; any extra space between paragraphs was put there by the author; the presence or absence of quotation marks for direct speech is the author's choice. While words glossed in the "Unusual Words or Meanings" section are not marked in the text, line numbers have been added in the margin to facilitate discussion. Following the convention of many literature texts, the original publication date appears in square brackets at the end of the story.

If readers want to read more when they have finished these stories, the book's purpose will have been achieved.

Acknowledgements

Many friends and colleagues have helped to make this book a reality. Indeed, the collaborative aspect was the greatest pleasure in preparing the manuscript. It is now my honor to name those who have contributed their talents and supportive concern to the project.

David R. Werner provided superb coaching at every stage of writing and production; his intelligence, understanding, and sense of humor have enriched the book. All in all, Dave and the boys kept both me and Mike (my computer) running smoothly throughout the process. My thanks for it all.

Winifred A. Falcon, Karla Jay, Laurie Lafferty, Jaime Mantilla, and Brett Sherman, as well as Heinle & Heinle readers, all helped in shaping the final selection of stories. Anne McCormick offered invaluable support in pursuing permissions, which are gratefully acknowledged at the back of the book. In addition, the authors Mari Evans, Mark Steven Hess, Lucy Honig, Judy Troy, W. D. Wetherell, and Hisaye Yamamoto responded graciously and generously to the queries of a stranger. My thanks to them, and indeed to all the writers whose stories and poems have provided me with such intense pleasure over the past two years.

Laurie Lafferty and Dave Werner patiently read successive drafts; their creative criticism and perceptive comments strengthened every chapter. One or more chapters also benefitted from the insights of Winnie Falcon, Jaime Mantilla, and Pat Rigg, as well as my editor Amy Lawler, and the following reviewers commissioned by Heinle & Heinle:

Lynne Barsky, *Suffolk Community College, New York*
Meggie Courtright, *University of Illinois, Urbana-Champaign*
Kay Ferrell, *Rancho Santiago Community College, California*
Judith Garcia, *Miami-Dade Community College*
Thomas Hardy, *University of Southern Mississippi*

Virginia Herringer, *Pasadena City College*
Joe McVeigh, *University of Southern California*
Melissa Munroe, *Boston University*
Karen Richelli-Kolbert, *Manhattanville College*
Ross Savage, *North Hennepin Community College,
    Minnesota*
Diane Starke, *El Paso Community College*
Mark Stepner, *Boston University*
Mo-Shuet Tam, *San Francisco Community College*

Additional field-testing was generously provided by Lise Winer and her Southern Illinois University graduate students Lori Brown, Tenley Chambliss, Randy Cotten, Simone DeVito, Laura Halliday, Robert Lee, and Paula Tabor, who tried out many of the stories with their undergraduate students. My thanks to all.

For additional clarification of assorted points, I am indebted to Judith Bauduy, Paul Cochran, Sergio Gaitán, Janet Ghattas, John Lafferty, George Marino, Shirley Miller, Tina Pratt, Allan Rabinowitz, Muriel Shine, Tippy Schwabe, and Patricia and Sidney Wittenberg, as well as to Jane Knowles, reference librarian at Radcliffe College. At Pace University's Henry Birnbaum Library, I benefitted from the creative determination of reference librarians Michelle Fanelli and Tom Snyder and from the legacy of the late Bruce Bergman, whose passion for acquisition has enriched us all.

Also at Pace University, Sherman Raskin, chair, Department of English, offered unstinting encouragement throughout the manuscript preparation, and Charles Masiello, dean, Dyson College of Arts and Sciences, kindly granted me a one-semester sabbatical leave to complete the manuscript. My thanks to both of them.

At Heinle & Heinle, Erik Gundersen proposed this revision and expansion of the original text, Amy Lawler tactfully suggested editorial improvements, Kristin Thalheimer and Margaret Cleveland meticulously supervised production, and Andreas Martin developed a creative marketing plan. I am grateful to all of them for enabling me to benefit from their professional expertise. For friendly and reliable technical support, Sanford Fox and his crew at Foxy Copy were, as always, indispensible.

The initial impetus for this book came, many years ago, from my colleague and friend Gary Gabriel, whom I thank once again.

No Speak English

"I believe she doesn't come out because she is afraid to speak English."

No Speak English

Sandra Cisneros
(born 1954)

In the last decade of the twentieth century, Sandra Cisneros has established herself as one of the important new voices in American literature. Cisneros, who now lives in San Antonio, Texas, was born and raised in Chicago. The daughter of a Mexican father and Mexican American mother, she grew up in a largely Spanish-speaking neighborhood and spent her childhood "being quiet," as was expected of a daughter in a Latino household and of a Latina girl in the society at large.*

Even in graduate school, Cisneros found that teachers paid little attention to women and that discussions excluded anyone who wasn't from a white middle-class family. When talking about the literary symbolism of houses, for example, one teacher spoke of attics (the storage space under the roof) as symbols of a family's past. Cisneros' family had always lived in an apartment and, as she says, "the third floor front doesn't come with an attic." Gradually, however, she realized there were subjects on which *she* was the expert. When other students talked about cupolas (a tiny room with windows on four sides on the roof of a Victorian house), she thought about narrow wooden back porches (a common feature of older three-story apartment buildings in Chicago). When others talked of swans, she thought about rats. Whatever her

---

*These direct quotations are reconstructed from notes taken during Cisneros' plenary address at the twenty-seventh annual convention of Teachers of English to Speakers of Other Languages, Atlanta, Georgia, 1993.

classmates wrote about, she presented the opposite. Gradually, Cisneros found herself with a number of stories about growing up in a Mexican American community, stories that were valuable precisely because they weren't like anyone else's. Teaching high school dropouts in Chicago the next year, Cisneros gathered additional stories from her students. Soon she had a collection of forty-four, including "No Speak English." Several years later, they were published by Women of Color Press under the title *The House on Mango Street.*

Although Cisneros by then really wanted to be a writer, she took another teaching job to support herself. Trying to be "perfect" as a teacher brought her to near-suicidal despair, but she was rescued by a National Endowment for the Arts Fellowship. "It reminded me that I was a writer," Cisneros says, "and it gave me *attitude.*" This self-confidence was supported by critics' praise for *The House on Mango Street* when it was reissued by a major publisher in 1989. Since that time, she has published *Woman Hollering Creek and Other Stories* (1991), set mainly in San Antonio, and *My Wicked Wicked Ways* (1992), her first book of poetry.

The stories in *The House on Mango* Street are very short, some less than a page. All of them are narrated by fourteen-year-old Esperanza Cordero, a girl whose first name means "Hope." Some of the stories are about her and some are about her girlfriend Rachel; others, including "No Speak English," are about their neighbors. What do you suppose that title means? Who do you suppose says it?

Mamacita is the big mama of the man across the street, third-floor front. Rachel says her name ought to be *Mamasota*, but I think that's mean.

The man saved his money to bring her here. He saved and
5 saved because she was alone with the baby boy in that country. He worked two jobs. He came home late and he left early. Every day.

Then one day Mamacita and the baby boy arrived in a yellow taxi. The taxi door opened like a waiter's arm. Out stepped
10 a tiny pink shoe, a foot soft as a rabbit's ear, then the thick ankle, a flutter of hips, fuchsia roses and green perfume. The man had to pull her, the taxi driver had to push. Push, pull. Push, pull. Poof!

All at once she bloomed. Huge, enormous, beautiful to
15 look at, from the salmon-pink feather on the tip of her hat down to the little rosebuds of her toes. I couldn't take my eyes off her tiny shoes.

Up, up, up the stairs she went with the baby boy in a blue blanket, the man carrying her suitcases, her lavender hatboxes,
20 a dozen boxes of satin high heels. Then we didn't see her.

Somebody said it's because she's too fat, somebody because of the three flights of stairs, but I believe she doesn't come out because she is afraid to speak English, and maybe this is so since she only knows eight words. She knows to say:
25 *He not here* for when the landlord comes. *No speak English* if anybody else comes, and *Holy smokes.* I don't know where she learned this, but I heard her say it one time and it surprised me.

My father says when he came to this country he ate hamandeggs for three months. Breakfast, lunch, and dinner. Haman-
30 deggs. That was the only word he knew. He doesn't eat hamandeggs anymore.

Whatever her reasons, whether she is fat, or can't climb the stairs, or is afraid of English, she won't come down. She sits all day by the window and plays the Spanish radio show and sings
35 all the homesick songs about her country in a voice that sounds like a seagull.

Home. Home. Home is a house in a photograph, a pink house, pink as hollyhocks with lots of startled light. The man paints the walls of the apartment pink, but it's not the same you know. She still sighs for her pink house, and then I think she cries. I would.

Sometimes the man gets disgusted. He starts screaming and you can hear it all the way down the street.

Ay, she says, she is sad.

Oh, he says, not again.

¿Cuándo, cuándo, cuándo? she asks.

¡Ay, Caray! We *are* home. This *is* home. Here I am and here I stay. Speak English. Speak English. Christ!

¡Ay! Mamacita, who does not belong, every once in a while lets out a cry, hysterical, high, as if he had torn the only skinny thread that kept her alive, the only road out to that country.

And then to break her heart forever, the baby boy who has begun to talk, starts to sing the Pepsi commercial he heard on T.V.

No speak English, she says to the child who is singing in the language that sounds like tin. No speak English, no speak English, and bubbles into tears. No, no, no as if she can't believe her ears.

[1989]

Uncommon Words or Meanings

Words or phrases from the story are explained if they are cultural references (including words in a language other than English), idioms, or slang, or if the meaning is not the first listed in a standard dictionary. The words or phrases appear in their order of first use in the story.

A note on translation: The Spanish words in this story (marked in this list with a star) are explained according to their meaning in Mexican Spanish; the meaning or implications in other Spanish-language communities may be different.

*Mamacita ("*Mamacita* is the big mama")—"little mother"; a term of endearment that shows both love and respect for the mother's authority.

a big mama ("Mamacita is the *big mama*")—(slang) a man's wife or lover, his "number one woman."

*Mamasota ("her name ought to be *Mamasota*")—(vulgar slang) a woman with big buttocks or "a large rear end."

mean ("I think that's *mean.*")—deliberately unkind.

a yellow taxi ("arrived in a *yellow taxi*")—an officially licensed taxicab.

fuchsia ("*fuchsia* roses")—a deep purplish-red color.

*Poof!—an interjection (sometimes spelled *¡Puf!* or *¡Pfffs!*) roughly equivalent to "Ouf!"; said when a strenuous physical effort suddenly succeeds.

lavender ("her *lavender* hatboxes")—a pale purple color.

Holy smokes—(slang) an exclamation of surprise; some say "holy smoke."

*¿Cuándo?—When?

*¡Ay, Caray!—An exclamation of impatience, with the sense of "That doesn't make any difference! That's how it is."

skinny ("the only *skinny* thread")—very thin.

tin ("the language that sounds like *tin*")—a soft silver-white metal with a dull, flat sound.

Popular Mechanics

"He reached
across the stove
and tightened his
hands on the
baby."

Popular Mechanics

Raymond Carver
(1938–1988)

Raymond Carver identified himself as "a full-time member of the working poor." Born in Clatskanie, Oregon, Carver grew up thinking that, like his father, he would go to work in a lumber mill after high school. But six months in the mills was enough; he knew he wanted more. With his wife and their two young children, Carver moved to northern California, where he began college on a partial scholarship.

One of his teachers, the novelist John Gardner, helped Carver to revive his childhood interest in making up stories and encouraged him to find his own voice as a writer. Working nights at a succession of blue-collar jobs, Carver used the days to learn to write. Because the house was always noisy, he often worked in the family car. Because his writing time was limited, he concentrated on short pieces—a poem or story—that could be finished in one sitting. Carver also worked to strip the stories down to the bare minimum— "cutting them to the bone, and then cutting them a bit more," he joked. His first collection of stories—*Will You Please Be Quiet, Please* (1976)—led reviewers to speak of "Carver country," a fictional world in which working-class people struggle to make sense of their lives, or failing that, simply to get through them. But Carver had also been troubled by alcoholism, which finally led him to stop writing and destroyed his family life.

In 1977, realizing that he was drinking himself to death, Carver took his last drink and began what he later identified as his "second life." (He and his first wife separated that year and were divorced five years later.) Carver started writing again the following year, after meeting the poet Tess Gallagher. His next book, *What We Talk About When We Talk About Love* (1981), brought him world-wide recognition, with translations in more than twenty languages. His following collection, *Cathedral* (1983), marked a new direction in his work, with much longer stories that also carried a sense of hope. In 1988, Carver married Gallagher, was elected to the American Academy and Institute of Arts and Letters, and won two awards for his story "Errand," which is based on the death of the Russian writer Anton Chekov. However, he also suffered a relapse of lung cancer, for which he had been treated earlier, and died at home in Port Angeles, Washington, leaving five collections of short stories, five books of poetry, and one collection of prose and poetry.

"Popular Mechanics" first appeared in *What We Talk About When We Talk About Love* and was reprinted under the title "Little Things" in *Where I'm Calling From* (1988). Asked once about the sense of menace—of impending danger—in his stories, Carver said, "The people I've chosen to write about *do* feel menace, and I think many, if not most, people feel the world is a menacing place. . . . Try living on the other side of the tracks for a while. Menace is there, and it's palpable. "*The characters of "Popular Mechanics" certainly live on the wrong side of the tracks, in a three-room house heated only by a free-standing stove in the kitchen. For this young couple and their baby, what do you suppose the menace will prove to be?

*Larry McCaffrey and Sinda Gregory, "An Interview with Raymond Carver," reprinted in *Conversations with Raymond Carver,* edited by Marshall Bruce Gentry and William L. Stull (1990).

Early that day the weather turned and the snow was melting into dirty water. Streaks of it ran down from the little shoulder-high window that faced the backyard. Cars slushed by on the street outside, where it was getting dark. But it was getting
5 dark on the inside too.

He was in the bedroom pushing clothes into a suitcase when she came to the door.

I'm glad you're leaving! I'm glad you're leaving! she said. Do you hear?
10 He kept on putting his things into the suitcase.

Son of a bitch! I'm so glad you're leaving! She began to cry. You can't even look me in the face, can you?

Then she noticed the baby's picture on the bed and picked it up.
15 He looked at her and she wiped her eyes and stared at him before turning and going back to the living room.

Bring that back, he said.

Just get your things and get out, she said.

He did not answer. He fastened the suitcase, put on his
20 coat, looked around the bedroom before turning off the light. Then he went out to the living room.

She stood in the doorway of the little kitchen, holding the baby.

I want the baby, he said.
25 Are you crazy?

No, but I want the baby. I'll get someone to come by for his things.

You're not touching this baby, she said.

The baby had begun to cry and she uncovered the blanket
30 from around his head.

Oh, oh, she said, looking at the baby.

He moved toward her.

For God's sake! she said. She took a step back into the kitchen.
35 I want the baby.

Get out of here!

She turned and tried to hold the baby over in a corner behind the stove.

But he came up. He reached across the stove and tightened
40   his hands on the baby.

Let go of him, he said.

Get away, get away! she cried.

The baby was red-faced and screaming. In the scuffle they knocked down a flowerpot that hung behind the stove.

45   He crowded her into the wall then, trying to break her grip. He held on to the baby and pushed with all his weight.

Let go of him, he said.

Don't, she said. You're hurting the baby, she said.

I'm not hurting the baby, he said.

50   The kitchen window gave no light. In the near-dark he worked on her fisted fingers with one hand and with the other hand he gripped the screaming baby up under an arm near the shoulder.

She felt her fingers being forced open. She felt the baby
55   going from her.

No! she screamed just as her hands came loose.

She would have it, this baby. She grabbed for the baby's other arm. She caught the baby around the wrist and leaned back.

60   But he would not let go. He felt the baby slipping out of his hands and he pulled back very hard.

In this manner, the issue was decided.

[1981]

ncommon Words or Meanings

Popular Mechanics (title)—The name of a magazine dedicated to electronics, automobiles, wood-working projects, and other "manly" pursuits.

slush ("Cars *slushed* by")—partly melted snow; Carver has turned the noun into a verb.

a scuffle ("In the *scuffle*")—a rough, confused struggle or fight.

a fist ("Her *fisted* fingers")—a tightly closed hand, with the fingers turned under; Carver has turned the noun into an adjective.

The Unicorn in the Garden

"'The unicorn is a mythical beast,' she said, and turned her back on him."

The Unicorn in the Garden

James Thurber
(1894–1961)

James Thurber spent his boyhood in Columbus, Ohio, in a family that was delightfully crazy. As he described the family in *My Life and Hard Times* (1933), his grandmother worried about electricity leaking out of light fixtures and wall sockets. His grandfather used to disappear for days at time, returning with late-breaking news of the Civil War, which had ended forty years before. Aunt Gracie Shoaf lived in fear of burglars. She was sure that they would come when she was asleep and use chloroform to keep her from waking up. To drive them away, she threw shoes down the hallway in the middle of the night. "Some nights," Thurber wrote, "she threw them all."

A childhood accident left Thurber blind in one eye and with only limited vision in the other. Some might say that his unusual view of the world is reflected in the style of his drawings, one of which appears with this story, as well as in the content of his stories. For over thirty years, Thurber's cartoons and stories about his family and other topics appeared in *The New Yorker,* a witty and sophisticated American magazine founded by Harold Ross. Thurber presented his version of working on *The New Yorker's* staff in *The Years with Ross* (1959). A representative selection of his work appears in *The Thurber Carnival* (1945).

Thurber stands beside Mark Twain as one of the most popular American humorists and satirists of his time. He has also joined the ancient Greek slave Aesop and the seventeenth-century French nobleman Jean de La Fontaine as a noted writer of fables. Fables, which often have animals who act like human beings as the main characters, illustrate morals that are stated directly at the end like proverbs. Thurber's *Fables for Our Time* (1940) includes "The Unicorn in the Garden." This fable illustrates a recurring theme in Thurber's work: the battle of the sexes, pitting timid but imaginative men against scheming and possessive women. In this story, a typical Thurber man finds his long-suffering existence dramatically altered. How? By the arrival of a unicorn—the medieval symbol of romantic love and sexual power.

The Unicorn in the Garden

Once upon a sunny morning a man who sat in a breakfast nook looked up from his scrambled eggs to see a white unicorn with a gold horn quietly cropping the roses in the garden. The man went up to the bedroom where his wife was still asleep and woke her. "There's a unicorn in the garden," he said. "Eating roses." She opened one unfriendly eye and looked at him. "The unicorn is a mythical beast," she said, and turned her back on him. The man walked slowly downstairs and out into the garden. The unicorn was still there; he was now browsing among the tulips. "Here, unicorn," said the man, and he pulled up a lily and gave it to him. The unicorn ate it gravely. With a high heart, because there was a unicorn in his garden, the man went upstairs and roused his wife again. "The unicorn," he said, "ate a lily." His wife sat up in bed and looked at him, coldly. "You are a booby," she said, "and I am going to have you put in the booby hatch." The man, who had never liked the words "booby" and "booby-hatch," and who liked them even less on a shining morning when there was a unicorn in the garden, thought for a moment. "We'll see about that," he said. He walked over to the door. "He has a golden horn in the middle of his forehead," he told her. Then he went back to the garden to watch the unicorn; but the unicorn had gone away. The man sat down among the roses and went to sleep.

As soon as the husband had gone out of the house, the wife got up and dressed as fast as she could. She was very excited and there was a gloat in her eye. She telephoned the police and she telephoned a psychiatrist; she told them to hurry to her house and bring a straight-jacket. When the police and the psychiatrist arrived they sat down in chairs and looked at her, with great interest. "My husband," she said, "saw a unicorn this morning." The police looked at the psychiatrist and the psychiatrist looked at the police. "He told me it ate a lily," she said. The psychiatrist looked at the police and the police looked at the psychiatrist. "He told me it had a golden horn in the middle of its forehead," she said. At a solemn signal from the psychiatrist, the police leaped from their chairs and seized the wife. They had a hard time subduing her, for she put up a terrific struggle, but they finally subdued her. Just as they got her into the straight-jacket, the husband came back into the house.

40   "Did you tell your wife you saw a unicorn?" asked the police. "Of course not," said the husband. "The unicorn is a mythical beast." "That's all I wanted to know," said the psychiatrist. "Take her away. I'm sorry, sir, but your wife is as crazy as a jay bird." So they took her away, cursing and screaming,

45 and shut her up in an institution. The husband lived happily ever after.

    MORAL: Don't count your boobies until they are hatched.

[1939]

Uncommon Words or Meanings

Once upon a (*"Once upon a* sunny morning"*)*—the conventional opening for a fairy tale is "Once upon a time." The conventional ending is "They all lived happily ever after."

a breakfast nook ("sat in a *breakfast nook*")—a corner of the kitchen with a small table and chairs.

a booby ("You are a *booby.*")—(slang) a foolish or mentally retarded person.

a booby-hatch ("put in the *booby hatch*")—(slang) an insane asylum, a hospital for people who are mentally ill. Thurber later makes a play on words with the verb *hatch*, to break out of a shell.

a gloat ("a *gloat* in her eye")—the verb *gloat* means to look at with selfish or malicious pleasure; here, the verb is used as a noun.

a straight-jacket ("got her into the *straight-jacket*")—a white jacket with very long sleeves used to control a mental patient.

a jay-bird ("as crazy as a *jay bird*")—a blue jay, a common crested bird with a harsh cry. (The usual comparison is "as crazy as a loon.")

Don't count . . . . ("Don't count your chickens until they are hatched.")—a play on the words of the proverb the moral of the fable.

The Summer of the Beautiful White Horse

"If you were crazy

about horses the

way my cousin

Mourad and I

were, it wasn't

stealing."

The Summer of the Beautiful White Horse

William Saroyan
(1908–1981)

The Armenian American writer William Saroyan grew up in poverty in Sacramento, California. After leaving school in his early teens, he worked at a variety of jobs, always with the idea of becoming a writer, and at the age of twenty-six published his first story. "The Daring Young Man on the Flying Trapeze" (1934) tells of a penniless young writer who merrily starves to death in San Francisco in the middle of the Great Depression. Like all of Saroyan's stories, that one has autobiographical elements. However, rather than starving, Saroyan became famous overnight, "the literary equivalent of a movie star," as one critic puts it. Soon he had two successful Broadway plays—*My Heart's in the Highlands* (1939) and *The Time of Your Life* (1940), both of them portraying gentle, eccentric, and homesick Armenian immigrants in California. In 1940, he also published *My Name Is Aram,* the collection of anecdotes in which "The Summer of the Beautiful White Horse" appears. Two years later, Saroyan published his best-known novel, *The Human Comedy,* also a story of Armenian immigrants in California.

Armenian history forms the background of all of these stories. This ancient kingdom of Asia Minor was located in the "fertile crescent" between the Black Sea and the Caspian Sea. Over the centuries, Armenia was invaded by one army after another and in the early 1800s, it disappeared as a country when the territory and people were divided among

Russia, Turkey, and Iran. The Turkish sultan then began a nearly successful effort to exterminate all of the Armenians under his control, by either deporting or killing them. After the great massacre of 1894, many Turkish Armenians—Saroyan's parents among them—fled Turkey and settled in California's San Joaquin Valley, raising grapes, walnuts, olives, and other crops.

In 1911, Saroyan's father died suddenly at the age of thirty-six, leaving a wife and four children, the youngest of whom was three-year-old William. Left without money, Mrs. Saroyan placed the children in an orphanage for the next five years while she worked as a maid. William's son believes that this experience left his father emotionally "frozen" in his childhood, delighting in fantasy but unable to deal with complex emotions.

"The Summer of the Beautiful White Horse" is Saroyan's reinventing of his childhood as a time of bliss rather than deep sorrow. It begins with a variation on the traditional opening of a fairy tale—"Once upon a time"—when a boy is awakened early one morning by his cousin, who is mounted on a beautiful white horse. Both boys love horses, but their families are very poor and could never buy a horse. Where has the horse come from? What will the boys do with it? And how will the matter of the horse be related to the older characters in the story, who long for their lost homelands?

The Summer of the Beautiful White Horse

One day back there in the good old days when I was nine
and the world was full of every imaginable kind of magnifi-
cence, and life was still a delightful and mysterious dream, my
cousin Mourad, who was considered crazy by everybody who
5   knew him except me, came to my house at four in the morning
and woke me up by tapping on the window of my room.
     Aram, he said.
     I jumped out of bed and looked out the window.
     I couldn't believe what I saw.
10   It wasn't morning yet, but it was summer and with day-
break not many minutes around the corner of the world it was
light enough for me to know I wasn't dreaming.
     My cousin Mourad was sitting on a beautiful white horse.
     I stuck my head out of the window and rubbed my eyes.
15   Yes, he said in Armenian. It's a horse. You're not dreaming.
Make it quick if you want to ride.
     I knew my cousin Mourad enjoyed being alive more than
anybody else who had ever fallen into the world by mistake,
but this was more than even I could believe.
20   In the first place, my earliest memories had been memories
of horses and my first longings had been longings to ride.
     This was the wonderful part.
     In the second place, we were poor.
     This was the part that wouldn't permit me to believe what
25   I saw.
     We were poor. We had no money. Our whole tribe was
poverty-stricken. Every branch of the Garoghlanian family was
living in the most amazing and comical poverty in the world.
Nobody could understand where we ever got money enough to
30   keep us with food in our bellies, not even the old men of the
family. Most important of all, though, we were famous for our
honesty. We had been famous for our honesty for something
like eleven centuries, even when we had been the wealthiest
family in what we liked to think was the world. We were proud
35   first, honest next, and after that we believed in right and wrong.
None of us would take advantage of anybody in the world, let
alone steal.

Consequently, even though I could *see* the horse, so magnificent; even though I could *smell* the horse, so lovely; even though I could *hear* it breathing, so exciting; I couldn't *believe* the horse had anything to do with my cousin Mourad or with me or with any of the other members of our family, asleep or awake, because I *knew* my cousin Mourad couldn't have *bought* the horse, and if he couldn't have bought it he must have *stolen* it, and I refused to believe he had stolen it.

No member of the Garoghlanian family could be a thief.

I stared first at my cousin and then at the horse. There was a pious stillness and humor in each of them which on the one hand delighted me and on the other frightened me.

Mourad, I said, where did you steal this horse?

Leap out of the window, he said, if you want to ride.

It was true, then. He *had* stolen the horse. There was no question about it. He had come to invite me to ride or not, as I chose.

Well, it seemed to me stealing a horse for a ride was not the same thing as stealing something else, such as money. For all I knew, maybe it wasn't stealing at all. If you were crazy about horses the way my cousin Mourad and I were, it wasn't stealing. It wouldn't become stealing until we offered to sell the horse, which of course I knew we would never do.

Let me put on some clothes, I said.

All right, he said, but hurry.

I leaped into my clothes.

I jumped down to the yard from the window and leaped up onto the horse behind my cousin Mourad.

That year we lived at the edge of town, on Walnut Avenue. Behind our house was the country: vineyards, orchards, irrigation ditches, and country roads. In less than three minutes we were on Olive Avenue, and then the horse began to trot. The air was new and lovely to breathe. The feel of the horse running was wonderful. My cousin Mourad who was considered one of the craziest members of our family began to sing. I mean, he began to roar.

Every family has a crazy streak in it somewhere, and my cousin Mourad was considered the natural descendant of the crazy streak in our tribe. Before him was our uncle Khosrove, an enormous man with a powerful head of black hair and the largest mustache in the San Joaquin Valley, a man so furious in temper, so irritable, so impatient that he stopped anyone from

80 talking by roaring, *It is no harm; pay no attention to it.*

That was all, no matter what anybody happened to be talking about. Once it was his own son Arak running eight blocks to the barber shop where his father was having his mustache trimmed to tell him that their house was on fire. This man

85 Khosrove sat up in the chair and roared, It is no harm; pay no attention to it. The barber said, But the boy says your house is on fire. So Khosrove roared, Enough, it is no harm, I say.

My cousin Mourad was considered the natural descendant of this man, although Mourad's father was Zorab, who

90 was practical and nothing else. That's how it is in our tribe. A man could be the father of his son's flesh, but that did not mean that he was also the father of his spirit. The distribution of the various kinds of spirit of our tribe had been from the beginning capricious and vagrant.

95 We rode and my cousin Mourad sang. For all anybody knew we were still in the old country where, at least according to some of our neighbors, we belonged. We let the horse run as long as it felt like running.

At last my cousin Mourad said, Get down. I want to ride

100 alone.

Will you let me ride alone? I said.

That is up to the horse, my cousin said. Get down.

The *horse* will let me ride, I said.

We shall see, he said. Don't forget that I have a way with a

105 horse.

Well, I said, any way you have with a horse, I have also.

For the sake of your safety, he said, let us hope so. Get down.

All right, I said, but remember you've got to let me try to

110 ride alone.

I got down and my cousin Mourad kicked his heels into the horse and shouted, *Vazire*, run. The horse stood on its hind legs, snorted, and burst into a fury of speed that was the loveliest thing I had ever seen. My cousin Mourad raced the horse

115 across a field of dry grass to an irrigation ditch, crossed the ditch on the horse, and five minutes later returned, dripping wet.

The sun was coming up.

Now it's my turn to ride, I said.

120   My cousin Mourad got off the horse.

Ride, he said.

I leaped to the back of the horse and for a moment knew the awfulest fear imaginable. The horse did not move.

Kick into his muscles, my cousin Mourad said. What are
125   you waiting for? We've got to take him back before everybody in the world is up and about.

I kicked into the muscles of the horse. Once again it reared and snorted. Then it began to run. I didn't know what to do. Instead of running across the field to the irrigation ditch the
130   horse ran down the road to the vineyard of Dikran Halabian where it began to leap over vines. The horse leaped over seven vines before I fell. Then it continued running.

My cousin Mourad came running down the road.

I'm not worried about you, he shouted. We've got to get
135   that horse. You go this way and I'll go this way. If you come upon him, be kindly. I'll be near.

I continued down the road and my cousin Mourad went across the field toward the irrigation ditch.

It took him half an hour to find the horse and bring him
140   back.

All right, he said, jump on. The whole world is awake now.

What will we do? I said.

Well, he said, we'll either take him back or hide him until tomorrow morning.

145   He didn't sound worried and I knew he'd hide him and not take him back. Not for a while, at any rate.

Where will we hide him? I said.

I know a place, he said.

How long ago did you steal this horse? I said.

150   It suddenly dawned on me that he had been taking these early morning rides for some time and had come for me this morning only because he knew how much I longed to ride.

Who said anything about stealing a horse? he said.

Anyhow, I said, how long ago did you begin riding every
155   morning?

Not until this morning, he said.

Are you telling the truth? I said.

Of course not, he said, but if we are found out, that's what you're to say. I don't want both of us to be liars. All you know
160   is that we started riding this morning.

All right, I said.

He walked the horse quietly to the barn of a deserted vine-yard which at one time had been the pride of a farmer named Fetvajian. There were some oats and dry alfalfa in the barn.

We began walking home.

It wasn't easy, he said, to get the horse to behave so nicely. At first it wanted to run wild, but, as I've told you, I have a way with a horse. I can get it to want to do anything *I* want it to do. Horses understand me.

How do you do it? I said.

I have an understanding with a horse, he said.

Yes, but what sort of an understanding? I said.

A simple and honest one, he said.

Well, I said, I wish I knew how to reach an understanding like that with a horse.

You're still a small boy, he said. When you get to be thirteen you'll know how to do it.

I went home and ate a hearty breakfast.

That afternoon my uncle Khosrove came to our house for coffee and cigarettes. He sat in the parlor, sipping and smoking and remembering the old country. Then another visitor arrived, a farmer named John Byro, an Assyrian who, out of loneliness, had learned to speak Armenian. My mother brought the lonely visitor coffee and tobacco and he rolled a cigarette and sipped and smoked, and then at last, sighing sadly, he said, My white horse which was stolen last month is still gone. I cannot understand it.

My uncle Khosrove became very irritated and shouted, It's no harm. What is the loss of a horse? Haven't we all lost a homeland? What is this crying over a horse?

That may be all right for you, a city dweller, to say, John Byro said, but what of my surrey? What good is a surrey without a horse?

Pay no attention to it, my uncle Khosrove roared.

I walked ten miles to get here, John Byro said.

You have legs, my uncle Khosrove shouted.

My left leg pains me, the farmer said.

Pay no attention to it, my uncle Khosrove roared.

That horse cost me sixty dollars, the farmer said.

I spit on money, my uncle Khosrove said.

He got up and stalked out of the house, slamming the screen door.

My mother explained.

He has a gentle heart, she said. It is simply that he is homesick and such a large man.

The farmer went away and I ran over to my cousin
Mourad's house.

He was sitting under a peach tree, trying to repair the hurt
wing of a young robin which could not fly. He was talking to
the bird.

What is it? he said.

The farmer, John Byro, I said. He visited our house. He
wants his horse. You've had it a month. I want you to promise
not to take it back until I learn to ride.

It will take you *a year* to learn to ride, my cousin Mourad
said.

We could keep the horse a year, I said.

My cousin Mourad leaped to his feet.

What? he roared. Are you inviting a member of the Garoghlanian family to steal? The horse must go back to its true
owner.

When? I said.

In six months at the latest, he said.

He threw the bird into the air. The bird tried hard, almost
fell twice, but at last flew away, high and straight.

Early every morning for two weeks my cousin Mourad and
I took the horse out of the barn of the deserted vineyard where
we were hiding it and rode it, and every morning the horse,
when it was my turn to ride alone, leaped over grape vines and
small trees and threw me and ran away. Nevertheless, I hoped
in time to learn to ride the way my cousin Mourad rode.

One morning on the way to Fetvajian's deserted vineyard
we ran into the farmer John Byro who was on his way to town.

Let me do the talking, my cousin Mourad said. I have a way
with farmers.

Good morning, John Byro, my cousin Mourad said to the
farmer.

The farmer studied the horse eagerly.

Good morning, sons of my friends, he said. What is the
name of your horse?

My Heart, my cousin Mourad said in Armenian.

A lovely name, John Byro said, for a lovely horse. I could
swear it is the horse that was stolen from me many weeks ago.
May I look into its mouth?

245   Of course, Mourad said.

The farmer looked into the mouth of the horse.

Tooth for tooth, he said. I would swear it *is* my horse if I didn't know your parents. The fame of your family for honesty is well known to me. Yet the horse is the twin of my horse. A
250   suspicious man would believe his eyes instead of his heart. Good day, my young friends.

Good day, John Byro, my cousin Mourad said.

Early the following morning we took the horse to John Byro's vineyard and put it in the barn. The dogs followed us
255   around without making a sound.

The dogs, I whispered to my cousin Mourad. I thought they would bark.

They would at somebody else, he said. I have a way with dogs.

260   My cousin Mourad put his arms around the horse, pressed his nose into the horse's nose, patted it, and then we went away.

That afternoon John Byro came to our house in his surrey and showed my mother the horse that had been stolen and
265   returned.

I do not know what to think, he said. The horse is stronger than ever. Better-tempered, too. I thank God.

My uncle Khosrove, who was in the parlor, became irritated and shouted, Quiet, man, quiet. Your horse has been
270   returned. Pay no attention to it.

[1940]

U ncommon Words or Meanings

a streak ("Every family has a crazy *streak* in it somewhere")—a characteristic, element.

to be up to ("That *is up to* the horse")—to be (someone's) responsibility to decide.

to have a way with ("I *have a way with* a horse")—to be skillful and persuasive in dealing with.

to dawn on ("suddenly *dawned on* me")—to become clear to the mind.

hearty ("ate a *hearty* breakfast")—abundant and nourishing.

Assyrian ("an *Assyrian* who, out of loneliness, had learned to speak Armenian")—a citizen of Assyria, an ancient country of Asia Minor that lost its independent existence in the eighth century B.C. In another story, Saroyan identified a well-known Armenian as "Assyrian." When asked why he had done that, Saroyan answered that "in a sense everybody in the world is an Assyrian, a remnant of a once-mighty race, now all but extinct" (*Letters from 74 rue Taitbout,* 1969).

Samuel

"The boys opened
their eyes wide at
each other and
laughed."

Samuel

Grace Paley
(born 1922)

Grace Paley was born in the Bronx, one of the five boroughs of New York City. Like many other Bronx residents at the time, her parents were Russian Jewish immigrants. The family members were lively story-tellers in three languages—Russian, Yiddish, and English. "I loved to listen," Paley has said of her childhood, "and soon I loved to talk and tell." She entered Hunter College at the age of fifteen and later attended New York University but never completed a degree. "I really went to school on poetry," Paley later explained. "I learned whatever I know about language and craft from writing poems."

Paley moved from writing poetry to writing stories during her years as a wife, mother, and political activist in the part of Manhattan (another borough of New York) called Greenwich Village. In the mid-twentieth century, "the Village" was favored by artists and political liberals. The streets were narrow, the buildings were not more than five stories high, and people talked comfortably with their neighbors. Meeting other women in the shops, on the playgrounds, and at anti-war demonstrations, Paley realized that they were not represented in contemporary literature. She began to write stories to give these women "a voice," winning high praise for her first collection, *The Little Disturbances of Man* (1959). Then Paley put aside literary concerns and devoted her energies to supporting the peace movement and campaigning for the nuclear freeze, environmentalism, feminism, and prison reform. (Paley has described herself as a "somewhat combative pacifist and cooperative anarchist.")

Despite her total of only three books in thirty years—the second and third are *Enormous Changes at the Last Minute* (1974), which includes "Samuel," and *Later the Same Day* (1985), Paley has become a writer with a large reputation. (The three were reissued in a single volume in 1994.) Since the early 1960s, Paley has taught university courses in writing because, as she explains, "teaching always puts you in contact with new historical experience—not just with people but with the nature of their lives." Paley has a gift for understanding this nature and capturing it in fiction. Beneath the "tough-kid" New York voice of the stories is an unfailing interest in and understanding of the enormous variety of people who comprise New York City. And through this understanding, Paley identifies feelings and experiences that every reader can share.

For "Samuel," Paley has chosen a location where the widest variety of people meet—the subway. The subway train in this story is traveling from Manhattan (the island that many people—including the men in the story—mean when they refer to "New York") to the Bronx, the northernmost of the city's five boroughs. To follow the story, it's useful to know something about the tracks and trains of the subway system. First, the tracks are underground in almost all of Manhattan but are elevated in the Bronx. Second, the cars of the subway train are joined by couplings similar to freight trains or passenger trains. A foot or so above these couplings are steel platforms that allow passengers to walk from one car to the next. (The doors at the ends of the cars began to be locked as air-conditioning was introduced in preparation for the 1964 World's Fair.) On either side of these platforms, at waist-height, are chains to keep passengers from falling between the cars. Come for a subway ride to meet Samuel and his friends, with the warning that Paley has the power to make her readers both laugh and cry in the course of one story.

Samuel

Some boys are very tough. They're afraid of nothing. They are the ones who climb a wall and take a bow at the top. Not only are they brave on the roof, but they make a lot of noise in the darkest part of the cellar where even the super hates to go. They also jiggle and hop on the platform between the locked doors of the subway cars.

Four boys are jiggling on the swaying platform. Their names are Alfred, Calvin, Samuel, and Tom. The men and the women in the cars on either side watch them. They don't like them to jiggle or jump but don't want to interfere. Of course some of the men in the cars were once brave boys like these. One of them had ridden the tail of a speeding truck from New York to Rockaway Beach without getting off, without his sore fingers losing hold. Nothing happened to him then or later. He had made a compact with other boys who preferred to watch: Starting at Eighth Avenue and Fifteenth Street, he would get to some specified place, maybe Twenty-third and the river, by hopping the tops of moving trucks. This was hard to do when one truck turned a corner in the wrong direction and the nearest truck was a couple of feet too high. He made three or four starts before succeeding. He had gotten this idea from a film at school called *The Romance of Logging*. He had finished high school, married a good friend, was in a responsible job and going to night school.

These two men and others looked at the four boys jumping and jiggling on the platform and thought, It must be fun to ride that way, especially now the weather is nice and we're out of the tunnel and way high over the Bronx. Then they thought, These kids do seem to be acting sort of stupid. They *are* little. Then they thought of some of the brave things they had done when they were boys and jiggling didn't seem so risky.

The ladies in the car became very angry when they looked at the four boys. Most of them brought their brows together and hoped the boys could see their extreme disapproval. One of the ladies wanted to get up and say, Be careful you dumb kids, get off that platform or I'll call a cop. But three of the boys were Negroes and the fourth was something else she couldn't tell for sure. She was afraid they'd be fresh and laugh at her and

embarrass her. She wasn't afraid they'd hit her, but she was
40 afraid of embarrassment. Another lady thought, Their mothers
never know where they are. It wasn't true in this particular case.
Their mothers all knew that they had gone to see the missile
exhibit on Fourteenth Street.

Out on the platform, whenever the train accelerated, the
45 boys would raise their hands and point them up to the sky to
act like rockets going off, then they rat-tat-tatted the shatterproof glass pane like machine guns, although no machine guns
had been exhibited.

For some reason known only to the motorman, the train
50 began a sudden slowdown. The lady who was afraid of embarrassment saw the boys jerk forward and backward and grab
the swinging guard chains. She had her own boy at home. She
stood up with determination and went to the door. She slid it
open and said, "You boys will be hurt. You'll be killed. I'm
55 going to call the conductor if you don't just go into the next car
and sit down and be quiet."

Two of the boys said, "Yes'm," and acted as though they
were about to go. Two of them blinked their eyes a couple of
times and pressed their lips together. The train resumed its
60 speed. The door slid shut, parting the lady and the boys. She
leaned against the side door because she had to get off at the
next stop.

The boys opened their eyes wide at each other and
laughed. The lady blushed. The boys looked at her and laughed
65 harder. They began to pound each other's back. Samuel
laughed the hardest and pounded Alfred's back until Alfred
coughed and the tears came. Alfred held tight to the chain
hook. Samuel pounded him even harder when he saw the
tears. He said, "Why you bawling? You a baby, huh?" and
70 laughed. One of the men whose boyhood had been much more
watchful than brave became angry. He stood up straight and
looked at the boys for a couple of seconds. Then he walked in
a citizenly way to the end of the car, where he pulled the emergency cord. Almost at once, with a terrible hiss, the pressure
75 of air abandoned the brakes and the wheels were caught
and held.

People standing in the most secure places fell forward,
then backward. Samuel had let go of his hold on the chain so
he could pound Tom as well as Alfred. All the passengers in the

80   car whipped back and forth, but he pitched only forward and
fell head first to be crushed and killed between the cars.

The train had stopped hard, halfway into the station, and
the conductor called at once for the trainmen who knew about
this kind of death and how to take the body from the wheels
85   and brakes. There was silence except for passengers from
other cars who asked, What happened! What happened! The
ladies waited around wondering if he might be an only child.
The men recalled other afternoons with very bad endings. The
little boys stayed close to each other, leaning and touching
90   shoulders and arms and legs.

When the policeman knocked at the door and told her
about it, Samuel's mother began to scream. She screamed all
day and moaned all night, though the doctors tried to quiet her
with pills.

95   Oh, oh, she hopelessly cried. She did not know how she
could ever find another boy like that one. However, she was a
young woman and she became pregnant. Then for a few
months she was hopeful. The child born to her was a boy. They
brought him to be seen and nursed. She smiled. But immedi-
100   ately she saw that this baby wasn't Samuel. She and her husband together have had other children, but never again will a
boy exactly like Samuel be known.

[1960]

⊔ncommon Words or Meanings

to take a bow ("the ones who climb a wall and *take a bow* at the
top")—(idiom) to acknowledge applause or verbal admiration by
bowing.

a super ("where even the *super* hates to go")—New York City
abbreviation for "superintendent," a building caretaker.

to jiggle ("*jiggle* and hop on the platform between the locked
doors of the subway cars")—(informal) to move sideways and up
and down (as the subway train moves rapidly along the tracks).

from New York to Rockaway Beach ("had ridden the tail of a speeding truck *from New York to Rockaway Beach*")—a distance of twelve or thirteen miles. Here "New York" means Manhattan; Rockaway Beach is in the borough of Queens, also part of New York City.

Eighth Avenue and Fifteenth Street . . . Twenty-third [Street] and the [Hudson] river ("Starting at *Eighth Avenue and Fifteenth Street,* he would get to some specified place, maybe *Twenty-third and the river*")—a distance of slightly over a mile. This is a commercial part of Manhattan with many warehouses and a lot of truck traffic.

logging ("a film at school called *The Romance of* Logging")—cutting down trees for lumber. At the time of the film, North American loggers, or lumberjacks, had one of the world's most dangerous jobs: as logs floated downriver to a sawmill, the lumberjacks could be called on to walk from one free-floating log to another to locate and loosen the key log in a logjam.

way high over the Bronx ("we're out of the tunnel and *way high over the Bronx*")—The train is going north from Manhattan, under the Harlem River, to the Bronx, where it runs as an elevated train.

fresh ("was afraid they'd be *fresh* and laugh at her")—impolite, especially used of children.

rat-tat-tatted ("then they *rat-tat-tatted* the shatterproof glass pane like machine guns")—made a sound like a machine gun.

shatterproof ("rat-tat-tatted the *shatterproof* glass pane)—treated to resist **shattering,** breaking violently into small pieces.

a motorman ("For some reason known only to the *motorman,* the train began a sudden slowdown.")—the "driver" in the first car of a subway train.

to pound ("Samuel laughed the hardest and *pounded* Alfred's back")—to hit heavily and repeatedly.

the emergency cord ("where he pulled *the emergency cord*")—the rope at the end of the subway car that enabled a passenger to stop the train.

The Chaser

"Young people

who need a love

potion very

seldom have five

thousand dollars."

The Chaser

John Collier
(1901–1980)

The short stories of John Collier, who was born and educated in England, were regularly published in leading American magazines from the 1930s through the 1950s. During that time, Collier also worked as a screenwriter in Hollywood. (He wrote the first draft for the script of *The African Queen,* which starred Humphrey Bogart and Katharine Hepburn.) Collier's stories have been collected in several books (including *Fancies and Goodnights,* 1951, and *The Best of John Collier,* 1975) and they continue to appear in short-story anthologies in English and in translation. A comprehensive study of his life and work appears in *John Collier* by Betty Richardson (1981).

As novelist Anthony Burgess notes in his introduction to *The Best of John Collier,* both the film scripts and short stories show Collier's skill in writing dialogue and his gift for sharp observation. Burgess also remarks that Collier "makes literature out of the intrusion of fantasy, or quiet horror, into a real world closely observed," often making fun of both the Hollywood films and the popular fiction of his day, particularly their portrayal of romantic love.

In "The Chaser," a young man adores a woman who doesn't return his affection. Though he is "as nervous as a kitten," the young man goes in search of a way to win the young woman's love. (Like many of Collier's light-hearted heroines, she is named Diana, after the Roman goddess of the hunt. Diana was also the goddess of the moon, which was believed to affect emotions.) What do you suppose the fantasy element in this story will be? A "chaser" is a mild beverage drunk after a stronger one, such as beer used to "chase" whiskey. What do you think the first drink will be in this story? And the chaser?

This is a story filled with irony—an intended or unintended contrast between what is expected and what actually happens, or between what is said and what is meant. For example, the young man wants to change the young woman without considering all the possible effects of the changes. As you read, look for other examples.

The Chaser

Alan Austen, as nervous as a kitten, went up certain dark and creaky stairs in the neighbourhood of Pell Street, and peered about for a long time on the dim landing before he found the name he wanted written obscurely on one of the
5 doors.

He pushed open this door, as he had been told to do, and found himself in a tiny room, which contained no furniture but a plain kitchen table, a rocking-chair, and an ordinary chair. On one of the dirty buff-coloured walls were a couple of shelves,
10 containing in all perhaps a dozen bottles and jars.

An old man sat in the rocking-chair, reading a newspaper. Alan, without a word, handed him the card he had been given. "Sit down, Mr. Austen," said the old man very politely. "I am glad to make your acquaintance."
15 "Is it true," asked Alan, "that you have a certain mixture that has—er—quite extraordinary effects?"

"My dear sir," replied the old man, "my stock in trade is not very large—I don't deal in laxatives and teething mixtures— but such as it is, it is varied. I think nothing I sell has effects
20 which could be precisely described as ordinary."

"Well, the fact is—" began Alan.

"Here, for example," interrupted the old man, reaching for a bottle from the shelf. "Here is a liquid as colourless as water, almost tasteless, quite imperceptible in coffee, milk, wine, or
25 any other beverage. It is also quite imperceptible to any known method of autopsy."

"Do you mean it is a poison?" cried Alan, very much horrified.

"Call it a glove-cleaner if you like," said the old man indif-
30 ferently. "Maybe it will clean gloves. I have never tried. One might call it a life-cleaner. Lives need cleaning sometimes."

"I want nothing of that sort," said Alan.

"Probably it is just as well," said the old man. "Do you know the price of this? For one teaspoonful, which is suffi-
35 cient, I ask five thousand dollars. Never less. Not a penny less."

"I hope all your mixtures are not as expensive," said Alan apprehensively.

"Oh dear, no," said the old man. "It would be no good charging that sort of price for a love potion, for example. Young people who need a love potion very seldom have five thousand dollars. Otherwise they would not need a love potion."

"I am glad to hear that," said Alan.

"I look at it like this," said the old man. "Please a customer with one article, and he will come back when he needs another. Even if it *is* more costly. He will save up for it, if necessary."

"So," said Alan, "you really do sell love potions?"

"If I did not sell love potions," said the old man, reaching for another bottle, "I should not have mentioned the other matter to you. It is only when one is in a position to oblige that one can afford to be so confidential."

"And these potions," said Alan. "They are not just—just—er—"

"Oh, no," said the old man. "Their effects are permanent, and extend far beyond the mere casual impulse. But they include it. Oh, yes, they include it. Bountifully, insistently. Everlastingly."

"Dear me!" said Alan, attempting a look of scientific detachment. "How very interesting!"

"But consider the spiritual side," said the old man.

"I do indeed," said Alan.

"For indifference," said the old man, "they substitute devotion. For scorn, adoration. Give one tiny measure of this to the young lady—its flavour is imperceptible in orange juice, soup, or cocktails—and however gay and giddy she is, she will change altogether. She will want nothing but solitude and you."

"I can hardly believe it," said Alan. "She is so fond of parties."

"She will not like them anymore," said the old man. "She will be afraid of the pretty girls you may meet."

"She will actually be jealous?" cried Alan in a rapture. "Of me?"

"Yes, she will want to be everything to you."

"She is already. Only she doesn't care about it."

"She will, when she has taken this. She will care intensely. You will be her sole interest in life."

"Wonderful!" cried Alan.

"She will want to know all you do," said the old man. "All that has happened to you during the day. Every word of it. She will want to know what you are thinking about, why you smile suddenly, why you are looking sad."

80 "That is love!" cried Alan.

"Yes," said the old man. "How carefully she will look after you! She will never allow you to be tired, to sit in a draught, to neglect your food. If you are an hour late, she will be terrified. She will think you are killed, or that some siren has caught

85 you."

"I can hardly imagine Diana like that!" cried Alan, overwhelmed with joy.

"You will not have to use your imagination," said the old man. "And, by the way, since there are always sirens, if by any

90 chance you *should*, later on, slip a little, you need not worry. She will forgive you, in the end. She will be terribly hurt, of course, but she will forgive you—in the end."

"That will not happen," said Alan fervently.

"Of course not," said the old man. "But if it did, you need

95 not worry. She would never divorce you. Oh, no! And, of course, she herself will never give you the least, the very least grounds for—uneasiness."

"And how much," said Alan, "is this wonderful mixture?"

"It is not as dear," said the old man, "as the glove-cleaner,

100 or life-cleaner, as I sometimes call it. No. That is five thousand dollars, never a penny less. One has to be older than you are, to indulge in that sort of thing. One has to save up for it."

"But the love potion?" said Alan.

"Oh, that," said the old man, opening the drawer in the

105 kitchen table, and taking out a tiny, rather dirty-looking phial. "That is just a dollar."

"I can't tell you how grateful I am," said Alan, watching him fill it.

"I like to oblige," said the old man. "Then customers come

110 back, later in life, when they are rather better off, and want more expensive things. Here you are. You will find it very effective."

"Thank you again," said Alan. "Good-bye."

"*Au revoir*," said the old man.

[1940]

Uncommon Words or Meanings

Pell Street ("in the neighbourhood of *Pell Street*")—a principal street in New York's Chinatown.

gay ("no matter how *gay* and giddy she is")—light-hearted, cheerful.

giddy ("gay and *giddy*")—frivolously happy.

a draught ("to sit in a *draught*")—a current of air (*draft* in American spelling).

a siren ("some *siren* has caught you")—a seductive woman; a reference to the minor goddesses of Greek mythology who lived on an island and used their enchanting voices to lure sailors to their deaths upon the rocks.

grounds ("give you the least . . . *grounds* for—uneasiness")—(usually plural) basis or reason for a thought or action; commonly used in the phrase "grounds for divorce."

***Au revoir*—**(French) "Good-bye until we meet again."

The Brown House

"... and everyone

knows that a

white-snake

dream is a sure

omen of good luck

in games of

chance."

The Brown House

Hisaye Yamamoto
(born 1921)

Hisaye Yamamoto, one of the pioneers of Asian American literature, was born in Redondo Beach, California shortly after World War I. At the beginning of the U.S. involvement in World War II, which came with the Japanese attack on Pearl Harbor in December 1941, both Issei (first-generation Japanese immigrants like Yamamoto's parents) and Nisei (their American-born children) were suspected of being sympathetic to Japan. Even though they were American citizens, these people were forced to give up their homes and businesses—most of which were in some way related to raising fruits and vegetables—and to spend the war in camps called "relocation centers" in remote areas away from the coast. The effect on many was devastating, for they felt betrayed by the country they had come to love. (Yamamoto's brother was one of the young Japanese American men who volunteered for the U.S. Army. Sent to fight in Europe, the Nisei unit was among the most decorated in the history of the U.S. armed forces. Yamamoto's brother was killed in action.)

In the Arizona camp where her family was interned, Yamamoto wrote for the camp newspaper and published a serialized murder mystery. After the war, she became a "rewrite man" and columnist for the *Los Angeles Tribune,* a black weekly. Her first acceptance by a literary magazine came in 1948; two years later a John Hay Whitney Foundation Fellowship provided her an opportunity to write full-time for a year. Soon she had three award-winning stories: "Seventeen Syllables" (1949), "Yoneko's Earthquake" (l951), and "The Brown House" (1951). Several years later, while volunteering at a Catholic Worker rehabilitation farm on Staten Island, a part of New York City, Yamamoto met and married Anthony DeSoto. Together with her adopted son, they returned to Los Angeles, where four more sons were born to them. Yamamoto continued to write stories that were widely anthologized. "I guess I write (aside from compulsion), to reaffirm certain basic truths which seem to get lost in the shuffle from generation to generation," she has said. "If the reader is entertained, wonderful. If he learns something, that's a bonus."* Forty years after the first appearance of Yamamoto's work in a literary magazine, *Seventeen Syllables and Other Stories* was published by Women of Color Press.

"The Brown House" illustrates several themes that are characteristic of Yamamoto's work. As these themes are identified by King-Kok Cheung in her introduction to *Seventeen Syllables,* the first is "the interaction among various ethnic groups in the American West." What ethnic groups, besides Japanese Americans, do you suppose there will be in the story? The second theme is "the precarious relationship between Issei parents and their Nisei children." How delicate and difficult are the relations between the first and second generations of any immigrant group? The final theme is the hopes of first-generation Japanese immigrants in contrast to the difficulties and frustrations that they face in America. In "The Brown House," Mr. Hattori finds an escape from the difficulties and frustrations of his life in gambling. What do you suppose his problems are? Mrs. Hattori is very likely one of the "picture brides" sent from Japan to marry the Japanese bachelors who had established themselves in the U.S. What hopes do you suppose she had at the beginning of her marriage? What frustrations do you suppose she faces? And what could be the significance of the brown house?

* Quoted in Kai-yu Hsu and Helen Palubinskas, eds., *Asian American Authors* (1972).

The Brown House

In California that year the strawberries were marvelous. As large as teacups, they were so juicy and sweet that Mrs. Hattori, making her annual batch of jam, found she could cut down on the sugar considerably. "I suppose this is supposed to be the
5 compensation," she said to her husband, whom she always politely called Mr. Hattori.

"Some compensation!" Mr. Hattori answered.

At that time they were still on the best of terms. It was only later, when the season ended as it had begun, with the market
10 price for strawberries so low nobody bothered to pick number twos, that they began quarreling for the first time in their life together. What provoked the first quarrel and all the rest was that Mr. Hattori, seeing no future in strawberries, began casting around for a way to make some quick cash. Word some-
15 how came to him that there was in a neighboring town a certain house where fortunes were made overnight, and he hurried there at the first opportunity.

It happened that Mrs. Hattori and all the little Hattoris, five of them, all boys and born about a year apart, were with him
20 when he paid his first visit to the house. When he told them to wait in the car, saying he had a little business to transact inside and would return in a trice, he truly meant what he said. He intended only to give the place a brief inspection in order to familiarize himself with it. This was at two o'clock in the after-
25 noon, however, and when he finally made his way back to the car, the day was already so dim that he had to grope around a bit for the door handle.

The house was a large but simple clapboard, recently painted brown and relieved with white window frames. It sat
30 under several enormous eucalyptus trees in the foreground of a few acres of asparagus. To the rear of the house was a ramshackle barn whose spacious blue roof advertised in great yellow letters a ubiquitous brand of physic. Mrs. Hattori, peering toward the house with growing impatience, could not under-
35 stand what was keeping her husband. She watched other cars either drive into the yard or park along the highway and she saw all sorts of people—white, yellow, brown, and black—

enter the house. Seeing very few people leave, she got the idea that her husband was attending a meeting or a party.

40 So she was more curious than furious that first time when Mr. Hattori got around to returning to her and the children. To her rapid questions Mr. Hattori replied slowly, pensively: it was a gambling den run by a Chinese family under cover of asparagus, he said, and he had been winning at first, but his luck had
45 suddenly turned, and that was why he had taken so long—he had been trying to win back his original stake at least.

"How much did you lose?" Mrs. Hattori asked dully.

"Twenty-five dollars," Mr. Hattori said.

"Twenty-five dollars!" exclaimed Mrs. Hattori. "Oh, Mr.
50 Hattori, what have you done?"

At this, as though at a prearranged signal, the baby in her arms began wailing, and the four boys in the back seat began complaining of hunger. Mr. Hattori gritted his teeth and drove on. He told himself that this being assailed on all sides by
55 bawling, whimpering, and murderous glances was no less than he deserved. Never again, he said to himself; he had learned his lesson.

Nevertheless, his car, with his wife and children in it, was parked near the brown house again the following week. This
60 was because he had dreamed a repulsive dream in which a fat white snake had uncoiled and slithered about and everyone knows that a white-snake dream is a sure omen of good luck in games of chance. Even Mrs. Hattori knew this. Besides, she felt a little guilty about having nagged him so bitterly about the
65 twenty-five dollars. So Mr. Hattori entered the brown house again on condition that he would return in a half-hour, surely enough time to test the white snake. When he failed to return after an hour, Mrs. Hattori sent Joe, the oldest boy, to the front door to inquire after his father. A Chinese man came to open
70 the door of the grille, looked at Joe, said, "Sorry, no kids in here," and clacked it to.

When Joe reported back to his mother, she sent him back again and this time a Chinese woman looked out and said, "What you want, boy?" When he asked for his father, she asked
75 him to wait, then returned with him to the car, carrying a plate of Chinese cookies. Joe, munching one thick biscuit as he led her to the car, found its flavor and texture very strange; it was unlike either its American or Japanese counterpart so that he could not decide whether he liked it or not.

80 Although the woman was about Mrs. Hattori's age, she immediately called the latter "mama," assuring her that Mr. Hattori would be coming soon, very soon. Mrs. Hattori, mortified, gave excessive thanks for the cookies which she would just as soon have thrown in the woman's face. Mrs. Wu, for so

85 she introduced herself, left them after wagging her head in amazement that Mrs. Hattori, so young, should have so many children and telling her frankly, "No wonder you so skinny, mama."

"Skinny, ha!" Mrs. Hattori said to the boys. "Well, perhaps.
90 But I'd rather be skinny than fat."

Joe, looking at the comfortable figure of Mrs. Wu going up the steps of the brown house, agreed.

Again it was dark when Mr. Hattori came back to the car, but Mrs. Hattori did not say a word. Mr. Hattori made a feeble
95 joke about the unreliability of snakes, but his wife made no attempt to smile. About halfway home she said abruptly, "Please stop the machine, Mr. Hattori. I don't want to ride another inch with you."

"Now, mother . . ." Mr. Hattori said. "I've learned my lesson.
100 I swear this is the last time."

"Please stop the machine, Mr. Hattori," his wife repeated.

Of course the car kept going, so Mrs. Hattori, hugging the baby to herself with one arm, opened the door with her free hand and made as if to hop out of the moving car.

105 The car stopped with a lurch and Mr. Hattori, aghast, said, "Do you want to kill yourself?"

"That's a very good idea," Mrs. Hattori answered, one leg out of the door.

"Now, mother . . ." Mr. Hattori said. "I'm sorry; I was wrong
110 to stay so long. I promise on my word of honor never to go near that house again. Come let's go home now and get some supper."

"Supper!" said Mrs. Hattori. "Do you have any money for groceries?"

115 "I have enough for groceries," Mr. Hattori confessed.

Mrs. Hattori pulled her leg back in and pulled the door shut. "You see!" she cried triumphantly. "You see!"

The next time, Mrs. Wu brought out besides the cookies a paper sackful of Chinese firecrackers for the boys. "This is
120 America," Mrs. Wu said to Mrs. Hattori. "China and Japan have

war, all right, but (she shrugged) it's not our fault. You understand?"

Mrs. Hattori nodded, but she did not say anything because she did not feel her English up to the occasion.

125 "Never mind about the firecrackers or the war," she wanted to say. "Just inform Mr. Hattori that his family awaits without."

Suddenly Mrs. Wu, who out of the corner of her eye had been examining another car parked up the street, whispered,
130 "Cops!" and ran back into the house as fast as she could carry her amplitude. Then the windows and doors of the brown house began to spew out all kinds of people—white, yellow, brown, and black—who either got into cars and drove frantically away or ran across the street to dive into the field of tall
135 dry weeds. Before Mrs. Hattori and the boys knew what was happening, a Negro man opened the back door of their car and jumped in to crouch at the boys' feet.

The boys, who had never seen such a dark person at close range before, burst into terrified screams, and Mrs. Hattori
140 began yelling too, telling the man to get out, get out. The panting man clasped his hands together and beseeched Mrs. Hattori, "Just let me hide in here until the police go away! I'm asking you to save me from jail!"

Mrs. Hattori made a quick decision. "All right," she said in
145 her tortured English. "Go down, hide!" Then, in Japanese, she assured her sons that this man meant them no harm and ordered them to cease crying, to sit down, to behave, lest she be tempted to give them something to cry about. The policemen had been inside the house about fifteen minutes when Mr. Hat-
150 tori came out. He had been thoroughly frightened, but now he managed to appear jaunty as he told his wife how he had cleverly thrust all incriminating evidence into a nearby vase of flowers and thus escaped arrest. "They searched me and told me I could go," he said. "A lot of others weren't so lucky. One lady
155 fainted."

They were almost a mile from the brown house before the man in back said, "Thanks a million. You can let me off here."

Mr. Hattori was so surprised that the car screeched when it stopped. Mrs. Hattori hastily explained, and the man, paus-
160 ing on his way out, searched for words to emphasize his gratitude. He had always been, he said, a friend of the Japanese

people; he knew no race so cleanly, so well-mannered, so downright nice. As he slammed the door shut, he put his hand on the arm of Mr. Hattori, who was still dumfounded, and promised never to forget this act of kindness.

"What we got to remember," the man said, "is that we all got to die sometime. You might be a king in silk shirts or riding a white horse, but we all got to die sometime."

Mr. Hattori, starting up the car again, looked at his wife in reproach. "A *kurombo!*" he said. And again, "A *kurombo!*" He pretended to be victim to a shudder.

"You had no compunctions about that, Mr. Hattori," she reminded him, "when you were inside that house."

"That's different," Mr. Hattori said.

"How so?" Mrs. Hattori inquired.

The quarrel continued through supper at home, touching on a large variety of subjects. It ended in the presence of the children with Mr. Hattori beating his wife so severely that he had to take her to the doctor to have a few ribs taped. Both in their depths were dazed and shaken that things should have come to such a pass.

A few weeks after the raid the brown house opened for business as usual, and Mr. Hattori took to going there alone. He no longer waited for weekends but found all sorts of errands to go on during the week which took him in the direction of the asparagus farm. There were nights when he did not bother to come home at all.

On one such night Mrs. Hattori confided to Joe, because he was the eldest, "Sometimes I lie awake at night and wish for death to overtake me in my sleep. That would be the easiest way." In response Joe wept, principally because he felt tears were expected of him. Mrs. Hattori, deeply moved by his evident commiseration, begged his pardon for burdening his childhood with adult sorrows. Joe was in the first grade that year, and in his sleep he dreamed mostly about school. In one dream that recurred he found himself walking in nakedness and in terrible shame among his closest schoolmates.

At last Mrs. Hattori could bear it no longer and went away. She took the baby, Sam, and the boy born before him, Ed (for the record, the other two were named Bill and Ogden), to one of her sisters living in a town about thirty miles distant. Mr. Hattori was shocked and immediately went after her, but her

sister refused to let him in the house. "Monster!" this sister
said to him from the other side of the door.

Defeated, Mr. Hattori returned home to reform. He worked
passionately out in the fields from morning to night, he kept
the house spick-and-span, he fed the remaining boys the best
food he could buy, and he went out of his way to keep several
miles clear of the brown house. This went on for five days, and
on the sixth day, one of the Hattoris' nephews, the son of the
vindictive lady with whom Mrs. Hattori was taking refuge,
came to bring Mr. Hattori a message. The nephew, who was
about seventeen at the time, had started smoking cigarettes
when he was thirteen. He liked to wear his amorphous hat on
the back of his head, exposing a coiffure neatly parted in the
middle which looked less like hair than a painted wig, so
unstintingly applied was the pomade which held it together.
He kept his hands in his pockets, straddled the ground, and let
his cigarette dangle to one side of his mouth as he said to Mr.
Hattori, "Your wife's taken a powder."

The world actually turned black for an instant for Mr. Hattori as he searched giddily in his mind for another possible
interpretation of this ghastly announcement. "Poison?" he
queried, a tremor in his knees.

The nephew cackled with restraint. "Nope, you dope," he
said. "That means she's leaving your bed and board."

"Talk in Japanese," Mr. Hattori ordered, "and quit trying to
be so smart."

Abashed, the nephew took his hands out of his pockets and
assisted his meager Japanese with nervous gestures. Mrs. Hattori, he managed to convey, had decided to leave Mr. Hattori
permanently and had sent him to get Joe and Bill and Ogden.

"Tell her to go jump in the lake," Mr. Hattori said in English,
and in Japanese, "Tell her if she wants the boys, to come back
and make a home for them. That's the only way she can ever
have them."

Mrs. Hattori came back with Sam and Ed that same night,
not only because she had found she was unable to exist without her other sons but because the nephew had glimpsed certain things which indicated that her husband had seen the
light. Life for the family became very sweet then because it
had lately been so very bitter, and Mr. Hattori went nowhere
near the brown house for almost a whole month. When he did
resume his visits there, he spaced them frugally and remem-

bered (although this cost him cruel effort) to stay no longer than an hour each time.

One evening Mr. Hattori came home like a madman. He sprinted up the front porch, broke into the house with a bang, and began whirling around the parlor like a human top. Mrs. Hattori dropped her mending and the boys their toys to stare at this phenomenon.

"Yippee," said Mr. Hattori, "banzai, yippee, banzai." Thereupon, he fell dizzily to the floor.

"What is it, Mr. Hattori, are you drunk?" Mrs. Hattori asked, coming to help him up.

"Better than that, mother," Mr. Hattori said, pushing her back to her chair. It was then they noticed that he was holding a brown paper bag in one hand. And from this bag, with the exaggerated ceremony of a magician pulling rabbits from a hat, he began to draw out stack after stack of green bills. These he deposited deliberately, one by one, on Mrs. Hattori's tense lap until the sack was empty and she was buried under a pile of money.

"Explain . . ." Mrs. Hattori gasped.

"I won it! In the lottery! Two thousand dollars! We're rich!" Mr. Hattori explained.

There was a hard silence in the room as everyone looked at the treasure on Mrs. Hattori's lap. Mr. Hattori gazed raptly, the boys blinked in bewilderment, and Mrs. Hattori's eyes bulged a little. Suddenly, without warning, Mrs. Hattori leaped up and vigorously brushed off the front of her clothing, letting the stacks fall where they might. For a moment she clamped her lips together fiercely and glared at her husband. But there was no wisp of steam that curled out from her nostrils and disappeared toward the ceiling; this was just a fleeting illusion that Mr. Hattori had. Then, "You have no conception, Mr. Hattori!" she hissed. "You have absolutely no conception!"

Mr. Hattori was resolute in refusing to burn the money, and Mrs. Hattori eventually adjusted herself to his keeping it. Thus, they increased their property by a new car, a new rug, and their first washing machine. Since these purchases were all made on the convenient installment plan and the two thousand dollars somehow melted away before they were aware of it, the car and the washing machine were claimed by a collection agency after a few months. The rug remained, however, as it

was a fairly cheap one and had already eroded away in spots to show the bare weave beneath. By that time it had become
290 an old habit for Mrs. Hattori and the boys to wait outside the brown house in their original car and for Joe to be commissioned periodically to go to the front door to ask for his father. Joe and his brothers did not mind the long experience too much because they had acquired a taste for Chinese cookies.
295 Nor, really, did Mrs. Hattori, who was pregnant again. After a fashion, she became quite attached to Mrs. Wu who, on her part, decided she had never before encountered a woman with such bleak eyes.

[1951]

Uncommon Words or Meanings

a clapboard ("a large but simple *clapboard*")—a wooden house with the outer walls covered by overlapping long narrow boards.

physic ("brand of *physic*")—an old-fashioned term for medicine.

a den ("it was a gambling *den*")—a secret meeting-place, where people meet for illegal activities.

to be up to ("did not feel her English [was] *up to* the occasion")—(idiom) to be adequate.

a stake ("trying to win back his original *stake*")—money risked, an amount placed on a bet.

to spew ("began to *spew* out all kinds of people")—to send out in a stream.

a *kurombo* (". . . looked at his wife in reproach. "A *kurombo!*" he said.")—(Japanese) a derogatory term for a Negro.

pomade ("so unstintingly applied was the *pomade*")—a perfumed cream for the hair and scalp.

banzai ("'*banzai,* yippee, *banzai*'")—a Japanese battle cry.

a lottery ("'I won it! In the *lottery*'")—an activity whose outcome depends on fate rather than chance or skill, often used to select winners of prizes.

bleak ("with such *bleak* eyes")—without hope.

Love

"'A snake is an enemy to me,' my father snapped. 'I hate a snake.'"

Love

Jesse Stuart
(1907–1984)

Jesse Stuart—a farmer, teacher, and master story-teller—was born in a log cabin in the foothills of the Appalachian Mountains in eastern Kentucky, one of the poor-est parts of the United States. Stuart's mother had two years of schooling; his father was a coal miner and farmer who never had the opportunity to learn to read or write. Jesse Stuart was the first in his family to finish high school, and he then worked his way through college. But he remained true to his roots, returning to live on the land where he had been raised and celebrating his life and the lives of those around him in fifty-seven books of poetry and prose.

"I am a farmer singing at the plow," Stuart wrote in one of his early poems. Before that, he had also been a teacher. It wasn't an easy job, for the Kentucky public school system paid the lowest wages in the country and the parents were suspicious of anything to do with education. But the pupils were eager and Stuart knew from experience that education was essential to break out of poverty. In a rural high school, Stuart was expected to teach everything from Latin to alge-bra, so he often had to work hard to keep ahead of his pupils. In the third week of Stuart's first year of teaching, a pupil came to him for help with an algebra problem. Stuart looked at the problem, then laughed and truthfully said that he couldn't work it. "Mr. Stuart, I understand," the boy responded earnestly. "You want your pupils to work these problems, don't you?" The boy then happily solved the problem by himself and brought it back. "I knew he was right after I had seen it worked," Stuart wrote in his autobiographical memoir, *The Thread that Runs So True* (1949). "But Billie Leonard never knew that I couldn't actually work this problem."

To support a wife and family, Stuart had to give up full-time teaching in favor of farming. But he continued writing and in 1937 won a Guggenheim Fellowship that enabled him to spend a year living in Scotland (his ancestral home) and visiting twenty-five other countries. Stuart also taught in poetry and writing programs at several American colleges, and he spent the 1960-61 academic year as a visiting professor of English at the American University in Cairo.

"Love" is characteristic of Stuart's work in being told in the first-person and using the "talk style" of American folklore. Just as urban writers use the names of real streets to provide a sense of reality, so Stuart names specific plants and tools and animals to present the harsh reality and great beauty of an Appalachian hill-country farm. This story also reflects Stuart's love and respect for the hill country and its people, as well as his mountain-man's easy acceptance of death as part of the natural world. Mitch Stuart held the same attitudes, as we see in this passage from *God's Oddling* (1960), Stuart's biography of his father, who also may have provided the idea for "Love":

> "A blacksnake is a pretty thing," he once said to me, "so shiny and black in the spring sun after he sheds his winter skin."
>
> He was the first man I ever heard say a snake was pretty. I never forgot his saying it. I can even remember the sumac thicket where he saw the blacksnake.*

A love story about a snake? Read on.

* From *God's Oddling* (1960), as reprinted in *A Jesse Stuart Reader* (1963).

Love

Yesterday when the bright sun blazed down on the wilted corn my father and I walked around the edge of the new ground to plan a fence. The cows kept coming through the chestnut oaks on the cliff and running over the young corn. They bit off
5 the tips of the corn and trampled down the stubble.

My father walked in the cornbalk. Bob, our Collie, walked in front of my father. We heard a ground squirrel whistle down over the bluff among the dead treetops at the clearing's edge. "Whoop, take him, Bob," said my father. He lifted up a young
10 stalk of corn, with wilted dried roots, where the ground squirrel had dug it up for the sweet grain of corn left on its tender roots. This has been a dry spring and the corn has kept well in the earth where the grain has sprouted. The ground squirrels love this corn. They dig up rows of it and eat the sweet grains. The
15 young corn stalks are killed and we have to replant the corn.

I could see my father keep sicking Bob after the ground squirrel. He jumped over the corn rows. He started to run toward the ground squirrel. I, too, started running toward the clearing's edge where Bob was jumping and barking. The dust
20 flew in tiny swirls behind our feet. There was a big cloud of dust behind us.

"It's a big bull blacksnake," said my father. "Kill him, Bob! Kill him, Bob!"

Bob was jumping and snapping at the snake so as to make
25 it strike and throw itself off guard. Bob has killed twenty-eight copperheads this spring. He knows how to kill a snake. He doesn't rush to do it. He takes his time and does the job well.

"Let's don't kill the snake," I said. "A blacksnake is a harmless snake. It kills poison snakes. It kills the copperhead. It
30 catches more mice from the fields than a cat."

I could see the snake didn't want to fight the dog. The snake wanted to get away. Bob wouldn't let it. I wondered why it was crawling toward a heap of black loamy earth at the bench of the hill. I wondered why it had come from the chest-
35 nut oak sprouts and the matted greenbriars on the cliff. I looked as the snake lifted its pretty head in response to one of Bob's jumps. "It's not a bull blacksnake," I said. "It's a she-snake. Look at the white on her throat."

"A snake is an enemy to me," my father snapped. "I hate a
40 snake. Kill it, Bob. Go in there and get that snake and quit playing with it!"

Bob obeyed my father. I hated to see him take this snake
by the throat. She was so beautifully poised in the sunlight.
Bob grabbed the white patch on her throat. He cracked her
45 long body like an ox whip in the wind. He cracked it against
the wind only. The blood spurted from her fine-curved throat.
Something hit against my legs like pellets. Bob threw the
snake down. I looked to see what had struck my legs. It was
snake eggs. Bob had slung them from her body. She was going
50 to the sand heap to lay her eggs, where the sun is the setting-
hen that warms them and hatches them.

Bob grabbed her body there on the earth where the red
blood was running down on the gray-piled loam. Her body was
still writhing in pain. She acted like a greenweed held over a
55 new-ground fire. Bob slung her viciously many times. He
cracked her limp body against the wind. She was now limber
as a shoestring in the wind. Bob threw her riddled body back
on the sand. She quivered like a leaf in the lazy wind, then her
riddled body lay perfectly still. The blood covered the loamy
60 earth around the snake.

"Look at the eggs, won't you?" said my father. We counted
thirty-seven eggs. I picked an egg up and held it in my hand.
Only a minute ago there was life in it. It was an immature seed.
It would not hatch. Mother sun could not incubate it on the
65 warm earth. The egg I held in my hand was almost the size of a
quail's egg. The shell on it was thin and tough and the egg
appeared under the surface to be a watery egg.

"Well, Bob, I guess you see now why this snake couldn't
fight," I said. "It is life. Stronger devour the weaker even
70 among human beings. Dog kills snake. Snake kills birds. Birds
kill the butterflies. Man conquers all. Man, too, kills for sport."

Bob was panting. He walked ahead of us back to the
house. His tongue was out of his mouth. He was tired. He was
hot under his shaggy coat of hair. His tongue nearly touched
75 the dry dirt and white flecks of foam dripped from it. We
walked toward the house. Neither my father nor I spoke. I still
thought of the dead snake. The sun was going down over the
chestnut ridge. A lark was singing. It was late for a lark to sing.
The red evening clouds floated above the pine trees on our
80 pasture hill. My father stood beside the path. His black hair

was moved by the wind. His face was red in the blue wind of day. His eyes looked toward the sinking sun.

"And my father hates a snake," I thought.

I thought about the agony women know of giving birth. I thought about how they will fight to save their children. Then, I thought of the snake. I thought it was silly of me to think such thoughts.

This morning my father and I got up with the chickens. He says one has to get up with the chickens to do a day's work. We got the posthole digger, ax, spud, measuring pole and the mattock. We started for the clearing's edge. Bob didn't go along.

The dew was on the corn. My father walked behind with the posthole digger across his shoulder. I walked in front. The wind was blowing. It was a good morning wind to breathe and a wind that makes one feel like he can get under the edge of a hill and heave the whole hill upside down.

I walked out the corn row where we had come yesterday afternoon. I looked in front of me. I saw something. I saw it move. It was moving like a huge black rope winds around a windlass. "Steady," I says to my father. "Here is the bull blacksnake." He took one step up beside me and stood. His eyes grew wide apart.

"What do you know about this," he said.

"You have seen the bull blacksnake now," I said. "Take a good look at him! He is lying beside his dead mate. He has come to her. He, perhaps, was on her trail yesterday."

The male snake had trailed her to her doom. He had come in the night, under the roof of stars, as the moon shed rays of light on the quivering clouds of green. He had found his lover dead. He was coiled beside her, and she was dead.

The bull blacksnake lifted his head and followed us as we walked around the dead snake. He would have fought us to his death. He would have fought Bob to his death. "Take a stick," said my father, "and throw him over the hill so Bob won't find him. Did to you ever see anything to beat that? I've heard they'd do that. But this is my first time to see it." I took a stick and threw him over the bank into the dewy sprouts on the cliff.

[1940]

new ground ("the edge of the *new ground*")—land that hasn't ever been cultivated.

a cornbalk ("walked in the *cornbalk*")—rows of planted corn.

bull ("a big *bull* blacksnake")—male (animal).

a copperhead ("killed twenty-eight *copperheads*")—a poisonous snake.

a bench ("at the *bench* of the hill")—a level, narrow stretch of land.

a greenweed ("like a *greenweed* held over a new-ground fire")—a small shrub with yellow flowers that shrivels and twists when thrown on a fire.

a pellet ("hit against my legs like *pellets*")—a small piece of lead for a shotgun.

riddled ("threw her *riddled* body")—filled with holes.

a quail ("about the size of a *quail's* egg")—a game bird whose eggs are about one-third the size of a chicken's egg.

to get up with the chickens ("This morning my father and I *got up with the chickens*.")—to get up as the sun is rising.

posthole digger, ax, spud, measuring pole, mattock ("We got the *posthole digger, ax, spud, measuring pole* and the *mattock*.")—tools used in building a fence.

I says ("'Steady,' *I says* to my father.")—a storyteller's shift to "historic present" tense for dramatic emphasis; "I says," suggesting a challenge, is also common in that context.

to beat ("'Did you ever see anything to *beat* that?'")—(informal) to excel or surpass.

The Use of Force

"... it was up to

me to tell them;

that's why they

were spending

three dollars on

me."

The Use of Force

William Carlos Williams
(1883–1963)

William Carlos Williams was born and raised in Rutherford, New Jersey. He was the son of an international marriage—his father was an Englishman who traveled in Europe and Latin America as a sales representative for an American drug company; his mother came from a well-to-do Puerto Rican family. Williams attended preparatory schools in New York and Switzerland, then studied to become a doctor, like his mother's brother Carlos, for whom he was named. After graduating from the University of Pennsylvania Medical School, Williams returned to his hometown as a school doctor and general practitioner. In that capacity, Williams held office hours in the morning and evening; in the afternoon, he visited schools and made house calls to see sick patients. When Williams went to Leipzig, Germany, to study for the new specialty in pediatrics (the medical care of infants and children), he joked that he was specializing to cut down on his practice.

While working more than full-time as a school and family doctor, Williams was also becoming one of the most prolific of twentieth-century American authors. He published his first volume of poems at the age of twenty-three, and in his lifetime published six hundred poems, fifty-two short stories, four novels, an opera libretto, and *The Autobiography of William Carlos Williams* (1951), as well as other non-fiction works. He found the energy to do his writing at night and at odd moments during the day, explaining that in concentrating on his patients' illnesses he "became *them*," allowing his own self to rest. "For the moment, I myself did not exist. Nothing of myself affected me. As a consequence, I came back to myself, as from any other sleep, rested."

"The Use of Force" is one of Williams' thirteen stories based directly on his experiences as a small town doctor, visiting a family that he hasn't met before.* The family doesn't have much money (the kitchen is the only room in the house that is heated) and they are suspicious of doctors. Yet they fear that their daughter may have diphtheria, which has already been diagnosed in other children in her school. In the 1930s, when the story first appeared, readers would have recognized the signs and danger of that highly contagious disease. Diphtheria normally begins with a coating of membrane in the throat. While some forms of the disease are mild, most are severe and can result in heart failure in as little as three days.

The story forcefully exemplifies Williams' comment in his *Autobiography* that "though I might be attracted or repelled, the professional attitude which every physician must call on would steady me, dictate the terms on which I was to proceed." The doctor in the story is steady in his approach. Yet in the *Autobiography,* Williams continues: "Many a time a man must watch the patient's mind as it watches him, distrusting him, ..." In "The Use of Force," he shows what the challenge of a strong patient's distrust may trigger in a doctor, who is, after all, a human being like any other.

*These stories, together with six doctor-related poems and a description of his practice from Williams' *Autobiography,* have been collected by Robert Coles in *William Carlos Williams: The Doctor Stories* (1984).

The Use of Force

They were new patients to me, all I had was the name, Olson. Please come down as soon as you can, my daughter is very sick.

When I arrived I was met by the mother, a big startled look-
5   ing woman, very clean and apologetic who merely said, Is this the doctor? and let me in. In the back, she added. You must excuse us, doctor, we have her in the kitchen where it is warm. It is very damp here sometimes.

The child was fully dressed and sitting on her father's lap
10   near the kitchen table. He tried to get up, but I motioned for him not to bother, took off my overcoat and started to look things over. I could see that they were all very nervous, eyeing me up and down distrustfully. As often, in such cases, they weren't telling me more than they had to, it was up to me to tell
15   them; that's why they were spending three dollars on me.

The child was fairly eating me up with her cold, steady eyes, and no expression to her face whatever. She did not move and seemed, inwardly, quiet; an unusually attractive little thing, and as strong as a heifer in appearance. But her face was
20   flushed, she was breathing rapidly, and I realized that she had a high fever. She had magnificent blond hair, in profusion. One of those picture children often reproduced in advertising leaflets and the photogravure sections of the Sunday papers.

She's had a fever for three days, began the father and we
25   don't know what it comes from. My wife has given her things, you know, like people do, but it don't do no good. And there's been a lot of sickness around. So we tho't you'd better look her over and tell us what is the matter.

As doctors often do I took a trial shot at it as a point of
30   departure. Has she had a sore throat?

Both parents answered me together, No . . . No, she says her throat don't hurt her.

Does your throat hurt you? added the mother to the child. But the little girl's expression didn't change nor did she move
35   her eyes from my face.

Have you looked?

I tried to, said the mother, but I couldn't see.

As it happens we had been having a number of cases of diphtheria in the school to which this child went during that month and we were all, quite apparently, thinking of that, though no one had as yet spoken of the thing.

Well, I said, suppose we take a look at the throat first. I smiled in my best professional manner and asking for the child's first name I said, come on, Mathilda, open your mouth and let's take a look at your throat.

Nothing doing.

Aw, come on, I coaxed, just open your mouth wide and let me take a look. Look, I said, opening both hands wide, I haven't anything in my hands. Just open up and let me see.

Such a nice man, put in the mother. Look how kind he is to you. Come on, do what he tells you to. He won't hurt you.

At that I ground my teeth in disgust. If only they wouldn't use the word "hurt" I might be able to get somewhere. But I did not allow myself to be hurried or disturbed but speaking quietly and slowly I approached the child again.

As I moved my chair a little nearer suddenly with one cat-like movement both her hands clawed instinctively for my eyes and she almost reached them too. In fact she knocked my glasses flying and they fell, though unbroken, several feet away from me on the kitchen floor.

Both the mother and father almost turned themselves inside out in embarrassment and apology. You bad girl, said the mother, taking her and shaking her by one arm. Look what you've done. The nice man . . .

For heaven's sake, I broke in. Don't call me a nice man to her. I'm here to look at her throat on the chance that she might have diphtheria and possibly die of it. But that's nothing to her. Look here, I said to the child, we're going to look at your throat. You're old enough to understand what I'm saying. Will you open it now by yourself or shall we have to open it for you?

Not a move. Even her expression hadn't changed. Her breaths however were coming faster and faster. Then the battle began. I had to do it. I had to have a throat culture for her own protection. But first I told the parents that it was entirely up to them. I explained the danger but said that I would not insist on a throat examination so long as they would take the responsibility.

If you don't do what the doctor says you'll have to go to the hospital, the mother admonished her severely.

80   Oh yeah? I had to smile to myself. After all, I had already fallen in love with the savage brat, the parents were contemptible to me. In the ensuing struggle they grew more and more abject, crushed, and exhausted while she surely rose to magnificent heights of insane fury of effort bred of her terror
85   of me.

The father tried his best, and he was a big man but the fact that she was his daughter, his shame at her behavior and his dread of hurting her made him release her just at the critical moment several times when I had almost achieved success, till
90   I wanted to kill him. But his dread also that she might have diphtheria made him tell me to go on, go on though he himself was almost fainting, while the mother moved back and forth behind us raising and lowering her hands in an agony of apprehension.

Put her in front of you on your lap, I ordered, and hold
95   both her wrists.

But as soon as he did the child let out a scream. Don't, you're hurting me. Let go of my hands. Let them go I tell you. Then she shrieked terrifyingly, hysterically. Stop it! Stop it! You're killing me!
100   Do you think she can stand it, doctor! said the mother.

You get out, said the husband to his wife. Do you want her to die of diphtheria?

Come on now, hold her, I said.

Then I grasped the child's head with my left hand and tried
105   to get the wooden tongue depressor between her teeth. She fought, with clenched teeth, desperately! But now I also had grown furious—at a child. I tried to hold myself down but I couldn't. I know how to expose a throat for inspection. And I did my best. When finally I got the wooden spatula behind the last
110   teeth and just the point of it into the mouth cavity, she opened up for an instant but before I could see anything she came down again and gripping the wooden blade between her molars she reduced it to splinters before I could get it out again.

Aren't you ashamed, the mother yelled at her. Aren't you
115   ashamed to act like that in front of the doctor?

Get me a smooth-handled spoon of some sort, I told the mother. We're going through with this. The child's mouth was already bleeding. Her tongue was cut and she was screaming in wild hysterical shrieks. Perhaps I should have desisted and

120 come back in an hour or more. No doubt it would have been better. But I have seen at least two children lying dead in bed of neglect in such cases, and feeling that I must get a diagnosis now or never I went at it again. But the worst of it was that I too had got beyond reason. I could have torn the child apart in

125 my own fury and enjoyed it. It was a pleasure to attack her. My face was burning with it.

The damned little brat must be protected against her own idiocy, one says to oneself at such times. Others must be protected against her. It is a social necessity. And all these things

130 are true. But a blind fury, a feeling of adult shame, bred of a longing for muscular release are the operatives. One goes on to the end.

In a final unreasoning assault I overpowered the child's neck and jaws. I forced the heavy silver spoon back of her

135 teeth and down her throat till she gagged. And there it was— both tonsils covered with membrane. She had fought valiantly to keep me from knowing her secret. She had been hiding that sore throat for three days at least and lying to her parents in order to escape just such an outcome as this.

140 Now truly she *was* furious. She had been on the defensive before but now she attacked. Tried to get off her father's lap and fly at me while tears of defeat blinded her eyes.

[1938]

Uncommon Words or Meanings

to eye (someone) up and down ("*eyeing* me *up and down* distrustfully")—(idiom) to look at (someone) carefully from head to foot.

to be up to (someone) ("it *was up to* me to tell them")—to be (someone's) responsibility.

photogravure ("the *photogravure* sections of the Sunday paper")—a printing process for reproducing pictures in color, recently invented at the time of the story.

tho't ("we *tho't* you'd better look her over")—"thought."

to look (someone) over ("we tho't you'd better *look* her *over*")—to examine.

to take a trial shot ("I *took a trial shot* at it")—(idiom) to make a first attempt at something.

a point of departure ("I took a trial shot at it as a *point of departure*")—a starting point, here for a diagnosis.

Nothing doing (". . . let's take a look at your throat. *Nothing doing.*")—(informal) a flat refusal; a firm "no."

aw ("*Aw*, come on, I coaxed")—an interjection, here used to be persuasive.

ground ("At that I *ground* my teeth in disgust.")—past tense of **grind,** to rub together with great pressure.

a culture ("I had to have a throat *culture* for her own protection.")—a sample of tissue to be examined for infection.

Oh yeah ("*Oh yeah?* I had to smile to myself.")—(idiom) casual pronunciation of "Oh, yes?" to show disbelief in what has just been said.

abject ("they grew more and more *abject,* crushed, and exhausted")—deserving contempt.

bred ("insane fury of effort *bred* of her terror of me")—past participle of **breed,** to be caused or produced by (something).

an operative ("a blind fury, a feeling of adult shame . . . are the *operatives*")—an essential factor in causing an action.

to gag ("down her throat till she *gagged*")—to choke because the throat is closing involuntarily.

The Lottery

"Bobby Martin

had already

stuffed his

pockets full of

stones."

The Lottery

Shirley Jackson
(1919–1965)

For most of her life (she died in her sleep at the age of forty-eight), Shirley Jackson felt like an outsider. As a child in San Francisco, she felt that her glamorous, socially ambitious mother was disappointed to have a plain, awkward daughter. As an adult married to a brilliant literary critic who taught at an expensive woman's college in Vermont, Jackson felt that her husband's colleagues and students saw her only as a plain, overweight faculty wife. She also felt that the townspeople of North Bennington, where they lived, regarded her as an outsider on many counts—she was from California, she was a woman writer, she was married to a New York Jewish intellectual, and they were associated with the college. Increasing her sense of "otherness" was Jackson's deep interest in witchcraft and her belief that she had supernatural powers.

Shirley Jackson also had a good mind, a quick sense of humor, and a great gift for writing. She turned her experiences in raising four lively children into humorous short stories, among them "Charles" (1948), and novels such as *Life Among the Savages* (1953). Jackson turned her fears of the outside world into chilling works of fiction, including the novel *We Have Always Lived in the Castle* (1962) and her most famous work, "The Lottery" (1948). The story came to her, she later said, one spring day on her way home from the morning grocery shopping. She was moving slowly because in addition to being four months pregnant, Jackson was pushing her two-year-old up the steep hill in a stroller while carrying two bags of groceries. But when she got home, she rapidly put away the groceries, settled the baby in the playpen, and sat down to write the story. By the time her five-year-old came home for lunch, the story was done. Jackson made a few minor changes that evening, then mailed the story to her literary agent in New York. *The New Yorker* quickly accepted it, asking only that the date of the lottery be made to coincide with the date of the issue in which it would appear—June 27.*

The story is set in a small New England farming community. As in North Bennington, a town common (common grazing land in Colonial times) is used for civic gatherings. Every year the townspeople hold a lottery—an activity in which people randomly draw "lots" to determine a winner. What do you suppose the prize will be? The setting and characters in the story seem realistic but the action, rather than being a factual report of a real event, is a portrayal of human nature. What aspects of human nature do you suppose it will show?

Evidently many readers recognize a part of themselves that they would rather not see. "The Lottery" brought the largest volume of mail that *The New Yorker* had ever received on a story, as well as puzzled and angry letters to Jackson's home—more than three hundred letters in all. Subsequently "The Lottery" has been dramatized for radio and TV, has been the subject of a ballet, and is regularly reprinted in anthologies. It is a story that a reader never forgets.

* Jackson recounts this in "Biography of a Story," a lecture reprinted in her posthumous collection *Come Along with Me,* edited by her husband, Stanley Edgar Hyman (1968). A carefully-documented and sympathetic treatment of Jackson's life can be found in Judy Oppenheimer, *Private Demons: The Life of Shirley Jackson* (1988).

The Lottery

The morning of June 27th was clear and sunny, with the fresh warmth of a full-summer day; the flowers were blossoming profusely and the grass was richly green. The people of the village began to gather in the square, between the post office and the bank, around ten o'clock; in some towns there were so many people that the lottery took two days and had to be started on June 26th, but in this village, where there were only about three hundred people, the whole lottery took less than two hours, so it could begin at ten o'clock in the morning and still be through in time to allow the villagers to get home for noon dinner.

The children assembled first, of course. School was recently over for the summer, and the feeling of liberty sat uneasily on most of them; they tended to gather together quietly for a while before they broke into boisterous play, and their talk was still of the classroom and the teacher, of books and reprimands. Bobby Martin had already stuffed his pockets full of stones, and the other boys soon followed his example, selecting the smoothest and roundest stones; Bobby and Harry Jones and Dicky Delacroix—the villagers pronounced this name "Dellacroy"— eventually made a great pile of stones in one corner of the square and guarded it against the raids of the other boys. The girls stood aside, talking among themselves, looking over their shoulders at the boys, and the very small children rolled in the dust or clung to the hands of their older brothers or sisters.

Soon the men began to gather, surveying their children, speaking of planting and rain, tractors and taxes. They stood together, away from the pile of stones in the corner, and their jokes were quiet and they smiled rather than laughed. The women, wearing faded house dresses and sweaters, came shortly after their menfolk. They greeted one another and exchanged bits of gossip as they went to join their husbands. Soon the women, standing by their husbands, began to call their children, and the children came reluctantly, having to be called four or five times. Bobby Martin ducked under his mother's grasping hand and ran, laughing, back to the pile of stones. His father spoke up sharply, and Bobby came quickly and took his place between his father and his oldest brother.

The lottery was conducted—as were the square dances, the teen-age club, the Halloween program—by Mr. Summers, who had time and energy to devote to civic activities. He was a round-faced jovial man and he ran the coal business, and people were sorry for him, because he had no children and his wife was a scold. When he arrived in the square, carrying the black wooden box, there was a murmur of conversation among the villagers, and he waved and called, "Little late today, folks." The postmaster, Mr. Graves, followed him, carrying a three-legged stool, and the stool was put in the center of the square and Mr. Summers set the black box down on it. The villagers kept their distance, leaving a space between them and the stool, and when Mr. Summers said, "Some of you fellows want to give me a hand?" there was a hesitation before two men, Mr. Martin and his oldest son, Baxter, came forward to hold the box steady on the stool while Mr. Summers stirred up the papers inside.

The original paraphernalia for the lottery had been lost long ago, and the black box now resting on the stool had been put into use even before Old Man Warner, the oldest man in town, was born. Mr. Summers spoke frequently to the villagers about making a new box, but no one liked to upset even as much tradition as was represented by the black box. There was a story that the present box had been made with some pieces from the box that had preceded it, the one that had been constructed when the first people settled down to make a village here. Every year, after the lottery, Mr. Summers began talking again about a new box, but every year the subject was allowed to fade off without anything's being done. The black box grew shabbier each year; by now it was no longer completely black but splintered badly along one side to show the original wood color, and in some places faded or stained.

Mr. Martin and his oldest son, Baxter, held the black box securely on the stool until Mr. Summers had stirred the papers thoroughly with his hand. Because so much of the ritual had been forgotten or discarded, Mr. Summers had been successful in having slips of paper substituted for the chips of wood that had been used for generations. Chips of wood, Mr. Summers had argued, had been all very well when the village was tiny, but now that the population was more than three hundred and likely to keep growing, it was necessary to use something that would fit more easily into the black box. The night before the lottery, Mr. Summers and Mr. Graves made up the slips of

paper and put them in the box, and it was then taken to the safe of Mr. Summers' coal company and locked up until Mr. Summers was ready to take it to the square the next morning. The rest of the year, the box was put away, sometimes one
85 place, sometimes another; it had spent one year in Mr. Graves' barn and another year underfoot in the post office, and sometimes it was set on a shelf in the Martin grocery and left there.

There was a great deal of fussing to be done before Mr. Summers declared the lottery open. There were the lists to
90 make up—of heads of families, heads of households in each family, members of each household in each family. There was the proper swearing-in of Mr. Summers by the postmaster, as the official of the lottery; at one time, some people remembered, there had been a recital of some sort, performed by the
95 official of the lottery, a perfunctory, tuneless chant that had been rattled off duly each year; some people believed that the official of the lottery used to stand just so when he said or sang it, others believed that he was supposed to walk among the people, but years and years ago this part of the ritual had been
100 allowed to lapse. There had been, also, a ritual salute, which the official of the lottery had had to use in addressing each person who came up to draw from the box, but this also had changed with time, until now it was felt necessary only for the official to speak to each person approaching. Mr. Summers
105 was very good at all this; in his clean white shirt and blue jeans, with one hand resting carelessly on the black box, he seemed very proper and important as he talked interminably to Mr. Graves and the Martins.

Just as Mr. Summers finally left off talking and turned to
110 the assembled villagers, Mrs. Hutchinson came hurriedly along the path to the square, her sweater thrown over her shoulders, and slid into place at the back of the crowd. "Clean forgot what day it was," she said to Mrs. Delacroix, who stood next to her, and they both laughed softly. "Thought my old man was
115 out back stacking wood," Mrs. Hutchinson went on, "and then I looked and the kids was gone and then I remembered it was the twenty-seventh and came a-running." She dried her hands on her apron, and Mrs. Delacroix said, "You're in time, though. They're still talking away up there."
120 Mrs. Hutchinson craned her neck to see through the crowd and found her husband and children standing near the front.

She tapped Mrs. Delacroix on the arm as a farewell and began to make her way through the crowd. The people separated good-humoredly to let her through; two or three people said, in voices just loud enough to be heard across the crowd, "Here comes your Missus, Hutchinson," and "Bill, she made it after all." Mrs. Hutchinson reached her husband, and Mr. Summers, who had been waiting, said cheerfully, "Thought we were going to have to get on without you, Tessie." Mrs. Hutchinson said, grinning, "Wouldn't have me leave m'dishes in the sink, now, would you, Joe?" and soft laughter ran through the crowd as the people stirred back into position after Mrs. Hutchinson's arrival.

"Well, now," Mr. Summers said soberly, "guess we better get started, get this over with, so's we can go back to work. Anybody ain't here?"

"Dunbar," several people said. "Dunbar, Dunbar."

Mr. Summers consulted his list. "Clyde Dunbar," he said. "That's right. He's broke his leg, hasn't he? Who's drawing for him?"

"Me, I guess," a woman said, and Mr. Summers turned to look at her. "Wife draws for her husband," Mr. Summers said. "Don't you have a grown boy to do it for you, Janey?" Although Mr. Summers and everyone else in the village knew the answer perfectly well, it was the business of the official of the lottery to ask such questions formally. Mr. Summers waited with an expression of polite interest while Mrs. Dunbar answered.

"Horace's not but sixteen yet," Mrs. Dunbar said regretfully. "Guess I gotta fill in for the old man this year."

"Right," Mr. Summers said. He made a note on the list he was holding. Then he asked, "Watson boy drawing this year?"

A tall boy in the crowd raised his hand. "Here," he said. "I'm drawing for m'mother and me." He blinked his eyes nervously and ducked his head as several voices in the crowd said things like "Good fellow, Jack," and "Glad to see your mother's got a man to do it."

"Well," Mr. Summers said, "guess that's everyone. Old Man Warner make it?" "Here," a voice said, and Mr. Summers nodded.

A sudden hush fell on the crowd as Mr. Summers cleared his throat and looked at the list. "All ready?" he called. "Now, I'll read the names of heads of families first and the men come up and take a paper out of the box. Keep the paper folded in your hand without looking at it until everyone has had a turn, everything clear?"

165   The people had done it so many times that they only half listened to the directions; most of them were quiet, wetting their lips, not looking around. Then Mr. Summers raised one hand high and said, "Adams." A man disengaged himself from the crowd and came forward. "Hi, Steve," Mr. Summers said,

170   and Mr. Adams said, "Hi, Joe." They grinned at one another humorlessly and nervously. Then Mr. Adams reached into the black box and took out a folded paper. He held it firmly by one corner as he turned and went hastily back to his place in the crowd, where he stood a little apart from his family, not look-

175   ing down at his hand.

"Allen," Mr. Summers said. "Anderson. . . . Bentham."

"Seems like there's no time at all between lotteries any more," Mrs. Delacroix said to Mrs. Graves in the back row. "Seems like we got through the last one only last week."

180   "Time sure goes fast," Mrs. Graves said.

"Clark. . . . Delacroix."

"There goes my old man," Mrs. Delacroix said. She held her breath while her husband went forward.

"Dunbar," Mr. Summers said, and Mrs. Dunbar went

185   steadily to the box while one of the woman said, "Go on, Janey," and another said, "There she goes."

"We're next," Mrs. Graves said. She watched while Mr. Graves came around from the side of the box, greeted Mr. Summers gravely, and selected a slip of paper from the box. By

190   now, all through the crowd there were men holding the small folded papers in their large hands, turning them over and over nervously. Mrs. Dunbar and her two sons stood together, Mrs. Dunbar holding the slip of paper.

"Harburt. . . . Hutchinson."

195   "Get up there, Bill," Mrs. Hutchinson said, and the people near her laughed.

"Jones."

"They do say," Mr. Adams said to Old Man Warner, who stood next to him, "that over in the north village they're talk-

200   ing of giving up the lottery."

Old Man Warner snorted. "Pack of crazy fools," he said. "Listening to the young folks, nothing's good enough for *them*. Next thing you know, they'll be wanting to go back to living in

caves, nobody work any more, live *that* way for a while. Used
to be a saying about 'Lottery in June, corn be heavy soon.' First
thing you know, we'd all be eating stewed chickweed and
acorns. There's *always* been a lottery," he added petulantly.
"Bad enough to see young Joe Summers up there joking with
everybody."

"Some places have already quit lotteries," Mrs. Adams said.

"Nothing but trouble in that," Old Man Warner said stoutly.
"Pack of young fools."

"Martin." And Bobby Martin watched his father go forward.
"Overdyke. . . . Percy."

"I wish they'd hurry," Mrs. Dunbar said to her older son. "I
wish they'd hurry."

"They're almost through," her son said.

"You get ready to run tell Dad," Mrs. Dunbar said.

Mr. Summers called his own name and then stepped forward precisely and selected a slip from the box. Then he
called, "Warner."

"Seventy-seventh year I been in the lottery," Old Man
Warner said as he went through the crowd. "Seventy-seventh
time."

"Watson." The tall boy came awkwardly through the crowd.
Someone said, "Don't be nervous, Jack," and Mr. Summers said,
"Take your time, son."

"Zanini."

After that, there was a long pause, a breathless pause, until
Mr. Summers, holding his slip of paper in the air, said, "All
right, fellows." For a minute, no one moved, and then all the
slips of paper were opened. Suddenly, all the women began to
speak at once, saying, "Who is it?" "Who's got it?" "Is it the
Dunbars?" "Is it the Watsons?" Then the voices began to say,
"It's Hutchinson. It's Bill," "Bill Hutchinson's got it."

"Go tell your father," Mrs. Dunbar said to her older son.

People began to look around to see the Hutchinsons. Bill
Hutchinson was standing quiet, staring down at the paper in his
hand. Suddenly, Tessie Hutchinson shouted to Mr. Summers,
"You didn't give him time enough to take any paper he wanted.
I saw you. It wasn't fair!"

"Be a good sport, Tessie," Mrs. Delacroix called, and Mrs.
Graves said, "All of us took the same chance."

"Shut up, Tessie," Bill Hutchinson said.

245 "Well, everyone," Mr. Summers said, "that was done pretty fast, and now we've got to be hurrying a little more to get done in time." He consulted his next list. "Bill," he said, "you draw for the Hutchinson family. You got any other households in the Hutchinsons?"

250 "There's Don and Eva," Mrs. Hutchinson yelled. "Make *them* take their chance!"

"Daughters draw with their husbands' families, Tessie," Mr. Summers said gently. "You know that as well as anyone else."

"It wasn't *fair*," Tessie said.

255 "I guess not, Joe," Bill Hutchinson said regretfully. "My daughter draws with her husband's family, that's only fair. And I've got no other family except the kids."

"Then, as far as drawing for families is concerned, it's you," Mr. Summers said in explanation, "and as far as drawing for 260 households is concerned, that's you, too. Right?"

"Right," Bill Hutchinson said.

"How many kids, Bill?" Mr. Summers asked formally.

"Three," Bill Hutchinson said. "There's Bill, Jr., and Nancy, and little Dave. And Tessie and me."

265 "All right, then," Mr. Summers said. "Harry, you got their tickets back?"

Mr. Graves nodded and held up the slips of paper. "Put them in the box, then," Mr. Summers directed. "Take Bill's and put it in."

270 "I think we ought to start over," Mrs. Hutchinson said, as quietly as she could. "I tell you it wasn't *fair*. You didn't give him time enough to choose. *Every*body saw that."

Mr. Graves had selected the five slips and put them in the box, and he dropped all the papers but those onto the ground, 275 where the breeze caught them and lifted off.

"Listen, everybody," Mrs. Hutchinson was saying to the people around her.

"Ready, Bill?" Mr. Summers asked, and Bill Hutchinson, with one quick glance around at his wife and his children, nodded.

280 "Remember," Mr. Summers said, "take the slips and keep them folded until each person has taken one. Harry, you help little Dave." Mr. Graves took the hand of the little boy, who came willingly with him up to the box. "Take a paper out of the box, Davy," Mr. Summers said. Davy put his hand into the 285 box and laughed. "Take just *one* paper," Mr. Summers said.

"Harry, you hold it for him." Mr. Graves took the child's hand and removed the folded paper from the tight fist and held it while little Dave stood next to him and looked up at him wonderingly.

290 "Nancy next," Mr. Summers said. Nancy was twelve, and her school friends breathed heavily as she went forward, switching her skirt, and took a slip daintily from the box. "Bill, Jr.," Mr. Summers said, and Billy, his face red and his feet over-large, nearly knocked the box over as he got a paper out.

295 "Tessie," Mr. Summers said. She hesitated for a minute, looking around defiantly, and then set her lips and went up to the box. She snatched a paper out and held it behind her.

"Bill," Mr. Summers said, and Bill Hutchinson reached into the box and felt around, bringing his hand out at last with the

300 slip of paper in it.

The crowd was quiet. A girl whispered, "I hope it's not Nancy," and the sound of the whisper reached the edges of the crowd.

"It's not the way it used to be," Old Man Warner said

305 clearly. "People ain't the way they used to be."

"All right," Mr. Summers said. "Open the papers. Harry, you open little Dave's."

Mr. Graves opened the slip of paper and there was a general sigh through the crowd as he held it up and everyone

310 could see that it was blank. Nancy and Bill, Jr., opened theirs at the same time, and both beamed and laughed, turning around to the crowd and holding their slips of paper above their heads.

"Tessie," Mr. Summers said. There was a pause, and then

315 Mr. Summers looked at Bill Hutchinson, and Bill unfolded his paper and showed it. It was blank.

"It's Tessie," Mr. Summers said, and his voice was hushed. "Show us her paper, Bill."

Bill Hutchinson went over to his wife and forced the slip of

320 paper out of her hand. It had a black spot on it, the black spot Mr. Summers had made the night before with the heavy pencil in the coal-company office. Bill Hutchinson held it up, and there was a stir in the crowd.

"All right, folks," Mr. Summers said. "Let's finish quickly."

325 Although the villagers had forgotten the ritual and lost the original black box, they still remembered to use stones. The pile of stones the boys had made earlier was ready; there were

stones on the ground with the blowing scraps of paper that had come out of the box. Mrs. Delacroix selected a stone so large that she had to pick it up with both hands and turned to Mrs. Dunbar. "Come on," she said. "Hurry up."

Mrs. Dunbar had small stones in both hands, and she said, gasping for breath, "I can't run at all. You'll have to go ahead and I'll catch up with you."

The children had stones already, and someone gave little Davy Hutchinson a few pebbles.

Tessie Hutchinson was in the center of a cleared space by now, and she held her hands out desperately as the villagers moved in on her. "It isn't fair," she said. A stone hit her on the side of the head.

Old Man Warner was saying, "Come on, come on, everyone." Steve Adams was in the front of the crowd of villagers, with Mrs. Graves beside him.

"It isn't fair, it isn't right," Mrs. Hutchinson screamed, and then they were upon her.

[1948]

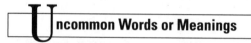

Uncommon Words or Meanings

a house dress ("faded *house dresses*")—an inexpensive cotton dress worn for working at home.

a recital ("a *recital* of some sort")—something said aloud from memory; a recitation.

a chant ("tuneless *chant*")—a monotonous, rhythmic recitation.

to lapse ("this part . . . had been allowed to *lapse*")—to pass away by neglect.

(someone's) old man ("'Thought my *old man* was out back'")—(informal) husband.

Missus ("'Here comes your *Missus*, Hutchinson.'")—(informal) wife.

stoutly ("said *stoutly*")—with determination.

a good sport ("'Be a *good sport,* Tessie'")—(idiom) someone who plays (a game) fairly and is willing to accept defeat without complaining.

A Blizzard Under Blue Sky

"When everything

in your life is

uncertain, there's

nothing quite like

the clarity and

precision of fresh

snow and blue

sky."

A Blizzard Under Blue Sky

Pam Houston
(born 1962)

Pam Houston has taught creative writing at Denison University in Ohio, where she completed her undergraduate studies, and her short stories have appeared in various literary magazines. Presently completing her doctoral studies at the University of Utah, Houston is also part of the world of women's fashion magazines as a contributing editor for *Elle* and a frequent contributor to *Mirabella* and *Mademoiselle*. For a number of years, Houston has also worked part-time as a river guide and hunting guide in the western United States and has written about those activities for the publications *Outside* and *Travel and Leisure*.

Houston's interest in the outdoors forms the core of the stories in *Cowboys Are My Weakness* (1992), stories that have been described as "exhilarating, like a swift ride through river rapids," as well as "beautifully written and funny." In "A Blizzard Under Blue Sky," the exhilaration comes from sharing a winter adventure in the foothills of the Rocky Mountains, while the beauty of the writing is exemplified by this magical description of snow: "[it] stopped being simply white and became translucent, hinting at other colors, reflections of purples and blues and grays." Much of the humor in the story is based on the American fondness for believing that pets think and act like humans. Another feature of Houston's style is that she reflects her generation's habit of referring to items by brand names. She also sometimes teases by not directly identifying a character's gender, using a name that could be either a man's or a woman's and letting a simple pronoun do the work, perhaps contradicting the reader's expectations.

A heavy snowstorm with high winds, the "blizzard" of the title, matches the narrator's mood at the beginning of the story. She tells us that "everyone in Park City," a resort area near Salt Lake City, Utah, was happy except her. Could that be literally true, or is she exaggerating to make fun of herself? What could have caused such self-pity and depression? And what do you suppose she did about it? How did she find the "blue sky" that is the proverbial symbol of happiness?

A Blizzard Under Blue Sky

The doctor said I was clinically depressed. It was February, the month in which depression runs rampant in the inversion-cloaked Salt Lake Valley and the city dwellers escape to Park City, where the snow is fresh and the sun is shining and
5 everybody is happy, except me. In truth, my life was on the verge of more spectacular and satisfying discoveries than I had ever imagined, but of course I couldn't see that far ahead. What I saw was work that wasn't getting done, bills that weren't getting paid, and a man I'd given my heart to week-
10 ending in the desert with his ex.

The doctor said, "I can give you drugs."

I said, "No way."

She said, "The machine that drives you is broken. You need something to help you get it fixed."

15 I said, "Winter camping."

She said, "Whatever floats your boat."

One of the things I love the most about the natural world is the way it gives you what's good for you even if you don't know it at the time. I had never been winter camping before, at least
20 not in the high country, and the weekend I chose to try and fix my machine was the same weekend the air mass they called the Alaska Clipper showed up. It was thirty-two degrees below zero in town on the night I spent in my snow cave. I don't know how cold it was out on Beaver Creek. I had listened to the
25 weather forecast, and to the advice of my housemate, Alex, who was an experienced winter camper.

"I don't know what you think you're going to prove by freezing to death," Alex said, "but if you've got to go, take my bivvy sack; it's warmer than anything you have."

30 "Thanks." I said.

"If you mix Kool-Aid with your water it won't freeze up," he said, "and don't forget lighting paste for your stove."

"Okay," I said.

"I hope it turns out to be worth it," he said, "because you
35 are going to freeze your butt."

When everything in your life is uncertain, there's nothing

quite like the clarity and precision of fresh snow and blue sky. That was the first thought I had on Saturday morning as I stepped away from the warmth of my truck and let my skis slap the snow in front of me. There was no wind and no clouds that morning, just still air and cold sunshine. The hair in my nostrils froze almost immediately. When I took a deep breath, my lungs only filled up halfway.

I opened the tailgate to excited whines and whimpers. I never go skiing without Jackson and Hailey: my two best friends, my yin and yang of dogs. Some of you might know Jackson. He's the oversized sheepdog-and-something-else with the great big nose and the bark that will shatter glass. He gets out and about more than I do. People I've never seen before come by my house daily and call him by name. He's all grace, and he's tireless; he won't go skiing with me unless I let him lead. Hailey is not so graceful, and her body seems in constant indecision when she runs. When we ski she stays behind me, and on the downhills she tries to sneak rides on my skis.

The dogs ran circles in the chest-high snow while I inventoried my backpack one more time to make sure I had everything I needed. My sleeping bag, my Thermarest, my stove, Alex's bivvy sack, matches, lighting paste, flashlight, knife. I brought three pairs of long underwear—tops and bottoms—so I could change once before I went to bed, and once again in the morning, so I wouldn't get chilled by my own sweat. I brought paper and pen, and Kool-Aid to mix with my water. I brought Mountain House chicken stew and some freeze-dried green peas, some peanut butter and honey, lots of dried apricots, coffee and Carnation instant breakfast for morning.

Jackson stood very still while I adjusted his backpack. He carries the dog food and enough water for all of us. He takes himself very seriously when he's got his pack on. He won't step off the trail for any reason, not even to chase rabbits, and he gets nervous and angry if I do. That morning he was impatient with me. "Miles to go, Mom," he said over his shoulder. I snapped my boots into my skis and we were off.

There are not too many good things you can say about temperatures that dip past twenty below zero, except this: They turn the landscape into a crystal palace and they turn your vision into Superman's. In the cold thin morning air the trees

and mountains, even the twigs and shadows, seemed to leap
out of the background like a 3-D movie, only it was better than
3-D because I could feel the sharpness of the air.

80   I have a friend in Moab who swears that Utah is the center
of the fourth dimension, and although I know he has in mind
something much different and more complicated than subzero
weather, it was there, on that ice-edged morning, that I felt on
the verge of seeing something more than depth perception in

85 the brutal clarity of the morning sun.

    As I kicked along the first couple of miles, I noticed the sun
crawling higher in the sky and yet the day wasn't really warming, and I wondered if I should have brought another vest,
another layer to put between me and the cold night ahead.

90   It was utterly quiet out there, and what minimal noise we
made intruded on the morning like a brass band: the squeaking
of my bindings, the slosh of the water in Jackson's pack, the
whoosh of nylon, the jangle of dog tags. It was the bass line
and percussion to some primal song, and I kept wanting to

95 sing to it, but I didn't know the words.

    Jackson and I crested the top of a hill and stopped to wait
for Hailey. The trail stretched out as far as we could see into
the meadow below us and beyond, a double track and pole
plants carving through softer trails of rabbit and deer.

100   "Nice place," I said to Jackson, and his tail thumped the
snow underneath him without sound.

    We stopped for lunch near something that looked like it
could be a lake in its other life, or maybe just a womb-shaped
meadow. I made peanut butter and honey sandwiches for all of

105 us, and we opened the apricots.

    "It's fabulous here," I told the dogs. "But so far it's not
working."

    There had never been anything wrong with my life that a
few good days in the wilderness wouldn't cure, but there I sat

110 in the middle of all those crystal-coated trees, all that dia-
mond-studded sunshine, and I didn't feel any better. Apparently clinical depression was not like having a bad day, it
wasn't even like having a lot of bad days, it was more like a
house of mirrors, it was like being in a room full of one-way

115 glass.

    "Come on, Mom," Jackson said. "Ski harder, go faster,
climb higher."

    Hailey turned her belly to the sun and groaned.

"He's right," I told her. "It's all we can do."

120 After lunch the sun had moved behind our backs, throwing a whole different light on the path ahead of us. The snow we moved through stopped being simply white and became translucent, hinting at other colors, reflections of blues and purples and grays. I thought of Moby Dick, you know, the

125 whiteness of the whale, where white is really the absence of all color, and whiteness equals truth, and Ahab's search is finally futile, as he finds nothing but his own reflection.

"Put your mind where your skis are," Jackson said, and we made considerably better time after that.

130 The sun was getting quite low in the sky when I asked Jackson if he thought we should stop to build the snow cave, and he said he'd look for the next good bank. About one hundred yards down the trail we found it, a gentle slope with eastern exposure that didn't look like it would cave in under any

135 circumstances. Jackson started to dig first.

Let me make one thing clear. I knew only slightly more about building snow caves than Jackson, having never built one, and all my knowledge coming from disaster tales of winter camping fatalities. I knew several things *not* to do when

140 building a snow cave, but I was having a hard time knowing what exactly to do. But Jackson helped, and Hailey supervised, and before too long we had a little cave built, just big enough for three. We ate dinner quite pleased with our accomplishments and set the bivvy sack up inside the cave just as the

145 sun slipped away and dusk came over Beaver Creek.

The temperature, which hadn't exactly soared during the day, dropped twenty degrees in as many minutes, and suddenly it didn't seem like such a great idea to change my long underwear. The original plan was to sleep with the dogs inside

150 the bivvy sack but outside the sleeping bag, which was okay with Jackson the super-metabolizer, but not so with Hailey, the couch potato. She whined and wriggled and managed to stuff her entire fat body down inside my mummy bag, and Jackson stretched out full-length on top.

155 One of the unfortunate things about winter camping is that it has to happen when the days are so short. Fourteen hours is a long time to lie in a snow cave under the most perfect of circumstances. And when it's thirty-two below, or forty, fourteen hours seems like weeks.

160   I wish I could tell you I dropped right off to sleep. In truth, fear crept into my spine with the cold and I never closed my eyes. Cuddled there, amid my dogs and water bottles, I spent half of the night chastising myself for thinking I was Wonder Woman, not only risking my own life but the lives of my dogs,
165   and other half trying to keep the numbness in my feet from crawling up to my knees. When I did doze off, I'd come back to my senses wondering if I had frozen to death, but the alternating pain and numbness that started in my extremities and worked its way into my bones convinced me I must still be alive.

170   It was a clear night, and every now and again I would poke my head out of its nest of down and nylon to watch the progress of the moon across the sky. There is no doubt that it was longest and most uncomfortable night of my life.

But then the sky began to get gray, and then it began to get
175   pink, and before too long the sun was on my bivvy sack, not warm, exactly, but holding the promise of warmth later in the day. And I ate apricots and drank Kool-Aid-flavored coffee and celebrated the rebirth of my fingers and toes, and the survival of many more important parts of my body. I sang "Rocky
180   Mountain High" and "If I Had a Hammer," and yodeled and whistled, and even danced the two-stop with Jackson and let him lick my face. And when Hailey finally emerged from the sleeping bag a full hour after I did, we shared a peanut butter and honey sandwich and she said nothing ever tasted so good.

185   We broke camp and packed up and kicked in the snow cave with something resembling glee.

I was five miles down the trail before I realized what had happened. Not once in that fourteen-hour night did I think about deadlines, or bills, or the man in the desert. For the first
190   time in many months I was happy to see a day beginning. The morning sunshine was like a present from the gods. What really happened, of course, is that I remembered about joy.

I know that one night out at thirty-two below doesn't sound like much to those of you who have climbed Everest or
195   run the Iditarod or kayaked to Antarctica, and I won't try to convince you that my life was like the movies where depression goes away in one weekend, and all of life's problems vanish with a moment's clear sight. The simple truth of the matter is this: On Sunday I had a glimpse outside of the house of mir-
200   rors, on Saturday I couldn't have seen my way out of a paper bag. And while I was skiing back toward the truck that morning,

a wind came up behind us and swirled the snow around our bodies like a blizzard under blue sky. And I was struck by the simple perfection of the snowflakes, and startled by the hopefulness of sun on frozen trees.

205

[1992]

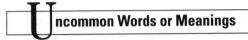

Uncommon Words or Meanings

clinically depressed ("The doctor said I was *clinically depressed.*")—suffering from a severe and continuing feeling of deep sadness.

to run rampant ("the month in which depression *runs rampant*")—to grow without limit.

an inversion ("the *inversion*-cloaked Salt Lake Valley")—an increase in air temperature with elevation that traps particles of dust and smoke at lower altitudes.

an ex ("weekending in the desert with his *ex*")—(informal) a previous romantic partner.

a housemate ("my *housemate,* Alex")—someone who shares the living space in a house.

a bivvy sack ("take my *bivvy sack*")—a large canvas bag.

Kool-Aid ("mix *Kool-Aid* with your water")—a brand of sugar and flavoring to be mixed with water to make a drink.

lighting paste ("don't forget *lighting paste* for your stove")—a sticky, flammable substance used to help wet wood burn.

a butt ("you are going to freeze your *butt*")—(informal) buttocks, the fleshy part of the body that one sits on.

yin and yang ("my *yin and yang* of dogs")—(Chinese philosophy) **yin,** the negative element, represents the female qualities of darkness and the sky; **yang,** the positive element, represents the male qualities of light and the earth.

a Thermarest ("My sleeping bag, my *Thermarest,* my stove")—a brand of inflatable, insulated mattress.

Mountain House ("*Mountain House* chicken stew")—a brand of freeze-dried food, eaten after boiling water is added.

Carnation instant breakfast (*"Carnation instant breakfast* for morning"*)—a brand of powered milk with flavoring and nutrients added, drunk after being mixed with water.

Miles to go (*"Miles to go,* Mom."*)—an **allusion** (an indirect reference) to the closing lines of the poem "Stopping by Woods on a Snowy Evening" by Robert Frost: "But I have promises to keep, / And miles to go before I sleep, / And miles to go before I sleep."

the fourth dimension ("swears that Utah is the center of the *fourth dimension*")—something beyond length, breadth, and thickness (height, width, and depth); usually taken to be time.

bindings ("the squeaking of my *bindings*")—the foot fastenings on a ski.

a dog tag (the jangle of *dog tags*")—a small metal disk attached to a dog's collar to identify the dog's owner.

primal ("the bass line and percussion of some *primal* song")—from the time of the first humans.

Moby Dick ("I thought of *Moby Dick,* you know, the whiteness of the whale")—in Herman Melville's 19th-century novel of the same name, a huge white whale pursued by Captain Ahab.

a fatality ("winter camping *fatalities*")—an accidental death.

couch potato ("not so with Hailey, the *couch potato*")—(slang) the sort of person who likes best to sit on a couch while watching TV and eating.

a mummy bag ("inside my *mummy bag*")—a sleeping bag that is wider at the head than at the foot.

to chastise ("I spent half the night *chastising* myself ")—to criticize severely.

Wonder Woman ("thinking I was *Wonder Woman*")—a comic book character with superhuman powers.

the Iditarod ("run the *Iditarod*")—the annual 1,200-mile Alaskan dog sled race from Anchorage to Nome.

to kayak ("*kayaked* to Antarctica")—to travel in a kayak, a light single-seat boat propelled with a double paddle.

The Sentinel

"... it was that

haunting doubt

that had driven

me forward. Well,

it was a doubt no

longer, but the

haunting had

scarcely begun."

The Sentinel

Arthur C. Clarke
(born 1917)

Known for his ability to explain scientific ideas clearly and accurately to a popular audience, Arthur C. Clarke is even more famous as a master of science fiction whose work has been translated into more than thirty languages. He was born during the First World War in an English seaside town and fell in love with science fiction as a boy. When he left school at the age of sixteen and took a civil service job, reading and writing science fiction remained his hobby. Then, in what he has described as "probably the most decisive act of my entire life," Clarke gave up his safe job to enlist in the British Royal Air Force at the beginning of World War II. While training to be a radar instructor, he taught himself mathematics and electronic theory and continued writing.

Clarke is unique as a science fiction writer, for he has not only dreamed of what could be but has specified how it could be done. In 1945, for example, he explained how a satellite could be placed in synchronous orbit to receive and retransmit radio signals; eighteen years later, when the communications satellite became a reality, Clarke was honored for conceiving the idea. After the war, he earned a college degree in physics and pure and applied mathematics and became an editor for a technical journal. Soon, however, the success of his books *The Exploration of Space* (1952) and *Childhood's End* (1953) enabled Clarke to give up the editing job to concentrate on his own writing. While primarily known for his science fiction works, Clarke has also written on underwater diving (an interest that led him to build a home on the Indian Ocean) and scientific mysteries.

Clarke's fiction often deals with themes of exploration and discovery, always firmly grounded in scientific possibility. For example, in "The Sentinel," published in 1951, a party of scientists exploring the moon have chosen the same landing site as that used eighteen years later by real-life American astronauts. Clarke makes readers feel the wonder of scientific inquiry as the narrator describes an unexpected discovery, but Clarke also enables readers to recognize their own reality with details such as breakfast sausages.

In the early 1960s, Clarke became a Hollywood screen writer when film director Stanley Kubrick asked him to collaborate on a science fiction movie. The script, which was four years in development, drew in part on "The Sentinel," the pyramidal structure turning into a black monolith. The result, which has been called "the most important science fiction film ever made," was *2001: A Space Odyssey.* This film about the voyage of the spaceship *Discovery,* under the control of the computer HAL 9000, appeared in 1968. The next year, the American astronaut Neil Armstrong took what he called "one small step for man, one giant leap for mankind" when he left the ladder of his spacecraft to set foot on the moon's powdery surface. Except that the powder proved to be thicker than Clarke had imagined and that there is no moisture to produce hoarfrost, the moon's surface is much as described it in "The Sentinel." Yes, this story is by an Englishman who now lives in Sri Lanka. But as the songwriter Paul Simon says in "American Tune," the United States is "the ship that sailed the moon." And until someone else plants their flag there, we're going to claim the story.

The Sentinel

The next time you see the full moon high in the south, look carefully at its right-hand edge and let your eye travel upward along the curve of the disk. Round about two o'clock you will notice a small, dark oval: anyone with normal eyesight can find
5   it quite easily. It is the great walled plain, one of the finest on the Moon, know as the Mare Crisium—the Sea of Crises. Three hundred miles in diameter, and almost completely surrounded by a ring of magnificent mountains, it had never been explored until we entered it in the late summer of 1996.
10   Our expedition was a large one. We had two heavy freighters which had flown our supplies and equipment from the main lunar base in the Mare Serenitatis; five hundred miles away. There were also three small rockets which were intended for short-range transport over regions which our sur-
15   face vehicles couldn't cross. Luckily, most of the Mare Crisium is very flat. There are none of the great crevasses so common and so dangerous elsewhere, and very few craters or mountains of any size. As far as we could tell, our powerful caterpillar tractors would have no difficulty in taking us wherever we
20   wished to go.
I was geologist—or selenologist, if you want to be pedantic—in charge of the group exploring the southern region of Mare. We had crossed a hundred miles of it in a week, skirting the foothills of the mountains along the shore of what was
25   once the ancient sea, some thousand million years before. When life was beginning on Earth, it was already dying here. The waters were retreating down the flanks of those stupendous cliffs, retreating into the empty heart of the Moon. Over the land which we were crossing, the tideless ocean had once
30   been half a mile deep, and now the only trace of moisture was the hoarfrost one could sometimes find in caves which the searing sunlight never penetrated.
We had begun our journey early in the slow lunar dawn, and still had almost a week of Earth-time before nightfall. Half
35   a dozen times a day we would leave our vehicle and go outside in the space suits to hunt for interesting minerals, or to place markers for the guidance of future travelers. It was an

Arthur C. Clarke

uneventful routine. There is nothing hazardous or even particularly exciting about lunar exploration. We could live comfortably for a month in our pressurized tractors, and if we ran into trouble, we could always radio for help and sit tight until one of the spaceships came to our rescue.

I said just now that there was nothing exciting about lunar exploration, but of course that isn't true. One could never grow tired of those incredible mountains, so much more rugged than the gentle hills of Earth. We never knew, as we rounded the capes and promontories of that vanished sea, what new splendors would be revealed to us. The whole southern curve of the Mare Crisium is a vast delta where a score of rivers once found their way into the ocean, fed perhaps by the torrential rains that must have lashed the mountains in the brief volcanic age when the Moon was young. Each of these ancient valleys was an invitation, challenging us to climb into the unknown uplands beyond. But we had a hundred miles still to cover, and could only look longingly at the heights which others must scale.

We kept Earth-time aboard the tractor, and precisely at 22:00 hours the final radio message would be sent out to Base and we would close down for the day. Outside, the rocks would still be burning beneath the almost vertical sun, but to us it would be night until we awoke again eight hours later. Then one of us would prepare breakfast, there would be a great buzzing of electric razors, and someone would switch on the shortwave radio from Earth. Indeed, when the smell of frying sausages began to fill the cabin, it was sometimes hard to believe that we were not back on our own world—everything was so normal and homely, apart from the feeling of decreased weight and the unnatural slowness with which objects fell.

It was my turn to prepare breakfast in the corner of the main cabin that served as a galley. I can remember that moment quite vividly after all these years, for the radio had just played one of my favorite melodies, the old Welsh air "David of the White Rock." Our driver was already outside in his space suit, inspecting our caterpillar treads. My assistant, Louis Garnett, was up forward in the control position, making some belated entries in yesterday's log.

As I stood by the frying pan, waiting, like any terrestrial housewife, for the sausages to brown, I let my gaze wander idly over the mountain walls which covered the whole of the

southern horizon, marching out of sight to east and west
80 below the curve of the Moon. They seemed only a mile or two
from the tractor, but I knew that the nearest was twenty miles
away. On the Moon, of course, there is no loss of detail with
distance—none of that almost imperceptible haziness which
softens and sometimes transfigures all far-off things on Earth.
85   Those mountains were ten thousand feet high, and they
climbed steeply out of the plain as if ages ago some subter-
ranean eruption had smashed them skyward through the
molten crust. The base of even the nearest was hidden from
sight by the steeply curving surface of the plain, for the Moon
90 is a very little world, and from where I was standing the horizon was only two miles away.
        I lifted my eyes toward the peaks which no man had ever
climbed, the peaks which, before the coming of terrestrial life,
had watched the retreating oceans sink sullenly into their
95 graves, taking with them the hope and the morning promise of
a world. The sunlight was beating against those ramparts with
a glare that hurt the eyes, yet only a little way above them the
stars were shining steadily in a sky blacker than a winter midnight on Earth.
100   I was turning away when my eye caught a metallic glitter
high on the ridge of a great promontory thrusting out into the
sea thirty miles to the west. It was a dimensionless point of
light, as if a star had been clawed from the sky by one of those
cruel peaks, and I imagined that some smooth rock surface
105 was catching the sunlight and heliographing it straight into my
eyes. Such things were not uncommon. When the Moon is in
her second quarter, observers on Earth can sometimes see the
great ranges in the Oceanus Procellarum burning with a blue-
white iridescence as the sunlight flashes from their slopes and
110 leaps again from world to world. But I was curious to know
what kind of rock could be shining so brightly up there, and I
climbed into the observation turret and swung our four-inch
telescope round to the west.
        I could see just enough to tantalize me. Clear and sharp in
115 the field of vision, the mountain peaks seemed only half a mile
away, but whatever was catching the sunlight was still too small
to be resolved. Yet it seemed to have an elusive symmetry, and
the summit upon which it rested was curiously flat. I stared for
a long time at that glittering enigma, straining my eyes into

120 space, until presently a smell of burning from the galley told me
that our breakfast sausages had made their quarter-million-mile
journey in vain.

All that morning we argued our way across the Mare Crisium while the western mountains reared higher in the sky.
125 Even when we were out prospecting in the space suits, the discussion would continue over the radio. It was absolutely certain, my companions argued, that there had never been any
form of intelligent life on the Moon. The only living things that
had ever existed there were a few primitive plants and their
130 slightly less degenerate ancestors. I knew that as well as anyone, but there are times when a scientist must not be afraid to
make a fool of himself.

"Listen," I said at last, "I'm going up there, if only for my
own peace of mind. That mountain's less than twelve thousand
135 feet high—that's only two thousand under Earth gravity—and
I can make the trip in twenty hours at the outside. I've always
wanted to go up into those hills, anyway, and this gives me an
excellent excuse."

"If you don't break your neck," said Garnett, "you'll be the
140 laughingstock of the expedition when we get back to Base. That
mountain will probably be called Wilson's Folly from now on."

"I won't break my neck," I said firmly. "Who was the first
man to climb Pico and Helicon?"

"But weren't you rather younger in those days?" asked
145 Louis gently.

"That," I said with great dignity, "is as good a reason as
any for going."

We went to bed early that night, after driving the tractor
to within half a mile of the promontory. Garnett was coming
150 with me in the morning; he was a good climber, and had often
been with me on such exploits before. Our driver was only too
glad to be left in charge of the machine.

At first sight, those cliffs seemed completely unscalable,
but to anyone with a good head for heights, climbing is easy on
155 a world where all weights are only a sixth of their normal value.
The real danger in lunar mountaineering lies in overconfidence;
a six-hundred-foot drop on the Moon can kill you just as thoroughly as a hundred-foot fall on Earth.

We made our first halt on a wide ledge about four thou-
160 sand feet above the plain. Climbing had not been very difficult,

but my limbs were stiff with the unaccustomed effort, and I was glad of the rest. We could still see the tractor as a tiny metal insect far down at the foot of the cliff, and we reported our progress to the driver before starting on the next ascent.

165   Inside our suits it was comfortably cool, for the refrigeration units were fighting the fierce sun and carrying away the body heat of our exertions. We seldom spoke to each other, except to pass climbing instructions and to discuss our best plan of ascent. I do not know what Garnett was thinking, prob-
170   ably that this was the craziest goose chase he had ever embarked upon. I more than half agreed with him, but the joy of climbing, the knowledge that no man had ever gone this way before, and the exhilaration of the steadily widening landscape gave me all the reward I needed.

175   I don't think I was particularly excited when I saw in front of us the wall of rock I had first inspected through the telescope from thirty miles away. It would level off about fifty feet above our heads, and there on the plateau would be the thing that had lured me over these barren wastes. It would be,
180   almost certainly, nothing more than a boulder splintered ages ago by a falling meteor, and with its cleavage planes still fresh and bright in this incorruptible, unchanging silence.

There were no handholds on the rock face, and we had to use a grapnel. My tired arms seemed to gain new strength as I
185   swung the three-pronged metal anchor round my head and sent it sailing up toward the stars. The first time it broke loose and came falling slowly back when we pulled the rope. On the third attempt, the prongs gripped firmly and our combined weights could not shift it.

190   Garnett looked at me anxiously. I could tell that he wanted to go first, but I smiled back at him through the glass of my helmet and shook my head. Slowly, taking my time, I began the final ascent.

Even with my space suit, I weighed only forty pounds
195   here, so I pulled myself up hand over hand without bothering to use my feet. At the rim I paused and waved to my companion, then I scrambled over the edge and stood upright, staring ahead of me.

You must understand that until this very moment I had
200   been almost completely convinced that there could be nothing strange or unusual for me to find here. Almost, but not quite; it

was that haunting doubt that had driven me forward. Well, it was doubt no longer, but the haunting had scarcely begun.

205 I was standing on a plateau perhaps a hundred feet across. It had once been smooth—too smooth to be natural—but falling meteors had pitted and scored its surface through immeasurable eons. It had been leveled to support a glittering, roughly pyramidal structure, twice as high as a man, that was set in the rock like a gigantic, many faceted jewel.

210 Probably no emotion at all filled my mind in those first few seconds. Then I felt a great lifting of my heart, and a strange, inexpressible joy. For I loved the Moon, and now I knew that the creeping moss of Aristarchus and Eratosthenes was not the only life she had brought forth in her youth. The

215 old, discredited dream of the first explorers was true. There had, after all, been a lunar civilization—and I was the first to find it. That I had come perhaps a hundred million years too late did not distress me; it was enough to have come at all.

My mind was beginning to function normally, to analyze

220 and to ask questions. Was this a building, a shrine—or something for which my language had no name? If a building, then why was it erected in so uniquely inaccessible a spot? I wondered it if might be a temple, and I could picture the adepts of some strange priesthood calling on their gods to preserve

225 them as the life of the Moon ebbed with the dying oceans, and calling on their gods in vain.

I took a dozen steps forward to examine the thing more closely, but some sense of caution kept me from going too near. I knew a little of archaeology, and tried to guess the cul-

230 tural level of the civilization that must have smoothed this mountain and raised the glittering mirror surfaces that still dazzled my eyes.

The Egyptians could have done it, I thought, if their workmen had possessed whatever strange materials these far more

235 ancient architects had used. Because of the thing's smallness, it did not occur to me that I might be looking at the handiwork of a race more advanced than my own. The idea that the Moon had possessed intelligence at all was still almost too tremendous to grasp, and my pride would not let me take the final,

240 humiliating plunge.

And then I noticed something that set the scalp crawling at the back of my neck—something so trivial and so innocent that many would never have noticed it at all. I have said that the plateau was scarred by meteors; it was also coated inches deep with the cosmic dust that is always filtering down upon the surface of any world where there are no winds to disturb it. Yet the dust and the meteor scratches ended quite abruptly in a wide circle enclosing the little pyramid as though an invisible wall was protecting it from the ravages of time and the slow but ceaseless bombardment from space.

There was someone shouting in my earphones, and I realized that Garnett had been calling me for some time. I walked unsteadily to the edge of the cliff and signaled him to join me, not trusting myself to speak. Then I went back toward that circle in the dust. I picked up a fragment of splintered rock and tossed it gently toward the shining enigma. If the pebble had vanished at that invisible barrier, I should not have been surprised, but it seemed to hit a smooth, hemispheric surface and slide gently to the ground.

I knew then that I was looking at nothing that could be matched in the antiquity of my own race. This was not a building, but a machine, protecting itself with forces that had challenged Eternity. Those forces, whatever they might be, were still operating, and perhaps I had already come too close. I thought of all the radiations man had trapped and tamed in the past century. For all I knew, I might be as irrevocably doomed as if I had stepped into the deadly, silent aura of an unshielded atomic pile.

I remember turning then toward Garnett, who had joined me and was now standing motionless at my side. He seemed quite oblivious to me, so I did not disturb him but walked to the edge of the cliff in an effort to marshal my thoughts. There below me lay the Mare Crisium—Sea of Crises, indeed—strange and weird to most men, but reassuringly familiar to me. I lifted my eyes toward the crescent Earth, lying in her cradle of stars, and I wondered what her clouds had covered when these unknown builders had finished their work. Was it the steaming jungle of the Carboniferous, the bleak shoreline over which the first amphibians must crawl to conquer the land—or, earlier still, the long loneliness before the coming of life?

Do not ask me why I did not guess the truth sooner—the truth that seems so obvious now. In the first excitement of my discovery, I had assumed without question that this crystalline apparition had been built by some race belonging to the Moon's remote past, but suddenly, and with overwhelming force, the belief came to me that it was as alien to the Moon as I myself.

In twenty years we had found no trace of life but a few degenerate plants. No lunar civilization, whatever its doom, could have left but a single token of its existence.

I looked at the shining pyramid again, and the more I looked the more remote it seemed from anything that had to do with the Moon. And suddenly I felt myself shaking with a foolish, hysterical laughter, brought on by excitement and overexertion: for I had imagined that the little pyramid was speaking to me and was saying, "Sorry, I'm a stranger here myself."

It has taken us twenty years to crack that invisible shield and to reach the machine inside those crystal walls. What we could not understand, we broke at last with the savage might of atomic power and now I have seen the fragments of the lovely, glittering thing I found up there on the mountain.

They are meaningless. The mechanisms—if indeed they are mechanisms—of the pyramid belong to a technology that lies far beyond our horizon, perhaps to the technology of paraphysical forces.

The mystery haunts us all the more now that the other planets have been reached and we know that only Earth has ever been the home of intelligent life in our Universe. Nor could any lost civilization of our own world have built that machine, for the thickness of the meteoric dust on the plateau has enabled us to measure its age. It was set there upon its mountain before life had emerged from the seas of Earth.

When our world was half its present age, *something* from the stars swept through the Solar System, left this token of its passage, and went again upon its way. Until we destroyed it, that machine was still fulfilling the purpose of its builders; and as to that purpose, here is my guess.

Nearly a hundred thousand million stars are turning in the circle of the Milky Way, and long ago other races on the worlds of other suns must have scaled and passed the heights that we have reached. Think of such civilizations, far back in time against the fading afterglow of Creation, masters of a universe so young that life as yet had come only to a handful of worlds. Theirs would have been a loneliness we cannot imagine, the loneliness of gods looking out across infinity and finding none to share their thoughts.

They must have searched the star clusters as we have searched the planets. Everywhere there would be worlds, but they would be empty or peopled with crawling, mindless things. Such was our own Earth, the smoke of the great volcanoes still staining the skies, when that first ship of the peoples of the dawn came sliding in from the abyss beyond Pluto. It passed the frozen outer worlds, knowing that life could play no part in their destinies. It came to rest among the inner planets, warming themselves around the fire of the Sun and waiting for their stories to begin.

Those wanderers must have looked on Earth, circling safely in the narrow zone between fire and ice, and must have guessed that it was the favorite of the Sun's children. Here, in the distant future, would be intelligence; but there were countless stars before them still, and they might never come this way again.

So they left a sentinel, one of millions they scattered throughout the Universe, watching over all worlds with the promise of life. It was a beacon that down the ages patiently signaled the fact that no one had discovered it.

Perhaps you understand now why that crystal pyramid was set upon the Moon instead of on the Earth. Its builders were not concerned with races still struggling up from savagery. They would be interested in our civilization only if we proved our fitness to survive—by crossing space and so escaping from the Earth, our cradle. That is the challenge that all intelligent races must meet, sooner or later. It is a double challenge, for it depends in turn upon the conquest of atomic energy and the last choice between life and death.

Once we had passed that crisis, it was only a matter of time before we found the pyramid and forced it open. Now its signals have ceased, and those whose duty it is will be turning their minds upon Earth. Perhaps they wish to help our infant civilization. But they must be very, very old, and the old are often insanely jealous of the young.

I can never look now at the Milky Way without wondering from which of those banked clouds of stars the emissaries are coming. If you will pardon so commonplace a simile, we have set off the fire alarm and have nothing to do but to wait.

365

I do not think we will have to wait for long.

Uncommon Words or Meanings

a sentinel (title)—a sentry, someone or something that stands guard.

two o'clock ("Round about *two o'clock* you will notice")—(military) the position where the two would be, if a clock face were superimposed on what you are looking at.

a caterpillar tractor ("our powerful *caterpillar tractors*")—a tractor with toothed wheels covered by a circular belt; used for heavy work on soft or uneven surfaces.

pedantic ("a geologist—or selenologist, if you want to be *pedantic*")—showing off academic knowledge.

a flank ("down the *flanks* of those stupendous cliffs")—the side of a mountain.

to sit tight ("radio for help and *sit tight*")—(informal) be patient and wait for the next event.

a score ("a *score* of rivers")—twenty.

homely ("so normal and *homely*")—(British usage) home-like.

a galley ("the corner . . . that served as a *galley*")—the kitchen on a ship or airplane.

a log ("entries in yesterday's *log*")—a book used on a ship or airplane for keeping a permanent daily record of events.

degenerate ("primitive plants and their slightly less *degenerate* ancestors")—(biology) having lost the normal or more highly developed characteristics of its type.

a laughingstock ("you'll be the *laughingstock* of the expedition")—a person or thing that is laughed at or made fun of.

a [wild] goose chase ("the craziest *goose chase* he had ever embarked on")—(idiom) a foolish or hopeless search (for something or somebody that can never be found).

a folly ("probably be called Wilson's *Folly*")—something foolish or ridiculous; here an allusion (an indirect reference) to "Seward's Folly," the mocking name given to the territory of Alaska in 1867, when Secretary of State Seward "wasted" $7,200,000 buying it from the Russian czar.

haunting ("*haunting* doubts had driven me forward")—returning to the mind repeatedly.

to score ("falling meteors had pitted and *scored*")—to mark with cuts, scratches, or lines.

to ebb ("as the life of the Moon *ebbed* with the dying oceans")—to become weak or faint.

to crawl ("set the scalp *crawling*")—to feel as though the flesh is covered with ants or another crawling thing.

an atomic pile ("an unshielded *atomic pile*")—the early name for a nuclear reactor.

an apparition ("crystalline *apparition*")—something strange that makes you doubt what you see.

banked ("those *banked* clouds of stars")—heaped up into a flat-topped mass.

Hills Like White Elephants

"'They just let the

air in and then it's

all perfectly

natural.'"

Hills Like
White Elephants

Ernest Hemingway
(1899–1961)

Ernest Hemingway almost single-handedly set the tone for twentieth-century American fiction. On the surface, his much-imitated style seems very easy to read and write. However, Hemingway challenges his readers to sense the emotion behind the words and to listen for the thoughts that the words either conceal or unintentionally (on the speaker's part) reveal.

Hemingway grew up in comfortable circumstances in Oak Park, Illinois, a suburb of Chicago. The family spent summers at their vacation home in Michigan, where young Ernest learned to hunt and fish. These activities reflected his ambitious and competitive spirit and remained important to him throughout his life. He found his way into World War I by convincing his father to let him volunteer as an ambulance driver for the American Red Cross in Italy. Six weeks after arriving in Italy, and two weeks before his nineteenth birthday, Hemingway was wounded under fire, thereby becoming something of a hero. He had long thrived on the companionship and admiration of other men; recovering from his wounds at the American Red Cross Hospital in Milan, he learned how attractive he was to women as well.

Hemingway returned to the U.S. briefly, married the first of his four wives, then returned to Europe. Living in Paris, he worked as a correspondent for the Toronto *Star* and established his position as one of the most celebrated writers of his generation. The novels he wrote during this time are modern classics, two of the most famous being *The Sun*

Also Rises (1926), about British and American expatriates in Paris and Spain, and *A Farewell to Arms* (1929), about doomed lovers in Italy during World War I. The heroes of these novels show physical courage in the face of danger, exemplifying Hemingway's admiration for "grace under pressure." The conversational style of his characters seems surprisingly modern. It can be said that Hemingway's characters, with their terse speech and lack of overt emotional involvement, served to define what is "cool" and American. Marlon Brando and James Dean would later personify this style in movies, and in turn would be imitated by teenagers to this day. The works also explore the complex relations between men and women, which seemed to puzzle Hemingway through all of his four marriages.

Fiction must be based on actual experience, Hemingway insisted, for "a writer's job is to tell the truth" and a good story "should produce a truer account than anything factual can be." According to the report of one of his friends,[*] Hemingway got the idea for "Hills Like White Elephants" (from Hemingway's 1927 collection *Men Without Women*) during an evening with American colleagues in an Italian café. They were speaking of birth control and of the cruelty of laws that made it a crime for a young unmarried woman to end an unwanted pregnancy. The man in the party who later wrote about it remembered an experience from his college days. At a time when abortion was both illegal and a forbidden topic in polite company, a young woman had spoken casually of having had an abortion. "Oh, it was nothing," the man remembered her saying. "The doctor just let the air in and a few hours later it was over." Four years later, Hemingway told the man that his remark had suggested the story "Hills Like White Elephants."

In what way could an American writer approach a subject that was shocking to many Americans at the time? And if the subject couldn't be discussed openly, how could the sentences in the story be—as Hemingway insisted they must be—"true"?

---

[*] Robert McAlmon, *Being Geniuses Together;* quoted by Carlos Baker in the major Hemingway biography to date—*Ernest Hemingway: A Life Story,* 1969.

Hills Like White Elephants

The hills across the valley of the Ebro were long and white.
On this side there was no shade and no trees and the station
was between two lines of rails in the sun. Close against the
side of the station there was the warm shadow of the building
5   and a curtain, made of strings of bamboo beads, hung across
the open door into the bar, to keep out flies. The American and
the girl with him sat at a table in the shade, outside the building. It was very hot and the express from Barcelona would
come in forty minutes. It stopped at this junction for two min-
10   utes and went on to Madrid.

"What should we drink?" the girl asked. She had taken off
her hat and put it on the table.

"It's pretty hot," the man said.

"Let's drink beer."

15   "Dos cervzas," the man said into the curtain.

"Big ones?" a woman asked from the doorway.

"Yes. Two big ones."

The woman brought two glasses of beer and two felt pads.
She put the felt pads and the beer glasses on the table and
20   looked at the man and the girl. The girl was looking off at the
line of hills. They were white in the sun and the country was
brown and dry.

"They look like white elephants," she said.

"I've never seen one," the man drank his beer.

25   "No, you wouldn't have."

"I might have," the man said. "Just because you say I
wouldn't have doesn't prove anything."

The girl looked at the bead curtain. "They've painted something on it," she said. "What does it say?"

30   "Anis del Toro. It's a drink."

"Could we try it?"

The man called "Listen" through the curtain. The woman
came out from the bar.

"Four reales."

35   "We want two Anis del Tor."

"With water?"

"Do you want it with water?"

"I don't know," the girl said. "Is it good with water?"

"It's all right."

40 "You want them with water?" asked the woman.

"Yes, with water."

"It tastes like licorice," the girl said and put the glass down.

"That's the way with everything."

"Yes," said the girl. "Everything tastes of licorice. Espe-
45 cially all the things you've waited so long for, like absinthe."

"Oh, cut it out."

"You started it," the girl said. "I was being amused. I was
having a fine time."

"Well, let's try and have a fine time."

50 "All right. I was trying. I said the mountains looked like
white elephants. Wasn't that bright?"

"That was bright."

"I wanted to try this new drink. That's all we do, isn't it—
look at things and try new drinks?"

55 "I guess so."

The girl looked across at the hills.

"They're lovely hills," she said. "They don't really look like
white elephants. I just meant the coloring of their skin through
the trees."

60 "Should we have another drink?"

"All right."

The warm wind blew the bead curtain against the table.

"The beer's nice and cool," the man said.

"It's lovely," the girl said.

65 "It's really an awfully simple operation, Jig," the man said.
It's not really an operation at all."

The girl looked at the ground the table legs rested on.

"I know you wouldn't mind it, Jig. It's really not anything.
It's just to let the air in."

70 The girl did not say anything.

"I'll go with you and I'll stay with you all the time. They just
let the air in and then it's all perfectly natural."

"Then what will we do afterward?"

"We'll be fine afterward. Just like we were before."

75 "What makes you think so?"

"That's the only thing that bothers us. It's the only thing
that's made us unhappy."

The girl looked at the bead curtain, put her hand out and took hold of two of the strings of beads.

80 "And you think then we'll be all right and be happy."

"I know we will. You don't have to be afraid. I've known lots of people that have done it."

"So have I," said the girl. "And afterward they were all so happy."

85 "Well," the man said, "if you don't want to you don't have to. I wouldn't have you do it if you didn't want to. But I know it's perfectly simple."

"And you really want to?"

"I think it's the best thing to do. But I don't want you to do 90 it if you don't really want to."

"And if I do it you'll be happy and things will be like they were and you'll love me?"

"I love you now. You know I love you."

"I know. But if I do it, then it will be nice again if I say 95 things are like white elephants, and you'll like it?"

"I'll love it. I love it now but I just can't think about it. You know how I get when I worry."

"If I do it you won't ever worry?"

"I won't worry about that because it's perfectly simple."

100 "Then I'll do it. Because I don't care about me."

"What do you mean?"

"I don't care about me."

"Well, I care about you."

"Oh yes. But I don't care about me. And I'll do it and then 105 everything will be fine."

"I don't want you to do it if you feel that way."

The girl stood up and walked to the end of the station. Across, on the other side, were fields of grain and trees along the banks of the Ebro. Far away, beyond the river, were moun- 110 tains. The shadow of a cloud moved across the field of grain and she saw the river through the trees.

"And we could have all this," she said. "And we could have everything and every day we make it more impossible."

"What did you say?"

115 "I said we could have everything."

"We can have everything."

"No, we can't."

"We can have the whole world."

"No, we can't."

120 "We can go everywhere."

"No, we can't. It isn't ours any more."

"It's ours."

"No, it isn't. And once they take it away, you never get it back."

125 "But they haven't taken it away."

"We'll wait and see."

"Come on back in the shade," he said. "You mustn't feel that way."

"I don't feel any way," the girl said. "I just know things."

130 "I don't want you to do anything that you don't want to do—"

"Nor that isn't good for me," she said. "I know. Could we have another beer?"

"All right. But you've got to realize—"

135 "I realize," the girl said. "Can't we maybe stop talking?"

They sat down at the table and the girl looked across at the hills on the dry side of the valley and the man looked at her and at the table.

"You've got to realize," he said, "that I don't want you to do
140 it if you don't want to. I'm perfectly willing to go through with it if it means anything to you."

"Doesn't it mean anything to you? We could get along."

"Of course it does. But I don't want anybody but you. I don't want any one else. And I know it's perfectly simple."

145 "Yes, you know it's perfectly simple."

"It's all right for you to say that, but I do know it."

"Would you do something for me now?"

"I'd do anything for you."

"Would you please please please please please please
150 please stop talking?"

He did not say anything but looked at the bags against the wall of the station. There were labels on them from all the hotels where they had spent nights.

"But I don't want you to," he said, "I don't care anything
155 about it."

"I'll scream," the girl said.

The woman came out through the curtains with two

glasses of beer and put them down on the damp felt pads. "The train comes in five minutes," she said.

160 "What did she say?" asked the girl.

"That the train is coming in five minutes."

The girl smiled brightly at the woman, to thank her.

"I'd better take the bags over to the other side of the station," the man said. She smiled at him.

165 "All right. Then come back and we'll finish the beer."

He picked up the two heavy bags and carried them around the station to the other tracks. He looked up the tracks but could not see the train. Coming back, he walked through the barroom, where people waiting for the train were drinking. He

170 drank an Anis at the bar and looked at the people. They were all waiting reasonably for the train. He went out through the bead curtain. She was sitting at the table and smiled at him.

"Do you feel better?" he asked.

"I feel fine," she said. "There's nothing wrong with me. I

175 feel fine."

[1925]

Uncommon Words or Meanings

Words or phrases from the story are explained if they are cultural references (including words in a language other than English), idioms, or slang, or if the meaning is not the first listed in a standard dictionary. The words or phrases appear in their order of first use in the story.

Ebro ("the valley of the *Ebro*")—a river in north-central Spain, about 150 miles north of Madrid.

a girl ("the American and the *girl* with him")—at the time this story was written, "girl" was commonly used to refer to any female who was not distinctly elderly.

a white elephant ("Hills Like *White Elephants*")—an expression used to describe something that is useless and expensive to keep but seems too valuable to throw away.

a real ("Four *reales*.")—a Spanish coin.

Anis del Toro ("We want two *Anis del Toro.*")—a brand of Spanish liqueur flavored with anise seed, which has a slightly bitter, slightly sweet taste. Anise seed is also the flavoring in **licorice,** a chewy black candy.

absinthe ("all the things you've waited so long for, like *absinthe*")—a French liqueur also flavored with anise seed. Since 1915, it has been illegal to produce absinthe in France because another ingredient, wormwood, has been found to cause delirium, hallucinations, and ultimately death.

bright ("I said the mountains looked like white elephants. Wasn't that *bright?*")—clever, original.

to cut (something) out ("Oh, *cut it out.*")—(idiom) to stop doing or saying (something that is annoying).

awfully ("an *awfully* simple operation")—very.

to let . . . in—("It's just to *let* the air *in.*")—to allow something to enter.

The Man to Send Rain Clouds

"'About the priest

sprinkling holy

water for Grandpa.

So he won't be

thirsty.'"

The Man to Send Rain Clouds

Leslie Marmon Silko
(born 1948)

Leslie Marmon Silko, who now lives in Tucson, Arizona, grew up in New Mexico in the Laguna Pueblo, the largest of the Rio Grande Pueblo Indian communities. (Laguna had a population of close to three thousand in the 1960s.) Like many Southwesterners, Silko's ancestry includes white speakers of English, Mexican speakers of Spanish, and American Indians. As a child, Silko loved listening to the stories told by her Laguna grandmother and great-aunt. "The best thing you can have in life," she has told an interviewer, "is to have someone tell you a story."* Years later, in her first creative writing class in college, Silko found she had so many ideas that she hardly knew where to begin. "The Man to Send Rain Clouds," which was based on an actual event at Laguna, was written during her college years. Silko's work gained national attention when that story, along with others of hers, appeared in 1974 in *The Man to Send Rain Clouds,* edited by Kenneth Rosen, one of the first anthologies of fiction written by American Indians. A collection of Silko's stories and poems was published as *Storyteller* (1981). In addition, she has published the novels *Ceremony* (1977) and *Almanac of the Dead* (1991), the latter written with the support of a MacArthur Foundation "genius" grant. All of Silko's fiction is concerned with the struggle of American Indians to live in two worlds, maintaining their traditional culture within the context of modern life.

*In Laura Coltelli, *Winged Words: American Indian Writers Speak* (1990).

The first American Indians arrived between 29,000 and 22,000 years ago, in a series of Ice Age of migrations from Asia. By 2000 B.C., some of those prehistoric immigrants were living in what is now the American Southwest. Fourteen centuries later, their descendants had settled in permanent villages with multi-story dwellings. When Spanish explorers arrived in the mid-1500s, they used *pueblo,* the Spanish word for "village" or "town," as their name for all the American Indian peoples of the region; that usage was later borrowed by English-speakers.

The Spanish brought with them diseases and a hunger for gold, with sad results that are well known. They also brought the Franciscan order of missionary priests, who were charged by the Pope to "save souls in the New World." The Franciscans, with the best and worst of intentions, gradually imposed the beliefs and rituals of Roman Catholicism on the "pagan" American Indians. In public, the Pueblos practiced the new European religion; in private they continued to follow their own religion, making sure that the ceremonies and beliefs were never revealed to outsiders. Understandably, one result was mutual wariness and a great potential for misunderstanding. In "The Man to Send Rain Clouds," this situation is presented in the context of differing beliefs about death and funeral customs. Who beyond family members needs to be told right away when someone has died? What ceremonies must be followed in disposing of a dead body? And what could a death have to do with life-giving rain?

The Man to Send Rain Clouds

ONE

They found him under a big cottonwood tree. His Levi jacket and pants were faded light-blue so that he had been easy to find. The big cottonwood tree stood apart from a small
5 grove of winterbare cottonwoods which grew in the wide, sandy arroyo. He had been dead for a day or more, and the sheep had wandered and scattered up and down the arroyo. Leon and his brother-in-law, Ken, gathered the sheep and left them in the pen at the sheep camp before they returned to the
10 cottonwood tree. Leon waited under the tree while Ken drove the truck through the deep sand to the edge of the arroyo. He squinted up at the sun and unzipped his jacket—it sure was hot for this time of year. But high and northwest the blue mountains were still deep in snow. Ken came sliding down the
15 low, crumbling bank about fifty yards down, and he was bringing the red blanket.

Before they wrapped the old man, Leon took a piece of string out of his pocket and tied a small gray feather in the old man's long white hair. Ken gave him the paint. Across the
20 brown wrinkled forehead he drew a streak of white and along the high cheekbones he drew a strip of blue paint. He paused and watched Ken throw pinches of corn meal and pollen into the wind that fluttered the small gray feather. Then Leon painted with yellow under the old man's broad nose, and
25 finally, when he had painted green across the chin, he smiled.

"Send us rain clouds, Grandfather." They laid the bundle in the back of the pickup and covered it with a heavy tarp before they started back to the pueblo.

They turned off the highway onto the sandy pueblo road.
30 Not long after they passed the store and post office they saw Father Paul's car coming toward them. When he recognized their faces he slowed his car and waved for them to stop. The young priest rolled down the car window.

"Did you find old Teofilo?" he asked loudly.
35 Leon stopped the truck. "Good morning, Father. We were just out to the sheep camp. Everything is O.K. now."

"Thank God for that. Teofilo is a very old man. You really shouldn't allow him to stay at the sheep camp alone."

"No, he won't do that any more now."

40 "Well, I'm glad you understand. I hope I'll be seeing you at Mass this week—we missed you last Sunday. See if you can get old Teofilo to come with you." The priest smiled and waved at them as they drove away.

TWO

45 Louise and Teresa were waiting. The table was set for lunch, and the coffee was boiling on the black iron stove. Leon looked at Louise and then at Teresa.

"We found him under a cottonwood tree in the big arroyo near the sheep camp. I guess he sat down to rest in the shade
50 and never got up again." Leon walked toward the old man's bed. The red plaid shawl had been shaken and spread carefully over the bed, and a new brown flannel shirt and pair of stiff new Levis were arranged neatly beside the pillow. Louise held the screen door open while Leon and Ken carried in the red
55 blanket. He looked small and shriveled, and after they dressed him in the new shirt and pants he seemed more shrunken.

It was noontime now because the church bells rang the Angelus. They ate the beans with hot bread, and nobody said anything until after Teresa poured the coffee.

60 Ken stood up and put on his jacket. "I'll see about the gravediggers. Only the top layer of soil is frozen. I think it can be ready before dark."

Leon nodded his head and finished his coffee. After Ken had been gone for a while, the neighbors and clanspeople
65 came quietly to embrace Teofilo's family and to leave food on the table because the gravediggers would come to eat when they were finished.

THREE

The sky in the west was full of pale-yellow light. Louise
70 stood outside with her hands in the pockets of Leon's green army jacket that was too big for her. The funeral was over, and the old men had taken their candles and medicine bags and were gone. She waited until the body was laid into the pickup before she said anything to Leon. She touched his arm, and he

noticed that her hands were still dusty from the corn meal that she had sprinkled around the old man. When she spoke, Leon could not hear her.

"What did you say? I didn't hear you."

"I said that I had been thinking about something."

"About what?"

"About the priest sprinkling holy water for Grandpa. So he won't be thirsty."

Leon stared at the new moccasins that Teofilo had made for the ceremonial dances in the summer. They were nearly hidden by the red blanket. It was getting colder, and the wind pushed gray dust down the narrow pueblo road. The sun was approaching the long mesa where it disappeared during the winter. Louise stood there shivering and watching his face. The he zipped up his jacket and opened the truck door. "I'll see if he's there."

FOUR

Ken stopped the pickup at the church, and Leon got out; and then Ken drove down the hill to the graveyard where people were waiting. Leon knocked at the old carved door with its symbols of the Lamb. While he waited he looked up at the twin bells from the king of Spain with the last sunlight pouring around them in their tower.

The priest opened the door and smiled when he saw who it was. "Come in! What brings you here this evening?"

The priest walked toward the kitchen, and Leon stood with his cap in his hand, playing with the earflaps and examining the living room—the brown sofa, the green armchair, and the brass lamp that hung down from the ceiling by links of chain. The priest dragged a chair out of the kitchen and offered it to Leon.

"No thank you, Father. I only came to ask you if you would bring your holy water to the graveyard."

The priest turned away from Leon and looked out the window at the patio full of shadows and the dining-room windows of the nuns' cloister across the patio. The curtains were heavy, and the light from within faintly penetrated; it was impossible to see the nuns inside eating supper. "Why didn't you tell me he was dead? I could have brought the Last Rites anyway."

115   Leon smiled. "It wasn't necessary, Father."

The priest stared down at his scuffed brown loafers and the worn hem of his cassock. "For a Christian burial it was necessary."

His voice was distant, and Leon thought that his blue eyes
120 looked tired.

"It's O.K. Father, we just want him to have plenty of water."

The priest sank down into the green chair and picked up a glossy missionary magazine. He turned the colored pages full
125 of lepers and pagans without looking at them.

"You know I can't do that, Leon. There should have been the Last Rites and funeral Mass at the very least."

Leon put on his green cap and pulled the flaps down over his ears. "It's getting late, Father. I've got to go."
130   When Leon opened the door Father Paul stood up and said, "Wait." He left the room and came back wearing a long brown overcoat. He followed Leon out the door and across the dim churchyard to the adobe steps in front of the church. They both stooped to fit through the low adobe entrance. And when
135 they started down the hill to the graveyard only half of the sun was visible above the mesa.

The priest approached the grave slowly, wondering how they had managed to dig into the frozen ground; and then he remembered that this was New Mexico, and saw the pile of
140 cold loose sand beside the hole. The people stood close to each other with little clouds of steam puffing from their faces. The priest looked at them and saw a pile of jackets, gloves, and scarves in the yellow, dry tumbleweeds that grew in the grave- yard. He looked at the red blanket, not sure that Teofilo was so
145 small, wondering if it wasn't some perverse Indian trick— something they did in March to ensure a good harvest—won- dering if maybe old Teofilo was actually at sheep camp corralling the sheep for the night. But there he was, facing into a cold dry wind and squinting at the last sunlight, ready to bury
150 a red wool blanket while the faces of his parishioners were in shadow with the last warmth of the sun on their backs.

His fingers were stiff, and it took him a long time to twist the lid off the holy water. Drops of water fell on the red blan- ket and soaked into dark icy spots. He sprinkled the grave and
155 the water disappeared almost before it touched the dim, cold

sand; it reminded him of something—he tried to remember
what it was, because he thought if he could remember he
might understand this. He sprinkled more water; he shook the
container until it was empty, and the water fell through the
160 light from the sundown like August rain that fell while the sun
was still shining, almost evaporating before it touched the
wilted squash flowers.

The wind pulled at the priest's brown Franciscan robe
and swirled away the corn meal and pollen that had been
165 sprinkled on the blanket. They lowered the bundle into the
ground, and they didn't bother to untie the stiff pieces of new
rope that were tied around the ends of the blanket. The sun
was gone, and over on the highway the eastbound lane was full
of headlights. The priest walked away slowly. Leon watched
170 him climb the hill, and when he had disappeared within the
tall, thick walls, Leon turned to look up at the high blue mountains in the deep snow that reflected a faint red light from the
west. He felt good because it was finished, and he was happy
about the sprinkling of the holy water; now the old man could
175 send them big thunderclouds for sure.

[1969]

Uncommon Words or Meanings

a cottonwood tree ("under a big *cottonwood* tree")—the poplar, a
tree with cottonlike tufts of white hair on its tiny seeds; the Southwestern varieties of the tree grow alongside streams.

an arroyo ("grew in the wide, sandy *arroyo*")—in the Southwestern United States, the dry bed of a stream.

to squint ("he *squinted* up at the sun")—to look with the eyes
partly closed.

corn meal, corn pollen ("throw pinches of *corn meal and
pollen*")—two forms of corn, both of which have religious significance for the Pueblos and would be carried in a medicine bag.
"Corn meal" is coarsely ground dried corn; "corn pollen" is the
fine yellowish powder on the silky strands of an ear of corn.

a tarp ("covered it with a heavy *tarp*")—short for "tarpaulin," a
sheet of canvas or other strong waterproof material, used as a
protective covering.

Father ("saw *Father* Paul's car")—"Father" is the term of address for a Roman Catholic priest.

the Angelus ("the church bells rang the *Angelus*")—a prayer said by Roman Catholics at morning, noon, and night.

clanspeople ("the neighbors and *clanspeople*")—members of the same clan, a group of relatives. The clans conduct religious ceremonies.

a medicine bag ("their candles and *medicine bags*")—a small leather or fabric sack used to carry small religious objects and corn pollen.

a pickup ("the body was laid into the *pickup*")—short for "pickup truck," a small light truck with an open back.

holy water ("sprinkling *holy water*")—water blessed by a priest for religious uses.

the Lamb ("its symbols of the *Lamb*")—with a capital letter, a Christian symbol for Jesus, "the Lamb of God," in the sense of a baby sheep who is sacrificed as an offering to God on behalf of a community.

cloister ("the nuns' *cloister* across the patio")—a building where nuns live in religious seclusion.

the Last Rites ("I could have brought the *Last Rites*")—the popular name for a ceremony performed by a Roman Catholic priest when a person is dying.

a tumbleweed ("the yellow, dry, *tumbleweeds*")—in the desert of the southwestern U.S., a plant that breaks off from its roots and is then blown about by the wind.

squash flowers ("the wilted *squash flowers*")—the large flower of a vinelike plant of the gourd family, one of the basic foods of the Pueblo culture; the flower grows limp from lack of water.

Franciscan ("the priest's brown *Franciscan* robe")—a religious order, for both men and women, founded by St. Francis of Assisi and dedicated to serving the poor and the sick. The Franciscans were the dominant order of missionaries in North America.

a pueblo ("off the highway onto the sandy *pueblo* road")—in the Southwestern United States, particularly the Rio Grande valley, an American Indian village.

The Man to Send Rain Clouds   129

The Somebody

"A spray can has

no heart. The

letters come out

very dead."

The Somebody

Danny Santiago
(1911–1988)

Reading "The Somebody," it seems clear that Danny Santiago must be a young, Mexican American author who grew up in Los Angeles. That's what reviewers said when Danny Santiago's first novel, *Famous All Over Town,* was published in 1984. In fact, the author was a man named Daniel James, a former screenwriter in his seventies who was the only son of a wealthy family from Kansas City. He was close to sixty when he wrote "The Somebody," which slowly developed into the novel. How did Dan James from Kansas City become Danny Santiago from Los Angeles?

Daniel James's grandfather (who was a cousin of the notorious outlaws Frank and Jesse James) became a wealthy man as an importer and seller of fine china in Kansas City. The business passed to his son, Daniel's father, a Yale graduate who wrote plays as a hobby and built a second home on the Pacific coast near Hollywood. Dan James also went to Yale, where he was the only member of the class of 1936 to major in classical Greek. After college, jobs in an Oklahoma oil field and as a traveling salesman for the family business gave Dan James his first glimpse of the lives of uneducated laborers and Depression-ruined middle-class families. Next he became an assistant to Charlie Chaplin, who was filming *The Great Dictator.* (James, six feet six inches tall, said years later that Chaplin "had a history of hiring tall, well-bred assistants who knew which fork to use.") As a member of Hollywood's newly-formed Screen Writers

Guild, James again saw how hard life was for the lower ranks of workers. To help improve working people's lives, he and many of his friends joined the Communist Party, though by 1948 he had dropped his membership as he became disenchanted with the Russian government.

In 1950, Wisconsin Senator Joseph McCarthy gained national attention by claiming that Communist agents in Hollywood were trying to overthrow the American government. After refusing to "cooperate" with McCarthy's investigating committee, Dan James and his wife found they could no longer work in Hollywood under their real names. (McCarthy was eventually censured by the Senate for making false claims, but only after he had ruined many people's careers.) Dan James wrote several monster pictures under an assumed name but he had lost confidence in himself as a writer. He also felt guilty about being able to live on inherited wealth.

James and his wife both spoke Spanish well and for some time they had been volunteer social workers in Eastside, a Los Angeles neighborhood of more than one and a half million Mexican Americans. They turned their energies to that project and became friendly with a dozen or more families. Gradually, Dan James began to write again, using the voice of his Chicano self and the Spanish version of his name. In 1968, he showed some of his stories to a younger friend who was a writer and who knew something about James's political past. The friend, John Gregory Dunne, sent the Danny Santiago stories to his literary agent, who soon placed them in national publications.*

One of the first published stories was "The Somebody," narrated by fourteen-year-old Chato Medina, a street-smart kid with an IQ of 135. "This is a big day in my life," Chato tells us, "because today I quit school and went to work as a writer." What kind of writer do you suppose he is going to be? Telling us of the adventures of his first day as a writer, Chato speaks of his home, his street, his school, the neighborhood playground, the juvenile court, the Boys' Club, and the business district near his home. How much security, understanding, and pleasure do you suppose he has found in each of those places? What disappointment or danger has he found in each?

* Much of the material in this introduction is from Dunne's splendid interview, "The Secret of Danny Santiago," *The New York Review of Books* (August 16, 1984).

The Somebody

This is Chato talking, Chato de Shamrock, from Eastside in old L.A., and I want you to know this is a big day in my life because today I quit school and went to work as a writer. I write on fences or buildings or anything that comes along. I
5   write my name, not the name I got from my father. I want no part of him. I write my gang name, Chato, which means Cat-face, because I have a flat nose like a cat. It's a Mexican word because that's what I am, a Mexican, and I'm not ashamed of it. I like that language, too. It's way better than English to say what
10 you mean. But German is the best. It's got a real rugged sound, and I'm going to learn to talk it someday.

After Chato I write "de Shamrock." That's the street where I live, and it's the name of the gang I belong to, but the others are all gone now. Their families had to move away, except
15 Gorilla is in jail and Blackie joined the navy because he liked swimming. But I still have our old arsenal. It's buried under the chickens and I dig it up when I get bored. There's tire irons and chains and pick handles with spikes and two zip guns we made but they don't shoot very straight.

20 In the good old days nobody cared to tangle with us. But now I'm the only one left.

Well, today started off like any other day. The toilet roars like a hot rod taking off. My father coughs and spits about nineteen times and hollers, "It's six-thirty." So I holler back,
25 "I'm quitting school." Things hit me like that—sudden.

"Don't you want to be a lawyer no more," he says in Span-ish, "and defend the Mexican people?"

My father thinks he is very funny, and next time I get an idea what I'm going to do in the world, he's sure not going to
30 hear about it.

"Don't you want to be a doctor," he says, "and cut off my leg for nothing when I ask you? How will you support me," he says, "when I retire? Or will you marry a rich old woman that owns a pool hall?"

35 "I'm leaving this dump! You'll never see me again!"

I hollered it at him, but he was already in the kitchen mak-

ing a big noise with his coffee. I could be dead and he would-
n't take me serious. So I laid there and waited for him to go off
to work. When I woke up again, it was way past eleven. So I
40   got out of bed and put on my khakis and my horsehide jacket
and combed myself very careful because already I had a feeling this was going to be a big day for me.

I had to wait for breakfast because the baby was sick and
throwing up milk on everything. There is always a baby vomit-
45   ing in my house. When they're born, everybody comes over
and says "*Qué* cute!" but nobody passes any comments on the
dirty way babies act.

When my mother finally served me, I had to hold my
breath, she smelled so bad of babies. I don't like to look at her
50   anymore. Her legs got those dark blue rivers running all over
them. I kept waiting for her to bawl me out for not going to
school, but I guess she forgot or something. So I cut out.

Every time I go out my front door I have to cry for what
they've done to old Shamrock Street. It used to be so fine,
55   man, with solid homes on both sides. Then the S.P. Railroad
bought up the whole street, every house except my father's.
He's real stubborn, to give him credit. But what good did it do?
The wreckers came rolling in with their trucks and bulldozer.
You could hear the houses scream when they ripped apart. So
60   now Shamrock Street is just front walks that lead to a hole in
the ground. And Pelón's house and Blackie's are just stacks of
old boards waiting to get hauled away. I hope that never happens to your street, man.

My first stop was the front gate and there was that sign
65   again, a big S wrapped around a cross like a snake, which is
the mark of the Sierra Street gang, as everybody knows. I
rubbed it off, but tonight they'll put it back again. In the old
days they wouldn't dare to pay any calls on Shamrock Street,
but without your gang you're nobody. And one of these fine
70   days they're going to catch up with me in person and that will
be the end of Chato de Shamrock.

So I cruised on down to Main Street like a ghost in the
graveyard. Just to prove I'm alive, I wrote my name on the
parking-lot fence at the corner. A lot of names you see in pub-
75   lic places are written very sloppy. Not me. I take my time. Like
my fifth-grade teacher used to say, "If others are going to see
your work, you owe it to yourself to do it right." Mrs. Cully was

her name and she was real nice, for an Anglo. My other teachers were cops, all of them, but one time Mrs. Cully drove me
80   home when some guys were after me. I think she wanted to
adopt me, too, but she never said anything about it. I owe a lot
to that lady, and especially my handwriting. You should see it,
man—it's real smooth and mellow, and curvy like a girl in a
bathing suit. Everybody says so. Except one time they had me
85   in Juvenile by mistake and some doctor looked at my writing.
He said it proved I had something wrong with me. That doctor
was crazy, because I made him show me *his* writing and it was
very ugly, like a barbed-wire fence with little chickens stuck on
the points and all flapping their wings.
90   So anyway, I signed myself very clean and neat on that corner. And then I thought, Why not go look for a job someplace?
But I was more in the mood to write my name, so I slid into the
dime store and helped myself to two boxes of crayons and
plenty of chalk. Some people lately have taken to writing their
95   name with spray cans, but they'll get over it. A spray can has
no heart. The letters come out very dead. Give me good old
chalk any day. And so I cruised down Main, writing as I went,
till a sudden question hit me. I wondered should I write more
than my name. Should I write, "Chato is a fine guy," or "Chato
100   is wanted by the police"? Things like that. But I decided no.
Better to keep them guessing.
      So I cut over to Forney Playground. It used to be Shamrock
territory, but now the Sierra have taken over there like everyplace else. Just to show them, I wrote on the tennis court and
105   the swimming pool and the gym. I left a fine little trail of Chato
de Shamrock in eight colors. Some places I used chalk, which
works better on brick or plaster. But crayons are the thing for
cement or anything smooth.
      I'm telling you, I was pretty famous at the Forney by the
110   time I cut out, and from there I continued my travels till a new
idea hit me. You know how you put your name on something
and that proves it belongs to you? Things like schoolbooks or
gym shoes? So I thought, how about that now? And I put my
name on the Triple A Market and on Morrie's Liquor Store and
115   on the Zócalo, which is a beer joint. Then I cruised on up
Broadway, getting rich. I took over a barber shop and a furniture store and the Plymouth agency. And the firehouse for
laughs, and the phone company so I could call all my girlfriends

and keep my dimes. And then there I was at Webster and Garcia's Funeral Home with the big white columns. At first I thought that might be bad luck, but then I said, Oh, well, we all got to die sometime. So I signed myself, and now I can eat good and live in style and have a big time all my life, and then kiss you all good-by and give myself the best funeral in L.A. for free.

And speaking of funerals, along came the Sierra guys right then, eight or twelve of them cruising down the street with that stupid walk which is their trademark. I ducked behind the hearse. Not that I'm a coward. Getting beat up doesn't bother me. What I hate is those blades. They're like a piece of ice cutting into your belly. But the Sierra didn't see me and went on by. I couldn't hear what they were saying but I knew they had me on their mind. So I ducked into the Boys' Club, where they don't let anybody get you, no matter who you are. To pass the time I shot some baskets and played a little pool and watched the television, but the story was boring, so it came to me, Why not write my name on the tube? Which I did with one of these squeaky pens. The cowboys sure looked fine with Chato de Shamrock pasted all over them. Everybody got a kick out of it. But of course up comes Mr. Calderon and makes me wipe it off. They're always spying on you up there. And he takes me into his office and closes the door.

"Well," he says, "and how is the last of the dinosaurs?"

"What's that?" I ask him.

He shows me their picture in a book, giant lizards and real ugly, worse than octopus, but they're all dead now, and he explains he called me that because of the Shamrocks. Then he goes into that voice with the church music in it and I look out the window.

"I know it's hard to lose your gang, Chato," he says, "but this is your chance to make new friends and straighten yourself out. Why don't you start coming to Boys' Club more?"

"It's too boring," I tell him.

"What about school?"

"I can't go," I said. "They'll get me."

"The Sierra's forgotten you're alive," he tells me.

"Then how come they put their mark on my house every night?"

"Do they?"

He stares at me very hard. I hate those eyes of his. He

160 thinks he knows everything. And what is he? Just a Mexican like everybody else.

"Maybe you put that mark there yourself," he says. "To make yourself big. Just like you wrote on the television."

"That was my name! I like to write my name!"

165 "So do dogs," he says. "On every lamppost they come to."

"You're a dog yourself," I told him, but I don't think he heard me. He just went on talking. Brother, how they love to talk up there! But I didn't bother to listen, and when he ran out of gas I left. From now on I'm scratching that Boys' Club off

170 my list.

Out on the street it was beginning to get dark, but I could still follow my trail back toward Broadway. It felt good to see myself written everyplace, but at the Zócalo I stopped dead. Around my name there was this big red heart in lipstick and

175 somebody's initials. To tell the truth, I didn't know how to feel. In one way I was mad to see my name molested, especially if by some guy for laughs. But if it was a girl, that could be more or less interesting. And who ever heard of a guy carrying lipstick?

A girl is what it turned out to be. I caught up with her at the

180 telephone building. There she is, standing in the shadows and drawing her heart around my name. She has a very pretty shape on her, too. I sneak up very quiet, thinking all kinds of crazy things. And my blood shoots around so fast it shakes me up and down all over. And then she turns around and it's only

185 Crusader Rabbit. That's what we called her since third grade, from the television show because of her big teeth in front.

When she sees me, she takes off down the alley, but in twenty feet I catch her. I grab for the lipstick, but she whips it behind her. I reach around and try to pull her fingers open, but

190 her hand is sweaty and so is mine. And then she loses her balance and falls against some garbage cans, so I get the lipstick away from her very easy.

"What right you got to my name?" I tell her. "I never gave you permission."

195 "You sign yourself real fine," she says.

I knew that already.

"Let's go writing together," she says.

"The Sierra's after me."

"I don't care," she says. "Come on, Chato—you and me can

200 have a lot of fun."

She came up close and giggled. She put her hand on my hand that had the lipstick in it. And you know what? I'm ashamed to say I almost told her yes. It would be a change to go writing with a girl. We could talk there in the dark. We could decide on the best places. And her handwriting wasn't too bad either. But then I remembered my reputation. Somebody would be sure to see us, and then they'd be laughing at me all over Eastside. So I pulled my hand away and told her off.

"Run along, Crusader," I told her. "I don't want no partners and especially you."

"Who you calling Crusader?" she yelled. "You ugly squash-nose punk!"

She called me everything. And spit in my face but missed. I didn't argue. I just cut out. And when I got to the first sewer, I threw away her lipstick. Then I drifted over to Broadway, which is a good street for writing because a lot of people pass by there. I don't mind crowds. The way I write, nobody notices till I'm finished, and I can smell a cop for half a mile.

You know me, I hate to brag but my work on Broadway was the best I've ever done in all my life. Under the street lamp my name shone out like solid gold. I stood to one side and checked the people as they walked past and inspected it. With some you can't tell just how they feel, but with others it rings out like a cash register. There was one man. He got out of a brand new Cadillac to buy a paper and when he saw my name he smiled. He was the age to be my father. I bet he'd give me a job if I asked him. I bet he'd take me to his home and to his office in the morning. Pretty soon I'd be sitting at my own desk and signing my name on letters and checks and things. But I would never buy a Cadillac. They burn too much gas.

Later a girl came by. She was around eighteen, I think, with green eyes. Her face was so pretty I didn't dare look at her shape. Do you want me to go crazy? That girl stopped and really studied my name like she fell in love with it. She wanted to know me, I could tell. She wanted to take my hand and we'd go off together just holding hands and nothing dirty. We'd go to Beverly Hills and nobody would look at us in the wrong way. I almost said "Hello" to that girl, and "How do you like my writing?" but not quite.

So here I am, standing on the corner of Broadway and Bailey with my chalk all gone and just one crayon left and it's an

ugly brown. My fingers are too cold to write, but that's nothing, man, nothing, because I just had a vision. I saw the Sincere Truth in flashing lights. I don't need to be a movie star or light-
245   weight boxing king. All I need is plenty of chalk and I'll be famous wherever there's a wall to write on. The Sierra will try to stop me, and the cops and everybody, but I'll be like a ghost, mysterious, and all they'll ever know of me is just my name, signed the way I always sign it, **CHATO DE SHAMROCK**,
250   with rays shooting out like from the Holy Cross.

[1970]

Uncommon Words or Meanings

de ("Chato *de* Shamrock")—"of"; in traditional Spanish family names, the *de* is a sign of aristocracy.

an arsenal ("I still have our old *arsenal*")—a stockpile of guns or other weapons.

a tire iron ("There's *tire irons* . . .")—a steel bar with a flattened end used in changing the tire on an automobile.

a hot rod ("roars like a *hot rod* taking off") (slang) an automobile that has been modified for greater speed and power.

a zip gun ("two *zip guns* we made")—a homemade "gun" that uses powerful rubber bands to shoot small pieces of lead.

a dump ("I'm leaving this *dump*!")—(slang) a poorly cared for, dirty place.

khakis ("put on my *khakis*")—slacks made of khaki, a sturdy light-brown cotton fabric.

Qué cute! ("everybody . . . says *'Qué cute!'*")—(a mixture of Spanish and English) "How cute!" "How adorable!"

to bawl (someone) out ("to *bawl* me *out* for not going to school")—(informal) to scold angrily.

to cut out ("So I *cut out*.")—(slang) to leave abruptly.

to pay a call ("wouldn't dare to *pay* any *calls* on Shamrock Street")—to come for a proper social visit, an old-fashioned term here used sarcastically.

S.P. Railroad ("the *S.P. Railroad* bought up the whole street")—the Southern Pacific Railroad.

to cruise ("So I *cruised* on down to Main Street ")—(slang) to move casually, with the idea of being noticed by others.

an Anglo ("real nice, for an *Anglo*")—Among Latinos, a white person who speaks English and is not of Latin descent.

Juvenile ("had me in *Juvenile* by mistake")—Short for "Juvenile Court," a court of law for offenders under a set age, sixteen in many states.

a dime store ("I slid into the *dime store*")—(informal) A place where only inexpensive merchandise is sold; originally, most prices were only five or ten cents—a nickel or a dime.

to help (one)self to ("*helped myself to* two boxes")—to take, rather than waiting to be served; here, to take without paying.

a spray can ("writing . . . with *spray cans*")—a pressurized can of paint.

a joint ("the Zócalo, which is a beer *joint*")—(slang) a cheap, disreputable bar.

Plymouth ("the *Plymouth* agency")—a medium-priced make of automobile.

to get a kick out of ("Everybody *got a kick out of* it.")—(slang) to be pleasantly surprised and amused by.

to whip ("she *whips* it behind her")—to move quickly or suddenly.

a sewer ("got to the first *sewer*")—an underground channel, with a metal grill opening onto the street, to carry off sewage or rainwater.

Beverly Hills ("We'd go to *Beverly Hills*")—the expensive residential area northwest of Los Angeles where many movie stars live.

Japanese Hamlet

"'Some day I'll be

the ranking

Shakespearean

actor,' he said."

Japanese Hamlet

Toshio Mori
(1910–1980)

Toshio Mori was a twentieth-century pioneer in Asian American literature, one who memorably recorded the experience of the seventh and eighth generations of Asian American citizens. He was the first Japanese American short story writer to be published in the U.S. and was one of the first published Asian American writers.

Mori's father had left Japan in the 1890s to prepare a new life for his wife and two sons in the United States, first working on a sugar plantation in Hawaii and then establishing a nursery in Oakland, California, where he grew plants and trees. In 1907, the American law changed to allow Japanese immigrants to bring wives from Japan, so long as the women didn't work. After Mrs. Mori joined her husband, Toshio and his younger brother were born. Then the two older sons were allowed to come from Japan. (For years, Toshio thought that his older brother was his father.) As a youngster, Mori was torn between a love of baseball and a love of reading. When his mother advised him to do less reading and more writing, Mori realized that he really wanted to be a writer and that he wanted to counteract the Asian stereotypes that he found in popular American fiction. Like the central character in "Japanese Hamlet," Mori knew that writers and other artists rarely make much money, so he accepted the idea of earning a living by working in the family nursery. His short story collection *Yokohama, California* was scheduled for publication in 1941, but the project was halted in response to the Japanese attack on Pearl Harbor and the book did not appear until 1949. During World War II, the Mori family, along with almost all other American citizens of Japanese ancestry, were regarded as potential spies and were forced to move to an internment center in a remote part of the American West. (Those Japanese Americans who volunteered for the American Army were sent to fight in Europe; one of Mori's older brothers served in Italy, where he received battle wounds that left him permanently paralyzed.)

When Mori's book appeared, the popular author William Saroyan (represented in volume 1) praised him as "a natural born writer." Some critics' complaints that Mori's English wasn't always perfect were gracefully answered by his friend and fellow-writer Hisaye Yamamoto (also represented in volume 1): "I think Toshio, just as I, was trying to use the very best English of which he was capable, and we have both run aground on occasion. Probably this was because we both spent the pre-kindergarten years speaking only Japanese, and, in such cases, *Sprachgefühl* [a feeling for the spoken language] is hard to come by."*

"Japanese Hamlet" first appeared in *Pacific Citizen,* the weekly publication of the Japanese-American Citizens League, in 1939. The story is set in Piedmont, a wealthy suburb of San Francisco. It seems to begin in the middle of a conversation, for the first six sentences refer to an unidentified "he," who proves to be the narrator's friend Tom Fukunaga. Many years before, Tom had defied the expectations of the Japanese American community in order to pursue a dream. As the narrator's tale unfolds, we learn about Tom's dream and the narrator's part in it. From the title, can you guess what the dream was? The conflict between dreams and reality is a theme in many works of literature. Perhaps it is also true of the lives of people whom you know.

* From Yamamoto's introduction to Mori's second short story collection, *The Chauvinist and Other Stories* (1979), which is also the source of the Saroyan quote later in "Making Connections."

He used to come to the house and ask me to hear him recite. Each time he handed me a volume of *The Complete Works of William Shakespeare*. He never forgot to do that. He wanted me to sit in front of him, open the book, and follow

5   him as he recited his lines. I did willingly. There was little for me to do in the evenings so when Tom Fukunaga came over I was ready to help out almost any time. And as his love for Shakespeare's plays grew with the years he did not want anything else in the world but to be a Shakespearean actor.

10   Tom Fukunaga was a schoolboy in a Piedmont home. He had been one since his freshman days in high school. When he was thirty-one he was still a schoolboy. Nobody knew his age but he and the relatives. Every time his relatives came to the city they put up a roar and said he was a good-for-nothing

15   loafer and ought to be ashamed of himself for being a schoolboy at this age.

"I am not loafing," he told his relatives. "I am studying very hard."

One of his uncles came often to the city to see him. He

20   tried a number of times to persuade Tom to quit stage hopes and schoolboy attitude. "Your parents have already disowned you. Come to your senses," he said. "You should go out and earn a man's salary. You are alone now. Pretty soon even your relatives will drop you."

25   "That's all right," Tom Fukunaga said. He kept shaking his head until his uncle went away.

When Tom Fukunaga came over to the house he used to tell me about his parents and relatives in the country. He told me in particular about the uncle who kept coming back to

30   warn and persuade him. Tom said he really was sorry for Uncle Bill to take the trouble to see him.

"Why don't you work for someone in the daytime and study at night?" I said to Tom.

"I cannot be bothered with such a change at this time," he

35   said. "Besides, I get five dollars a week plus room and board. That is enough for me. If I should go out and work for someone I would have to pay for room and board besides carfare so

I would not be richer. And even if I should save a little more it would not help me to become a better Shakespearean actor."

40 When we came down to the business of recitation there was no recess. Tom Fukunaga wanted none of it. He would place a cup of water before him and never touch it. "Tonight we'll begin with Hamlet," he said many times during the years. Hamlet was his favorite play. When he talked about Shake-
45 speare to anyone he began by mentioning Hamlet. He played parts in other plays but always he came back to Hamlet. This was his special role, the role which would establish him in Shakespearean history.

There were moments when I was afraid that Tom's energy
50 and time were wasted and I helped along to waste it. We were miles away from the stage world. Tom Fukunaga had not seen a backstage. He was just as far from the stagedoor in his thirties as he was in his high school days. Sometimes as I sat holding Shakespeare's book and listening to Tom I must have
55 looked worried and discouraged.

"Come on, come on!" he said. "Have you got the blues?"

One day I told him the truth: I was afraid we were not getting anywhere, that perhaps we were attempting the impossible. "If you could contact the stage people it might help," I
60 said. "Otherwise we are wasting our lives."

"I don't think so," Tom said. "I am improving every day. That is what counts. Our time will come later."

That night we took up Macbeth. He went through his parts smoothly. This made him feel good. "Some day I'll be the rank-
65 ing Shakespearean actor," he said.

Sometimes I told him I liked best to hear him recite the sonnets. I thought he was better with the sonnets than in the parts of Macbeth or Hamlet.

"I'd much rather hear you recite the sonnets, Tom." I said.

70 "Perhaps you like his sonnets best of all," he said. "Hamlet is my forte. I know I am at my best playing Hamlet."

For a year Tom Fukunaga did not miss a week coming to the house. Each time he brought a copy of Shakespeare's complete works and asked me to hear him say the lines. For better
75 or worse, he was not a bit downhearted. He still had no contact with the stage people. He did not talk about his uncle who kept coming back urging him to quit. I found out later that his uncle did not come to see him any more.

In the meantime Tom stayed at the Piedmont home as a
80 schoolboy. He accepted his five dollars a week just as he had
done years ago when he was a freshman at Piedmont High.
This fact did not bother Tom at all when I mentioned it to him.
"What are you worrying for?" he said. "I know I am taking
chances. I went into this with my eyes open so don't worry."

85 But I could not get over worrying about Tom Fukunaga's
chances. Every time he came over I felt bad for he was wasting his life and for the fact that I was mixed in it. Several times
I told him to go somewhere and find a job. He laughed. He kept
coming to the house and asked me to sit and hear him recite
90 Hamlet.

The longer I came to know Tom the more I wished to see
him well off in business or with a job. I got so I could not stand
his coming to the house and asking me to sit while he recited.
I began to dread his presence in the house as if his figure
95 reminded me of my part in the mock play that his life was, and
the prominence that my house and attention played.

One night I became desperate. "That book is destroying
you, Tom. Why don't you give this up for awhile?"

He looked at me curiously without a word. He recited sev-
100 eral pages and left early that evening.

Tom did not come to the house again. I guess it got so that
Tom could not stand me any more than his uncle and parents.
When he quit coming I felt bad. I knew he could never abandon
his ambition. I was equally sure that Tom would never rank
105 with the great Shakespearean actors, but I could not forget his
simple persistence.

One day, years later, I saw him on the Piedmont car at
Fourteenth and Broadway. He was sitting with his head buried
in a book and I was sure it was a copy of Shakespeare's. For a
110 moment he looked up and stared at me as if I were a stranger.
Then his face broke into a smile and he raised his hand. I
waved back eagerly.

"How are you, Tom?" I shouted.

He waved his hand politely again but did not get off, and
115 the car started up Broadway.

[1939]

Uncommon Words or Meanings

Hamlet (title)—*The Tragedy of Hamlet, Prince of Denmark* is the best-known of William Shakespeare's plays. Because of his father's sudden death, Hamlet has returned home from his studies. His mother has quickly married her late husband's brother, who has named himself king. A ghost appears to Hamlet, saying "I am your father's spirit, murdered by my own brother. You must avenge my death." Hamlet promises to do so. But then he worries that perhaps the ghost was the devil in disguise. What if his uncle/stepfather is innocent? Hamlet alternates between uncertainty and impulsive action that finally leads to many deaths, including his own.

a Piedmont home ("a schoolboy in a *Piedmont home*")—Piedmont is a well-to-do suburb of San Francisco. Tom was probably working as a gardener for an upper-middle-class family.

room and board ("pay for *room and board*")—a place to sleep and three meals a day.

carfare ("pay for . . . *carfare*")—the cost of daily public transportation, e.g., by trolley car.

the blues ("Have you got *the blues*?")—(informal) a feeling of sadness.

Macbeth ("That night we took up *Macbeth.*)—In *The Tragedy of Macbeth,* three witches tell Macbeth, a Scottish noble who is also a brave and victorious general, that he will one day become king of Scotland. Urged on by his ambitious wife, Lady Macbeth, he murders the present king and other innocent people to make the prophecy come true. In the end, however, Macbeth is defeated by his own ambition.

ranking ("the *ranking* Shakespearean actor")—leading, most important.

a forte ("Hamlet is my *forte.*")—something in which a person excels, a strong point.

Secrets

" . . . my life had

started to seem

like too much

trouble."

Secrets

Judy Troy
(born 1951)

Judy Troy sets her stories in many different parts of the country, reflecting her experience living in the South, Southwest, and West. The plot of "Secrets," which first appeared in *The New Yorker* magazine in 1992, is completely fictional. "On an emotional level, however," Troy affirms, "in the way Jean [the narrator] feels and in the things she notices and responds to, the story is very autobiographical."

As a child, Troy enjoyed both writing and acting. When she reached adolescence, she found that she was too self-conscious to perform but she did continue writing poems and stories in private. "I liked being able to become someone else, to create a different life from the one I was living, and I also liked being able to say what was secret within myself." Although she was twenty-six before she felt at all confident about her writing, Troy feels that the self-doubt was valuable. "I was able to be very critical of my own work," she says. "I never thought writing well would be easy, and I never minded rewriting." As a teacher of creative writing (at Indiana University, the University of Missouri-Columbia, and presently at Auburn University in Alabama), Troy helps her students to discover what every writer comes to learn—that writing a story is a much more intuitive than intellectual activity. "I have to get to know my characters," Troy explains, "to understand what they would realistically think and say. I don't always know what will happen, or how a story will end, until I write it. Then I have to revise it over and over again until it says what I want it to."

The characters in Troy's stories are small-town, blue-collar Americans struggling to find security, and perhaps some meaning, in their lives. "Secrets," the third of the four "Florida Stories" in *Mourning Doves* (1993), is narrated by a teenage girl. The girl's father has tried, and failed at, a succession of jobs in Indiana. Deciding that he should go into business with a relative in Key West, he packs up the family to move there. But by the time they reach Jacksonville, in northern Florida, they are out of money. "Secrets" tells some of what happens next. The narrator's voice seems rather flat—she doesn't show much emotion in telling about her life and she reports actions without analyzing people's motives. Yet this surface simplicity is deceptive. Along with the events of the twenty-four hour period from a Sunday evening to Monday evening, we learn about the family's history and also develop a sense of what the next few years may bring. What are the "secrets" of the title? Are they secrets that people have kept from other people? Could they be secrets that people have kept from themselves?

My father died in 1966, from a fall at a construction site where he was working, in Jacksonville, Florida. I was thirteen, and my brothers, Eddie and Lee, were eleven and eight. We had just moved from an apartment into a small house near Interstate 95, but our real home was South Bend, Indiana. We had only been in Florida for eight months. Both sets of grandparents wanted us to return to Indiana.

"They think I'm helpless," my mother said, "which makes me angry."

We were in the car on a Sunday night, two weeks after my father's funeral, driving home from the beach. My mother was working as a secretary at my brothers' elementary school, and her friends from work had invited us to a cookout. My mother said the cookout was to cheer us up. But, once her friends had got the fire going, they talked about how sad they felt for us. "What kind of food did your father like?" my mother's friend Grace Nolan asked us.

"Meat," Eddie said, "and not many kinds of vegetables."

Grace Nolan started to cry.

"Well, he liked potatoes, too," Lee told her.

"So," my mother said to us now, in the car, "I told your grandparents we'd be staying here."

"Good," Eddie said, from the back seat. Of the three of us—Eddie and Lee and me—he was the one who had made the most friends.

"I'm not sure I want to stay," I told my mother. "Or if Lee does." Lee was asleep, next to Eddie, with his head and shoulders on the seat and the rest of him limp on the floor.

"Lee wants to stay, Jean," my mother said. "I already know that." She pulled up in front of our house. It was ten o'clock, and we had forgotten to leave on any lights.

"Wake up, Lee," my mother said. She got out of the car and opened the back door and gently shook him. Sometimes he slept so soundly that it was impossible to wake him up. He opened his eyes for a moment and looked at the dark house.

"Why isn't Dad home yet?" he asked. My mother picked him up and carried him inside. He and Eddie were small for

their ages, whereas I was tall and too heavy. I watched my
mother put Lee into bed. Eddie lay down on his own bed,
against the opposite wall, and fell asleep with his clothes on.

My mother and I went into the kitchen. Spread out over the
table were letters from the construction company my father
had worked for, and forms from its insurance company. We
were supposed to receive twenty-five thousand dollars, and
my mother was planning to use this money to buy the house
we were in, which would allow us to live on the salary she
made. The problem was that there had been people around,
when the accident happened, who said the fall had been my
father's own fault, and not the fault of the construction company. So there was a chance the insurance company might not
pay us. My mother was worried about this, and now she sat
down at the table and began to fill out the forms.

I went into my room, next to the kitchen, which was really
meant to be a small utility room. My father had painted it yellow and put in carpeting for me. I changed into my nightgown
and got into bed. Every night since my father died, I had been
unable to fall asleep. During the day I didn't cry, and it didn't
upset me to hear about things my father had said or done. But
as soon as I was almost asleep, memories would come into my
mind that made our situation seem real to me. I stayed awake
all night, it seemed to me, listening to my mother in the kitchen
and to the distant noise of the cars on the highway.

In the morning, my mother made me get up and get ready
for school. My brothers and I had stayed home for a week after
my father died, and then my mother allowed me to stay home
for an additional week. I told her I didn't want to talk to people
at school yet, but the truth was also that I had got used to staying home—to being able to wear my nightgown all day if I
wanted to, or lie in bed all morning, reading a book. I didn't
want to go back to living my life, because my life had started to
seem like too much trouble. Each small thing, like brushing my
teeth or putting on knee-socks, now made me tired. I felt I had
to do fewer things each morning, in order to save energy for
some more important thing I might have to do in the afternoon.

After I ate breakfast, I walked to the end of our block and
waited for the bus with Nancy Dyer, who was in my class. It was
November, and she was wearing a blue corduroy jumper her
mother had made. She had brought over my assignments, for

the two weeks I had been home, and on the bus we went over
them. I made corrections according to the answers she remembered from class. "You did real well," she said when we were
finished. "But then, you're smarter than I am to begin with."

"That's not true," I told her. "I just do more homework."

"That's what I mean," she said. She had her eyes on her
boyfriend, who was getting on the bus. He was a thin boy, with
black hair. He sat in front of us. He ignored her and took out a
piece of notebook paper and shot spitballs at a red-haired boy
across the aisle.

"He's mad at me all the time now," Nancy whispered. "I
don't know why."

She had tears in her eyes, and I looked away and watched
the trees flashing past in the window. In the reflection, I could
see that three people on the bus were looking at me—the red-
haired boy, and two girls in the seat in front of him. When I
first got on the bus, one of these girls had said, "There was an
announcement in school about your dad."

"I know," I said. "Nancy told me."

"I can't believe that happened to you," she said, and whispered something that I couldn't hear to the other girl. Now, as I
turned away from the window and looked across the aisle, the
red-haired boy smiled at me and was about to say something
when he was hit in the forehead by a spitball.

When we got to school, I went to my locker to put away my
sweater, and then I went to science and algebra and history. In
each class, the teacher took me aside and talked to me about
my father, and two or three other people spoke to me about
him as well. The boys, especially, wanted to know exactly
what happened. "Did he step off the beam by accident," one
boy asked, "or was there something he tripped over?"

"I think he tripped," I told him.

"Wow," the boy said. "I can just picture that."

During lunch, the group of girls I sat with stopped talking
to each other when I walked up. "You can sit here, in the middle," Roberta Price said. Everyone moved over, and Carla Norris unwrapped my straw and put it in my milk. "We wondered
when you were coming back," Roberta said. "The principal
thought maybe last week."

"I decided to wait until today," I told her. We began to eat.
Most of us had bought hot lunches. We all had mothers who

120 were either too busy in the mornings to make us sandwiches or who felt we were old enough how to make them ourselves. Carla was the one exception. Her mother not only made her a sandwich but put a note in with her lunch every day.

"Here it is," Carla said. She unfolded a small piece of yel-
125 low paper. "Good luck on your geography quiz," she read out loud. "Your father and I are very proud of you." She and everybody else at the table looked down at their food.

"That's better than the one where she told you to wash off your mascara," I said, after a silence.
130 "It sure is," Roberta said quickly. "That one was sickening."

I had English class afterward, during fourth period. My English teacher, Mr. Thompson, was sitting at his desk when I walked in. I went to my seat and listened to a boy standing next to Mr. Thompson's desk talk to him about commas. "I don't
135 think we need them," the boy said. "Periods are good enough."

Other people were coming into the room, and Mr. Thompson went up to the blackboard and wrote down a sentence from *A Separate Peace*. The sentence was, "Perhaps I was stopped by that level of feeling, deeper than thought, which
140 contains the truth." After the bell rang, he stepped back from the board and asked, "What, exactly, does this sentence mean?"

Four people he called on said they didn't know. The fifth person said, "I think it means a feeling you keep to yourself."

"Why wouldn't you want anyone to know?" Mr. Thompson
145 asked.

"Because it's a secret," someone else said.

"Maybe it's a secret you keep from yourself," a girl in the back row said. "Maybe people don't want to know their own secrets."
150 "That doesn't make sense," a boy said.

"A lot of things don't make sense," Mr. Thompson told him, "but they're still true." He gave us an assignment, which we were to do in class, and then he sat on the radiator and watched us work. "Don't forget to use commas," he told us.
155 After class, I went downstairs to the girls' locker room to change my clothes for gym. Our teacher was already there, marking off our names as we walked in. She talked to me about my father, and then a girl I knew from another class said, "I don't know what I would do if my father died, even though I
160 hate him."

We all went out to the basketball court and shot baskets from the free-throw line. After gym, I went to the library for study hall, and then I met Nancy in front of my locker, and we walked out to the school bus. Her boyfriend, who got on the bus a few minutes after we did, sat down four rows ahead of us. He spent the whole bus ride talking loudly to a small, blond girl.

"Sometimes people try to hurt you just to see if they can do it," Nancy said.

"You don't know that for sure," I told her.

"Yes, I do," she said. "I've done it to people myself."

We got off at our block and stood for a moment at the corner before we each went home. The air was so still that the traffic from the highway seemed louder than usual. "I guess I don't need to talk to you about feeling sad," Nancy said. "I forgot for a minute."

"It's different with me," I told her. "It's not something you feel every second."

I walked across the neighbors' yard and into our own; I put Lee's bike in the shed and went into the house through the kitchen door. My mother was standing in Lee's doorway, and I heard Lee say, "I got an A in spelling. Dad gave me fifty cents last time."

My mother gave Lee two quarters, and then she walked past me into the kitchen, opened the kitchen door, and sat outside on our steps. I went out and sat beside her. "Did Dad really give Lee fifty cents?" she asked me.

"I thought it was a quarter," I told her, "but I might be remembering it wrong." She held my hand, and we watched a squirrel race around the shed.

"Would you give me a hug, honey?" she asked. I put my arms around her. In the past year, I had grown a lot, and now I was bigger than she was; when I hugged her, I was able to put my arms all the way around her.

"I wish I'd stop growing," I told her.

"You'll be tall, like Dad was," she said. "Someday you'll appreciate it." She stood up and walked down into the yard. She was still dressed in her work clothes—a skirt and blouse and high heels—and her shoes were invisible in the long grass. No one had mowed the yard since my father had died. "The

200 lawn will have to be Eddie's job now," my mother said. "You and Lee can do the raking." She looked up toward the clatter of a woodpecker in our sweetgum tree. "I'll find a gas station that will change the oil in the car, and then I'll teach myself to do the other things Dad did."

205 "That seems like a lot," I told her.

"I know it does, honey." She sat back down beside me and pulled up weeds that were growing out of the cracks in the steps. I looked around at the yard and the house—at the patches of bare ground under the trees, the peeling paint
210 around the windows, and all the small holes in the screens— and thought that it would take an army of men to fix everything that was broken.

My mother and I went inside to peel potatoes. At six o'clock, when Eddie came home from playing football with his
215 friends, we all had supper in the kitchen.

"I made a touchdown today," Eddie said.

"Well, good for you," my mother said, "I wish I could have seen it." She had eaten quickly, and she put her plate in the sink and drank a cup of instant coffee while she watched us finish.

220 Afterward, I cleared the table and washed the dishes. I forgot that it was Eddie's turn, and he didn't remind me until I was done. He and Lee were sitting on the floor in the living room, with Lee's toy soldiers all around them. They were watching television with my mother. I came in the room and said, "I
225 don't feel like watching TV."

"Who cares?" Eddie asked.

"We all care," my mother said sharply. "We're a family, even without Dad. We care what happens to each other." The way she spoke and the look on her face reminded me of my father, of the
230 times he'd lost his temper with us. Eddie and Lee looked surprised, and then, a second later, there were tears on their faces.

I was crying, too, because my mother had started to cry. But I wasn't upset about what Eddie had said or because my mother had got angry. I startled myself by feeling almost glad.
235 It seemed to me that all of a sudden our lives were ordinary again, except that my father wasn't there, and I felt like I was paying attention after being lost in a daydream, or like I was opening my eyes after seeing how long I could keep them closed. When my mother started to speak, I hoped she wouldn't

240 say something nice that would cancel out her angry words. But what she said was, "O.K. Pick up these toys. Then we're going to turn off the television and go to bed."

It was only seven-thirty, but we went into our rooms. I didn't bother to put on my nightgown. I took off my clothes and got 245 into bed in my underwear, and, even though it was early, I didn't have my same trouble falling asleep. I knew now that my father was dead and that we would live our lives without him, and I fell asleep right away, so that for a while I could not know these things.

[1993]

Uncommon Words or Meanings

Interstate 95 ("a small house near *Interstate 95*")—a highway running from Maine to Florida.

a cookout ("invited us to a *cookout*")—a picnic at which some foods are cooked outdoors.

heavy ("I was tall and too *heavy.*")—overweight, fat.

limp ("the rest of him *limp* on the floor")—with the muscles completely relaxed.

a utility room ("meant to be a small *utility room*")—a room for household appliances such as machines for washing and drying clothes.

a spitball ("shot *spitballs* at the red-haired boy")—(informal) a small piece of paper crumpled up and moistened with saliva (spit).

A Separate Peace ("a sentence from *A Separate Peace*")—a 1959 novel by John Knowles about a boy's coming of age in a New England boarding school.

to mark off ("*marking off* our names as we walked in")—here, to make a note that someone is present.

to shoot baskets from the freethrow line ("went to the basketball court and *shot baskets from the freethrow line*")—to throw a basketball through a hoop from a marked spot eight feet away.

a study hall ("went to the library for *study hall*")—in high school, a class period when students work quietly on their individual assignments.

a touchdown ("I made a *touchdown*")—in football, six points scored by carrying the ball over the opponents' goal line or throwing it to a teammate behind the goal line.

to cancel out ("something nice that would *cancel out* her angry words")—to make up for, neutralize, remove the impact of.

The Orphaned Swimming Pool

"True, late
splashes and
excited guffaws
did often keep
Mrs. Chace
awake. . . "

The Orphaned
Swimming Pool

John Updike
(born 1932)

A chronicler of contemporary middle-class and upper-middle-class American life, John Updike is the author of thirteen novels, nine collections of short stories, four children's books, and one play, as well as poetry, essays and criticism. How did such a writer develop from, as Updike has written of himself in *Self-Consciousness* (1989), "a very average little boy, and furthermore a boy who loved the average, the daily, the safely hidden"?

Updike was born in Shillington, a small town in eastern Pennsylvania, in 1932. His father was a high school math teacher who had previously been a telephone cable-splicer ("a telephone lineman" is mentioned in "The Orphaned Swimming Pool"). His parents and grandparents, like many Americans, had lost most of their money during the Depression. Nevertheless, Updike's mother, an unpublished writer, encouraged her son to plan a future in the arts—drawing or writing—rather than in a safe, ordinary job. Two other factors also influenced the unusual development of the "average little boy." The first factor was a pair of physical problems—a chronic skin disease and a stutter—that made Updike self-conscious about both his body and his speech. The second factor was his high intelligence, which enabled Updike to earn high grades in school, as well as a full scholarship to Harvard University and a one-year post-graduate fellowship to Oxford University.

At Harvard, Updike majored in English but wrote short stories only when they were required for a class, being much more interested in drawing cartoons and writing light verse. Yet the first story Updike wrote after graduating in 1954 was accepted by *The New Yorker,* and he worked as a staff writer there for a year when he returned from Oxford. In 1957, seeking a climate that would help him to control his skin problem, Updike moved to the Boston suburbs and became a full-time writer. There he has devoted his happiest hours to preparing words for print, "words as smooth in their arrangement and flow as repeated revision could make them."

"The voice of fiction speaks in images," Updike reminds us, noting that he finds his own fictional voice "when the images come abundantly, and interweave to make a continuous music." For "The Orphaned Swimming Pool," these images are based on the details of suburban American life. The story shows his characteristic use of brand names—for example, Triscuits (a salty wheat cracker), Agitrol (a chemical used to control algae), and Off! (a bug spray/insect repellent)—in creating a realistic setting. It also illustrates Updike's continuing interest in "the animating force of sexual desire behind polite appearances." What is the connection between sexual desire and a swimming pool? And what can the title mean? An orphan is a child who has lost both parents. How can a suburban swimming pool be "orphaned"?

The Orphaned Swimming Pool

Marriages, like chemical unions, release upon dissolution packets of the energy locked up in their bonding. There is the piano no one wants, the cocker spaniel no one can take care of. Shelves of books suddenly stand revealed as burdensomely dated and unlikely to be reread; indeed, it is difficult to remember who read them in the first place. And what of those old skis in the attic? Or the doll house waiting to be repaired in the basement? The piano goes out of tune, the dog goes mad. The summer that the Turners got their divorce, their swimming pool had neither a master nor a mistress, though the sun beat down day after day, and a state of drought was declared in Connecticut.

It was a young pool, only two years old, of the fragile type fashioned by laying a plastic liner within a carefully carved hole in the ground. The Turners' side yard looked infernal while it was being done; one bulldozer sank into the mud and had to be pulled free by another. But by midsummer the new grass was sprouting, the encircling flagstones were in place, the blue plastic tinted the water a heavenly blue, and it had to be admitted that the Turners had scored again. They were always a little in advance of their friends. He was a tall, hairy-backed man with long arms, and a nose flattened by football, and a sullen look of too much blood; she was a fine-boned blonde with dry blue eyes and lips usually held parted and crinkled as if about to ask a worrisome, or whimsical, question. They had never seemed happier, nor their marriage healthier, than those two summers. They grew brown and supple and smooth with swimming. Ted would begin his day with a swim, before dressing to catch the train, and Linda would hold court all day amid crowds of wet matrons and children, and Ted would return from work to find a poolside cocktail party in progress, and the couple would end their day at midnight, when their friends had finally left, by swimming nude, before bed. What ecstasy! In darkness the water felt mild as milk and buoyant as helium, and the swimmers became giants, gliding from side to side in a single languorous stroke.

The next May, the pool was filled as usual, and the usual after-school gangs of mothers and children gathered, but Linda, unlike her, stayed indoors. She could be heard within

the house, moving from room to room, but she no longer
40 emerged, as in the other summers, with a cheerful tray of ice
and brace of bottles, and Triscuits and lemonade for the children. Their friends felt less comfortable about appearing, towels in hand, at the Turners' on weekends. Though Linda had
lost some weight and looked elegant, and Ted was cumber-
45 somely jovial, they gave off the faint, sleepless, awkward-mak-
ing aroma of a couple in trouble. Then, the day after school
was out, Linda fled with the children to her parents in Ohio.
Ted stayed nights in the city, and the pool was deserted.
Though the pump that ran the water through the filter contin-
50 ued to mutter in the lilacs, the cerulean pool grew cloudy. The
bodies of dead horseflies and wasps dotted the still surface. A
speckled plastic ball drifted into a corner beside the diving
board and stayed there. The grass between the flagstones grew
lank. On the glass-topped poolside table, a spray can of Off!
55 had lost its pressure and a gin and tonic glass held a sere mint
leaf. The pool looked desolate and haunted, like a stagnant
jungle spring; it looked poisonous and ashamed. The postman,
stuffing overdue notices and pornography solicitations into
the mailbox, averted his eyes from the side yard politely.
60   Some June weekends, Ted sneaked out from the city. Families driving to church glimpsed him dolefully sprinkling chemical substances into the pool. He looked pale and thin. He
instructed Roscoe Chace, his neighbor on the left, how to
switch on the pump and change the filter, and how much chlo-
65 rine and Algitrol should be added weekly. He explained he
would not be able to make it out every weekend—as if the distance that for years he had traveled twice each day, gliding in
and out of New York, had become an impossibly steep climb
back into the past. Linda, he confided vaguely, had left her par-
70 ents in Akron and was visiting her sister in Minneapolis. As the
shock of the Turners' joint disappearance wore off, their pool
seemed less haunted and forbidding. The Murtaugh children—
the Murtaughs, a rowdy, numerous family, were the Turners'
right-hand neighbors—began to use it, without supervision. So
75 Linda's old friends, with their children, began to show up, "to
keep the Murtaughs from drowning each other." For if anything were to happen to a Murtaugh, the poor Turners (the
adjective had become automatic) would be sued for everything, right when they could least afford it. It became, then, a
80 kind of duty, a test of loyalty, to use the pool.

July was the hottest in twenty-seven years. People brought their own lawn furniture over in station wagons and set it up. Teenage offspring and Swiss *au-pair* girls were established as lifeguards. A nylon rope with flotation corks, meant to divide the wading end from the diving end of the pool, was found coiled in the garage and reinstalled. Agnes Kleefeld contributed an old refrigerator, which was wired to an outlet above Ted's basement workbench and used to store ice, quinine water, and soft drinks. An honor system shoebox containing change appeared beside it; a little lost-and-found—an array of forgotten sunglasses, flippers, towels, lotions, paperbacks, shirts, even underwear—materialized on the Turners' side steps. When people, that July, said, "Meet you at the pool," they did not mean the public pool past the shopping center, or the country-club pool beside the first tee. They meant the Turners'. Restrictions on admission were difficult to enforce tactfully. A visiting Methodist bishop, two Taiwanese economists, an entire girls' softball team from Darien, an eminent Canadian poet, the archery champion of Hartford, the six members of a black rock group called the Good Intentions, an ex-mistress of Aly Khan, the lavender-haired mother-in-law of a Nixon adviser not quite of Cabinet rank, an infant of six weeks, a man who was killed the next day on the Merritt Parkway, a Filipino who could stay on the pool bottom for eighty seconds, two Texans who kept cigars in their mouths and hats on their heads, three telephone linemen, four expatriate Czechs, a student Maoist from Wesleyan, and the postman all swam, as guests, in the Turners' pool, though not all at once. After the daytime crowd ebbed, and the shoebox was put back in the refrigerator, and the last *au-pair* girl took the last goose-fleshed, wrinkled child shivering home to supper, there was a tide of evening activity, trysts (Mrs. Kleefeld and the Nicholson boy, most notoriously) and what some called, overdramatically, orgies. True, late splashes and excited guffaws did often keep Mrs. Chace awake, and the Murtaugh children spent hours at their attic window with binoculars. And there was the evidence of the lost underwear.

One Saturday early in August, the morning arrivals found an unknown car with New York plates parked in the garage. But cars of all sorts were so common—the parking tangle frequently extended into the road—that nothing much was

thought of it, even when someone noticed that the bedroom
windows upstairs were open. And nothing came of it, except
that around suppertime, in the lull before the evening crowds
began to arrive in force, Ted and an unknown woman, of the
same physical type as Linda but brunette, swiftly exited from
the kitchen door, got into the car, and drove back to New York.
The few lingering babysitters and beaux thus unwittingly
glimpsed the root of the divorce. The two lovers had been
trapped inside the house all day; Ted was fearful of the legal
consequences of their being seen by anyone who might write
and tell Linda. The settlement was at a ticklish stage; nothing
less than terror of Linda's lawyers would have led Ted to sup-
press his indignation at seeing, from behind the window
screen, his private pool turned public carnival. For long there-
after, though in the end he did not marry the woman, he
remembered that day when they lived together like fugitives in
a cave, feeding on love and ice water, tiptoeing barefoot to the
depleted cupboards, which they, arriving late last night, had
hoped to stock in the morning, not foreseeing the onslaught of
interlopers that would pin them in. Her hair, he remembered,
had tickled his shoulders as she crouched behind him at the
window, and through the angry pounding of his own blood he
had felt her slim body breathless with the attempt not to giggle.

August drew in, with cloudy days. Children grew bored
with swimming. Roscoe Chace went on vacation to Italy; the
pump broke down, and no one repaired it. Dead dragonflies
accumulated on the surface of the pool. Small deluded toads
hopped in and swam around hopelessly. Linda at last returned.
From Minneapolis she had gone on to Idaho for six weeks, to
be divorced. She and the children had burnt faces from riding
and hiking; her lips looked drier and more quizzical than ever,
still seeking to frame that troubling question. She stood at the
window, in the house that already seemed to lack its furniture,
at the same side window where the lovers had crouched, and
gazed at the deserted pool. The grass around it was green from
splashing, save where a long-lying towel had smothered a rec-
tangle and left it brown. Aluminum furniture she didn't recognize lay strewn and broken. She counted a dozen bottles
beneath the glass-topped table. The nylon divider had parted,
and its two halves floated independently. The blue plastic
beneath the colorless water tried to make a cheerful, other-

worldly statement, but Linda saw that the pool in truth had no
bottom, it held bottomless loss, it was one huge blue tear.
165 Thank God no one had drowned in it. Except her. She saw that
she could never live here again. In September the place was
sold to a family with toddling infants, who for safety's sake
have not only drained the pool but have sealed it over with
iron pipes and a heavy mesh, and put warning signs around, as
170 around a chained dog.

[1970]

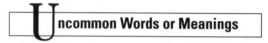

Uncommon Words or Meanings

dissolution ("Marriages, like chemical unions, release upon *dissolution* packets of energy")—decomposition into fragments or parts; termination of a formal or legal bond or contract.

bonding ("the energy locked up in their *bonding*")—the force that holds atoms together; when the bond is broken, energy (motion, heat, or light) is released.

to go mad ("the dog *goes mad*")—to become infected with rabies (a dog); to become insane.

to score ("the Turners had *scored* again")—to make a point in a contest.

to hold court ("would *hold court* all day")—to entertain visitors, as a queen receives courtiers.

a solicitation ("stuffing . . . pornography *solicitations* into the mailbox")—(1) a request made using persuasion; (2) an offer of sexual services. Both meanings apply here.

an au-pair girl ("Swiss *au-pair girls*")—a young woman who lives with a family and looks after the children in exchange for room and board.

an honor system ("an *honor system* shoebox containing change")—an informal agreement that, without supervision, people will follow a set of rules.

Darien ("softball team from *Darien*")—a very fashionable Connecticut suburb of New York.

Hartford ("archery champion of *Hartford*")—an unfashionable city in northern Connecticut.

Good Intentions ("rock group called the *Good Intentions*")—from the proverbial expression "The road to hell is paved with good intentions."

Aly Khan ("an ex-mistress of *Aly Khan*")—a Pakistani prince known as a playboy and sportsman in his youth; Pakistani ambassador to the United Nations, 1958–60.

lavender-haired ("the *lavender-haired* mother-in-law")—with white hair tinted a purplish-blue.

Nixon ("a *Nixon* adviser")—Richard M. Nixon, American president, 1969–74.

a parkway ("killed the next day on the Merritt *Parkway*")—a highway on which no trucks or commercial vehicles are allowed.

a Maoist ("a student *Maoist*")—a follower of Mao Zedong, the primary Chinese Communist organizer and theoretician from the 1920s to his death in 1979.

Wesleyan ("from *Wesleyan*")—a fashionable private university in western Connecticut.

beaux ("The few lingering babysitters and *beaux*")—Plural form of *beau,* a boyfriend.

ticklish ("The settlement was at a ticklish stage")—delicate, easy to upset.

The Sojourner

"Certainly his love

for his ex-wife was

long since past.

So why the

unhinged body,

the shaken

mind?"

The Sojourner

Carson McCullers
(1917–1967)

Born and raised in Georgia, Carson McCullers lived for most of her adult life in or near New York City. She was a promising pianist in her childhood but realized as a young adult that her real talent was for writing. McCullers became a literary celebrity with her first novel, *The Heart Is a Lonely Hunter* (1940), published when she was only twenty-three. Though chronic ill-health limited her output, she completed three other novels (including *The Member of the Wedding*, 1946, which was later turned into a successful play and film), twenty short stories, two plays, and a children's book, as well as poetry and essays.

All of McCullers's short stories deal in one way or another with rejection or unrequited love, and many of them have characters who share some of McCullers's personal history. In "The Sojourner," the title character, John Ferris, is a Southerner who, like McCullers, has chosen to live outside the South as an adult. Ferris also shares personality traits with Reeves McCullers, whom the author married twice and who ultimately committed suicide in Paris.

"The Sojourner" invites the reader into the sophisticated world of well-to-do Southerners now living in other parts of the world. John Ferris works in Paris as an international newspaper correspondent. He has lived for brief periods of time—"sojourned," as he says—in various European capitals, speaks French, and has had a series of mistresses since his divorce eight years earlier. He is undaunted by a twelve-hour (pre-jet) transatlantic flight, but he has been shaken by the death of his father, who had had a year of treatment at the prestigious Johns Hopkins Medical Center in Baltimore, a hospital well-known for its treatment of cancer, a disease not spoken of openly at the time the story was written.

Ferris's ex-wife lives with her second husband and their two children in a fashionable part of New York City. Their live-in housekeeper can easily prepare a Southern-style company meal on short notice. While the adults talk over cocktails, the housekeeper feeds the children and then serves dinner. The wife, like McCullers herself, is an amateur pianist who enjoys playing for others and is fond of the intricate music of Johann Sebastian Bach. After an early dinner, the couple can arrive at the theater for an 8:30 performance. What problems could there possibly be in such comfortable lives? And what connection do their lives have with those of less-privileged people?

The twilight border between sleep and waking was a Roman one this morning: splashing fountains and arched, narrow streets, the golden lavish city of blossoms and age-soft stone. Sometimes in this semi-consciousness he sojourned again in Paris, or war German rubble, or Swiss skiing and a snow hotel. Sometimes, also, in a fallow Georgia field at hunting dawn. Rome it was this morning in the yearless regions of dreams.

John Ferris awoke in a room in a New York hotel. He had the feeling that something unpleasant was awaiting him—what it was, he did not know. The feeling, submerged by matinal necessities, lingered even after he had dressed and gone downstairs. It was a cloudless autumn day and the pale sunlight sliced between the pastel skyscrapers. Ferris went into the next-door drugstore and sat at the end booth next to the window glass that overlooked the sidewalk. He ordered an American breakfast with scrambled eggs and sausage.

Ferris had come from Paris to his father's funeral which had taken place the week before in his home town in Georgia. The shock of death had made him aware of youth already passed. His hair was already receding and the veins in his now naked temples were pulsing and prominent and his body was spare except for an incipient belly bulge. Ferris had loved his father and the bond between them had once been extraordinarily close—but the years had somehow unraveled this filial devotion; the death, expected for a long time, had left him with an unforeseen dismay. He had stayed as long as possible to be near his mother and brothers at home. His plane for Paris was to leave the next morning.

Ferris pulled out his address book to verify a number. He turned the pages with growing attentiveness. Names and addresses from New York, the capitals of Europe, a few faint ones from his home state in the South. Faded, printed names, sprawled drunken ones. Betty Wills: a random love, married now. Charlie Williams: wounded in the Hürtgen Forest, unheard of since. Grand old Williams—did he live or die? Don Walker: a B.T.O., in television, getting rich. Henry Green: hit the skids

after the war, in a sanitarium now, they say. Cozie Hall: he had
heard that she was dead. Heedless, laughing Cozie—it was
strange to think that she too, silly girl, could die. As Ferris
40 closed the address book, he suffered a sense of hazard, transience, almost of fear.

It was then that his body jerked suddenly. He was staring
out of the window when there, on the sidewalk, passing by,
was his ex-wife. Elizabeth passed quite close to him, walking
45 slowly. He could not understand the wild quiver of his heart,
nor the following sense of recklessness and grace that lingered
after she was gone.

Quickly Ferris paid his check and rushed out to the sidewalk. Elizabeth stood on the corner waiting to cross Fifth
50 Avenue. He hurried toward her meaning to speak, but the
lights changed and she crossed the street before he reached
her. Ferris followed. On the other side he could easily have
overtaken her, but he found himself lagging unaccountably.
Her fair brown hair was plainly rolled, and as he watched her
55 Ferris recalled that once his father had remarked that Elizabeth had a "beautiful carriage." She turned at the next corner
and Ferris followed, although by now his intention to overtake
her had disappeared. Ferris questioned the bodily disturbance
that the sight of Elizabeth aroused in him, the dampness of his
60 hands, the hard heartstrokes.

It was eight years since Ferris had last seen his ex-wife. He
knew that long ago she had married again. And there were
children. During recent years he had seldom thought of her.
But at first, after the divorce, the loss had almost destroyed
65 him. Then after the anodyne of time, he had loved again, and
then again. Jeannine, she was now. Certainly his love for his
ex-wife was long since past. So why the unhinged body, the
shaken mind? He knew only that his clouded heart was oddly
dissonant with the sunny, candid autumn day. Ferris wheeled
70 suddenly, and walking with long strides, almost running, hurried back to the hotel.

Ferris poured himself a drink, although it was not yet
eleven o'clock. He sprawled out in an armchair like a man
exhausted, nursing his glass of bourbon and water. He had
75 a full day ahead of him as he was leaving by plane the next
morning for Paris. He checked over his obligations: take luggage

to Air France, lunch with his boss, buy shoes and an overcoat. And something—wasn't there something else? Ferris finished his drink and opened the telephone directory.

80   His decision to call his ex-wife was impulsive. The number was under Bailey, the husband's name, and he called before he had much time for self-debate. He and Elizabeth had exchanged cards at Christmastime, and Ferris had sent a carving set when he received the announcement of her wedding.
85 There was no reason *not* to call. But as he waited, listening to the ring at the other end, misgiving fretted him.

    Elizabeth answered; her familiar voice was a fresh shock to him. Twice he had to repeat his name, but when he was identified, she sounded glad. He explained he was only in
90 town for that day. They had a theater engagement, she said— but she wondered if he would come by for an early dinner. Ferris said he would be delighted.

    As he went from one engagement to another, he was still bothered at odd moments by the feeling that something neces-
95 sary was forgotten. Ferris bathed and changed in the late afternoon, often thinking about Jeannine: he would be with her the following night. "Jeannine," he would say, "I happened to run into my ex-wife when I was in New York. Had dinner with her. And her husband, of course. It was strange seeing
100 her after all these years."

    Elizabeth lived in the East Fifties, and as Ferris taxied uptown he glimpsed at intersections the lingering sunset, but by the time he reached his destination it was already autumn dark. The place was a building with a marquee and a doorman,
105 and the apartment was on the seventh floor.

    "Come in, Mr. Ferris."

    Braced for Elizabeth or even the unimagined husband, Ferris was astonished by the freckled red-haired child; he had known of the children, but his mind had failed somehow to
110 acknowledge them. Surprise made him step back awkwardly.

    "This is our apartment," the child said politely. "Aren't you Mr. Ferris? I'm Billy. Come in."

    In the living room beyond the hall, the husband provided another surprise; he too had not been acknowledged emotion-
115 ally. Bailey was a lumbering red-haired man with a deliberate manner. He rose and extended a welcoming hand.

"I'm Bill Bailey. Glad to see you. Elizabeth will be in, in a minute. She's finishing dressing."

The last words struck a gliding series of vibrations, memories of the other years. Fair Elizabeth, rosy and naked before
her bath. Half-dressed before the mirror of her dressing table,
brushing her fine, chestnut hair. Sweet, casual intimacy, the
soft-fleshed loveliness indisputably possessed. Ferris shrank
from the unbidden memories and compelled himself to meet
Bill Bailey's gaze.

"Billy, would you please bring that tray of drinks from the
kitchen table?"

The child obeyed promptly, and when he was gone Ferris
remarked conversationally, "Fine boy you have there."

"We think so."

Flat silence until the child returned with a tray of glasses
and a cocktail shaker of Martinis. With the priming drinks they
pumped up conversation: Russia, they spoke of, and the New
York rainmaking, and the apartment situation in Manhattan
and Paris.

"Mr. Ferris is flying all the way across the ocean tomorrow,"
Bailey said to the little boy who was perched on the arm of his
chair, quiet and well behaved. "I bet you would like to be a
stowaway in his suitcase."

Billy pushed back his limp bangs. "I want to fly in an airplane
and be a newspaperman like Mr. Ferris." He added with sudden
assurance, "That's what I would like to do when I am big."

Bailey said, "I thought you wanted to be a doctor."

"I do!" said Billy. "I would like to be both. I want to be a
atom-bomb scientist too."

Elizabeth came in carrying in her arms a baby girl.

"Oh, John!" she said. She settled the baby in the father's
lap. "It's grand to see you. I'm awfully glad you could come."

The little girl sat demurely on Bailey's knees. She wore a
pale pink crêpe de Chine frock, smocked around the yoke with
rose, and a matching silk hair ribbon tying back her pale soft
curls. Her skin was summer tanned and her brown eyes
flecked with gold and laughing. When she reached up and fin-
gered her father's horn-rimmed glasses, he took them
off and let her look through them a moment. "How's my
old Candy?"

Elizabeth was very beautiful, more beautiful perhaps than he had ever realized. Her straight clean hair was shining. Her face was softer, glowing and serene. It was a madonna loveliness, dependent on the family ambiance.

"You've hardly changed at all," Elizabeth said, "but it has been a long time."

"Eight years." His hand touched his thinning hair self-consciously while further amenities were exchanged.

Ferris felt himself suddenly a spectator—an interloper among these Baileys. Why had he come? He suffered. His own life seemed so solitary, a fragile column supporting nothing amidst the wreckage of the years. He felt he could not bear much longer to stay in the family room.

He glanced at his watch. "You're going to the theater?"

"It's a shame," Elizabeth said, "but we've had this engagement for more than a month. But surely, John, you'll be staying here one of these days before long. You're not going to be an expatriate, are you?"

"Expatriate," Ferris repeated. "I don't much like the word."

"What's a better word?" she asked.

He thought for a moment. "Sojourner might do."

Ferris glanced again at his watch, and again Elizabeth apologized. "If only we had known ahead of time—"

"I just had this day in town. I came home unexpectedly. You see, Papa died last week."

"Papa Ferris is dead?"

"Yes, at Johns Hopkins. He had been sick there nearly a year. The funeral was down home in Georgia."

"Oh, I'm so sorry, John. Papa Ferris was always one of my favorite people."

The little boy moved from behind the chair so that he could look into his mother's face. He asked, "Who is dead?"

Ferris was oblivious to apprehension; he was thinking of his father's death. He saw again the outstretched body on the quilted silk within the coffin. The corpse flesh was bizarrely rouged and the familiar hands lay massive and joined above a spread of funeral roses. The memory closed and Ferris awakened to Elizabeth's calm voice.

"Mr. Ferris' father, Billy. A really grand person. Somebody you didn't know."

"But why did you call him *Papa* Ferris?"

Bailey and Elizabeth exchanged a trapped look. It was Bailey who answered the questioning child. "A long time ago," he said, "your mother and Mr. Ferris were once married. Before you were born—a long time ago."

"Mr. Ferris?"

The little boy stared at Ferris, amazed and unbelieving. And Ferris' eyes, as he returned the gaze, were somehow unbelieving too. Was it indeed true that at one time he had called this stranger, Elizabeth, Little Butterduck during nights of love, that they had lived together, shared perhaps a thousand days and nights and—finally—endured in the misery of sudden solitude the fiber by fiber (jealousy, alcohol and money quarrels) destruction of the fabric of married love.

Bailey said to the children, "It's somebody's suppertime. Come on now."

"But Daddy! Mama and Mr. Ferris—I—"

Billy's everlasting eyes—perplexed and with a glimmer of hostility—reminded Ferris of the gaze of another child. It was the young son of Jeannine—a boy of seven with a shadowed little face and nobby knees whom Ferris avoided and usually forgot.

"Quick march!" Bailey gently turned Billy toward the door. "Say good night now, son."

"Good night, Mr. Ferris." He added resentfully, "I thought I was staying up for the cake."

"You can come in afterward for the cake," Elizabeth said. "Run along now with Daddy for your supper."

Ferris and Elizabeth were alone. The weight of the situation descended on those first moments of silence. Ferris asked permission to pour himself another drink and Elizabeth set the cocktail shaker on the table at his side. He looked at the grand piano and noticed the music on the rack.

"Do you still play as beautifully as you used to?"

"I still enjoy it."

"Please play, Elizabeth."

Elizabeth arose immediately. Her readiness to perform when asked had always been one of her amiabilities; she never hung back, apologized. Now as she approached the piano there was the added readiness of relief.

She began with a Bach prelude and fugue. The prelude was
as gaily iridescent as a prism in a morning room. The first voice
of the fugue, an announcement pure and solitary, was repeated
240   intermingling with a second voice, and again repeated within
an elaborated frame, the multiple music, horizontal and serene,
flowed with unhurried majesty. The principal melody was
woven with two other voices, embellished with countless inge-
nuities—now dominant, again submerged, it had the sublimity
245   of a single thing that does not fear surrender to the whole.
Toward the end, the density of the material gathered for the last
enriched insistence on the dominant first motif and with a
chorded final statement the fugue ended. Ferris rested his head
on the chair back and closed his eyes. In the following silence a
250   clear, high voice came from the room down the hall.

"Daddy, how *could* Mama and Mr. Ferris—" A door was
closed.

The piano began again—what was this music? Unplaced,
familiar, the limpid melody had lain a long while dormant in
255   his heart. Now it spoke to him of another time, another
place—it was the music Elizabeth used to play. The delicate air
summoned a wilderness of memory. Ferris was lost in the riot
of past longings, conflicts, ambivalent desires. Strange that the
music, catalyst for this tumultuous anarchy, was so serene and
260   clear. The singing melody was broken off by the appearance of
the maid.

"Miz Bailey, dinner is out on the table now."

Even after Ferris was seated at the table between his host
and hostess, the unfinished music still overcast his mood. He
265   was a little drunk.

"*L'improvisation de la vie humaine,*" he said. "There's
nothing that makes you so aware of the improvisation of human
existence as a song unfinished. Or an old address book."

"Address book?" repeated Bailey. Then he stopped, non-
270   committal and polite.

"You're still the same old boy, Johnny," Elizabeth said with
a trace of the old tenderness.

It was a Southern dinner that evening, and the dishes were
his old favorites. They had fried chicken and corn pudding and
275   rich, glazed candied sweet potatoes. During the meal Elizabeth
kept alive a conversation when the silences were overlong.
And it came about that Ferris was led to speak of Jeannine.

"I first knew Jeannine last autumn—about this time of the year—in Italy. She's a singer and she had an engagement in Rome. I expect we will be married soon."

The words seemed so true, inevitable, that Ferris did not at first acknowledge to himself the lie. He and Jeannine had never in that year spoken of marriage. And indeed, she was still married—to a White Russian money-changer in Paris from whom she had been separated for five years. But it was too late to correct the lie. Already Elizabeth was saying: "This really makes me glad to know. Congratulations, Johnny."

He tried to make amends with truth. "The Roman autumn is so beautiful. Balmy and blossoming." He added, "Jeannine has a little boy of seven. A curious trilingual little fellow. We go to the Tuileries sometimes."

A lie again. He had taken the boy once to the gardens. The sallow foreign child in shorts that bared his spindly legs had sailed his boat in the concrete pond and ridden the pony. The child had wanted to go in to the puppet show. But there was not time, for Ferris had an engagement at the Scribe Hotel. He had promised they would go to the guignol another afternoon. Only once had he taken Valentin to the Tuileries.

There was a stir. The maid brought in a white-frosted cake with pink candles. The children entered in their night clothes. Ferris still did not understand.

"Happy birthday, John," Elizabeth said. "Blow out the candles."

Ferris recognized his birthday date. The candles blew out lingeringly and there was the smell of burning wax. Ferris was thirty-eight years old. The veins in his temples darkened and pulsed visibly.

"It's time you started for the theater."

Ferris thanked Elizabeth for the birthday dinner and said the appropriate good-byes. The whole family saw him to the door.

A high, thin moon shone above the jagged, dark skyscrapers. The streets were windy, cold. Ferris hurried to Third Avenue and hailed a cab. He gazed at the nocturnal city with the deliberate attentiveness of departure and perhaps farewell. He was alone. He longed for flighttime and the coming journey.

The next day he looked down on the city from the air, burnished in sunlight, toylike, precise. Then America was left behind and there was only the Atlantic and the distant European shore. The ocean was milky pale and placid beneath the clouds. Ferris dozed most of the day. Toward dark he was thinking of Elizabeth and the visit of the previous evening. He thought of Elizabeth among her family with longing, gentle envy and inexplicable regret. He sought the melody, the unfinished air, that had so moved him. The cadence, some unrelated tones, were all that remained; the melody itself evaded him. He found instead the first voice of the fugue that Elizabeth had played—it came to him, inverted mockingly and in a minor key. Suspended above the ocean the anxieties of transience and solitude no longer troubled him and he thought of his father's death with equanimity. During the dinner hour the plane reached the shore of France.

At midnight Ferris was in a taxi crossing Paris. It was a clouded night and mist wreathed the lights of the Place de la Concorde. The midnight bistros gleamed on the wet pavements. As always after a transocean flight the change of continents was too sudden. New York at morning, this midnight Paris. Ferris glimpsed the disorder of his life: the succession of cities, of transitory loves; and time, the sinister glissando of the years, time always.

"*Vite! Vite!*" he called in terror. "*Dépêchez-vous.*"

Valentin opened the door to him. The little boy wore pajamas and an outgrown red robe. His gray eyes were shadowed and, as Ferris passed into the flat, they flickered momentarily.

"*J'attends Maman.*"

Jeannine was singing in a night club. She would not be home before another hour. Valentin returned to a drawing, squatting with his crayons over the paper on the floor. Ferris looked down at the drawing—it was a banjo player with notes and wavy lines inside a comic-strip balloon.

"We will go again to the Tuileries."

The child looked up and Ferris drew him closer to his knees. The melody, the unfinished music that Elizabeth had played, came to him suddenly. Unsought, the load of memory jettisoned—this time bringing only recognition and sudden joy.

"Monsieur Jean," the child said, "did you see him?"

Confused, Ferris thought only of another child—the freckled, family-loved boy. "See who, Valentin?"

"Your dead papa in Georgia." The child added, "Was he okay?"

Ferris spoke with rapid urgency: "We will go often to the Tuileries. Ride the pony and we will go into the guignol. We will see the puppet show and never be in a hurry any more."

"Monsieur Jean," Valentine said. "The guignol is now closed."

365 Again, the terror the acknowledgment of wasted years and death. Valentin, responsive and confident, still nestled in his arms. His cheek touched the soft cheek and felt the brush of the delicate eyelashes. With inner desperation, he pressed the child close—as though an emotion as protean as his love could
370 dominate the pulse of time.

[1950]

Uncommon Words or Meanings

a sojourner (title)—someone who stays for a brief time in each of a series of places.

Ferris ("John *Ferris* awoke")—a family name, reminiscent of "Ferris Wheel," a large upright, rotating wheel with suspended seats in which passengers ride for amusement.

matinal ("This feeling, submerged by *matinal* necessities")—part of the early hours of the day.

a belly bulge ("his body was spare except for an incipient *belly bulge*")—a softening of the stomach ("belly") muscles, as well as excess stomach fat.

to unravel ("*unraveled* his filial devotion")—(literally) to cause the threads of a piece of fabric to pull apart.

a B.T.O. ("a *B.T.O.* in television")—(slang) Big Time Operator, an important person.

to hit the skids ("*hit the skids* after the war")—(slang) to become headed for failure.

transience ("a sense of hazard, of *transience*")—the state or quality of being **transient,** that is, of (1) lasting only a brief time; (2) passing through on the way from one place to another. Both meanings apply here.

carriage ("Elizabeth had a 'beautiful *carriage*'")—one's manner of holding the head and body.

an anodyne ("the *anodyne* of time")—something that can relieve or soothe mental distress.

a carving set ("sent a *carving set* when he received an announcement of her wedding")—a heavy knife and fork used by the host to cut and serve meat at the dining table.

a marquee ("a building with a *marquee* and a doorman")—a canopy from the front door to the street, a sign of elegance for an apartment building.

lumbering ("a *lumbering*, red-haired man")—moving heavily.

a Martini ("a cocktail shaker of *Martinis*")—the most fashionable before-dinner drink at the time of the story; made of three parts gin and one part dry vermouth.

to prime ("With the *priming* drinks they pumped up conversation.")—to pour water into (a pump) to start its action.

crêpe de Chine ("a pale pink *crêpe de Chine* frock")—literally, China crêpe, a silk fabric.

to smock ("a pale pink crêpe de Chine frock, *smocked* around the yoke with rose")—to embroider with a decorative stitch that gathers the cloth tightly, used on expensive babies' clothes.

an expatriate ("be an *expatriate*")—a person living outside of his or her own country.

an amiability ("one of her *amiabilities*")—a good-natured, pleasant quality.

a prelude ("a Bach *prelude* and fugue")—an independent piece of moderate length that precedes a fugue.

a fugue ("a Bach prelude and *fugue*")—a musical form in which the same melody is repeated by different instruments or "voices," playing first one after the other, then in an overlapping fashion that blends them into a grand melodious whole.

a catalyst ("*catalyst* for this tumultuous anarchy")—something that causes a change.

anarchy ("this tumultuous *anarchy*")—disorder, confusion.

Miz ("*Miz* Bailey, dinner is out on the table now.")—"Mrs." in the Black English of the period.

an improvisation ("the *improvisation* of human existence")—
something improvised, done as needed, without previous preparation.

to know ("I first *knew* Jeannine last autumn")—here, to meet;
Ferris is unconsciously translating directly from French.

a White Russian ("married to a *White Russian*")—a Russian who
recognizes the former czarist government as the only legal government of Russia.

the guignol ("go to the *guignol*")—a comic puppet show for children, presented outdoors in warm weather.

the Tuileries ("go to *the Tuileries*")—a public park in the center of
Paris.

an air ("the melody, the unfinished *air*")—a melody or tune.

a cadence ("The *cadence,* some related tones")—the rhythm and
pacing of a musical work.

to jettison ("the load of memory *jettisoned*")—(literally) to throw
something overboard to lighten a ship in distress. (In this sentence, the load seems to jettison itself.)

Monsieur Jean ("'*Monsieur Jean,*' the child said")—"Mr. John";
in French, a polite way for a child to address an adult who is a
close family friend.

protean ("an emotion as *protean* as his love")—readily assuming
a different form or character (like the Greek god Proteus, who
could change his shape at will).

English as a Second Language

"'And Mama, you
are going for an
award for your
English, for all
you've learned, so
please speak
English!'"

English as a
Second Language

Lucy Honig
(born 1948)

Lucy Honig is a writer who has also taught English as a Second Language (ESL) in a number of adult education and intensive English-language programs in the New York City area. Her interests in teaching ESL and in writing fiction have emerged, she says, "from the same discomfort with 'mainstream' American culture—a need to get out of it, understand it, be with people who aren't in it either." Both interests are reflected in "English as a Second Language," which was honored by inclusion in *Prize Stories 1992: The O. Henry Awards.* "The story," Honig reports, "grew out of one of my first part-time teaching jobs, in a free adult education program. My students had come from all over the third world. In New York, they were struggling to live, struggling to be understood, and grasping for insider tips on how to fit in America."

Maria, the story's main character, is a middle-aged immigrant from Central America who lives in New York City and is enrolled in an ESL class at a community college. During a moment of relaxation at work, Maria's thoughts wander from the immediate present to other parts of her life. Then and at other times during the story, she suddenly relives the traumatic events of her last day at home in Guatemala, a country whose long and brutal civil strife reflects social, religious, and political differences within the country and the region. And at the end of a painful day, Maria finds herself remembering a classmate's description of tragic events that took place in the People's Republic of China during the social upheaval of the Cultural Revolution (1966–76).

The story moves back and forth in time: from New York in the present to Guatemala in the past. It also moves among several different locations in New York City: the Plaza Hotel on the southern edge of Central Park in Manhattan, Maria's apartment in the Bronx, and the auditorium of a community college near City Hall, an hour or more by subway from Maria's home.

Like many authors, Honig has used white space between paragraphs to signal changes of time and location. For additional emphasis, she has placed three asterisks (stars) after Maria's first memory of her last day at home in Guatemala. What do you suppose happened on that day? As you will see, the past and present become merged toward the end of the story. What do you suppose might cause that to happen? You may find that you recognize some of the students in Maria's ESL class. You may even recognize yourself.

Inside Room 824, Maria parked the vacuum cleaner, fastened all the locks and the safety chain and kicked off her shoes. Carefully she lay a stack of fluffy towels on the bathroom vanity. She turned the air conditioning up high and the
5   lights down low. Then she hoisted up the skirt of her uniform and settled all the way back on the king-sized bed with her legs straight out in front of her. Her feet and ankles were swollen. She wriggled her toes. She threw her arms out in each direction and still her hands did not come near the edges of the bed.
10 From here she could see, out the picture window, the puffs of green treetops in Central Park, the tiny people circling along the paths below. She tore open a small foil bag of cocktail peanuts and ate them very slowly, turning each one over separately with her tongue until the salt dissolved. She snapped on
15 the TV with the remote control and flipped channels.

The big mouth game show host was kissing and hugging a woman playing on the left-hand team. Her husband and children were right there with her, and *still* he encircled her with his arms. Then he sidled up to the daughter, a girl younger than
20 her own Guiliette, and *hugged* her and kept *holding* her, asking questions. None of his business, if this girl had a boyfriend back in Saginaw!

"Mama, you just don't understand." That's what Jorge always said when she watched TV at home. He and his
25 teenaged friends would sit around in their torn bluejeans dropping potato chips between the cushions of her couch and laughing, writhing with laughter while she sat like a stone.

Now the team on the right were hugging each other, squealing, jumping up and down. They'd just won a whole new
30 kitchen—refrigerator, dishwasher, clothes washer, microwave, *everything!* Maria could win a whole new kitchen too, someday. You just spun a wheel, picked some words. She could do that.

She saw herself on TV with Carmen and Guiliette and Jorge. Her handsome children were so quick to press the
35 buzzers the other team never had a chance to answer first. And they got every single answer right. Her children shrieked and clapped and jumped up and down each time the board lit up.

They kissed and hugged that man whenever they won a prize. That man put his hands on her beautiful young daughters. That man pinched and kissed *her*, an old woman, in front of the whole world! Imagine seeing *this* back home! Maria frowned, chewing on the foil wrapper. There was nobody left at home in Guatemala, nobody to care if a strange man squeezed her wrinkled flesh on the TV.

"Forget it, Mama. They don't let poor people on these programs," Jorge said one day.

"But poor people need the money, they can win it here!"

Jorge sighed impatiently. "They don't give it away because you *need* it!"

It was true, she had never seen a woman with her kids say on a show: My husband's dead. Jorge knew. They made sure before they invited you that you were the right kind of people and that you said the right things. Where would she put a new kitchen in her cramped apartment anyway? No hookups for a washer, no space for a two-door refrigerator.

She slid sideways off the bed, carefully smoothed out the quilted spread, and squeezed her feet into her shoes. Back out in the hall she counted the bath towels in her cart to see if there were enough for the next wing. Then she wheeled the cart down the corridor, silent on the deep blue rug.

Maria pulled the new pink dress on over her head, eased her arms into the sleeves, then let the skirt slide into place. In the mirror she saw a small dark protrusion from a large pink flower. She struggled to zip up in back, then she fixed the neck, attaching the white collar she had crocheted. She pinned the rhinestone brooch on next. Shaking the pantyhose out of the package, she remembered the phrase: the cow before the horse, wasn't that it? She should have put these on first. Well, so what. She rolled down the left leg of the nylons, stuck her big toe in, and drew the sheer fabric around her foot, unrolling it up past her knee. Then she did the right foot, careful not to catch the hose on the small flap of scar.

The right foot bled badly when she ran over the broken glass, over what had been the only window of the house. It had shattered from gunshots across the dirt yard. The chickens dashed around frantically, squawking, trying to fly, spraying brown feathers into the air. When she had seen Pedro's head turn to blood and the two oldest boys dragged away, she swallowed every word, every cry, and ran with the two girls. The fragments of glass stayed in her foot for all the days of hiding. They ran and ran and ran and somehow Jorge caught up and they were found by their own side and smuggled out. And still she was silent, until the nurse at the border went after the glass and drained the mess inside her foot. Then she had sobbed and screamed, "Aaiiee!"

*　　*　　*

"Mama, stop thinking and get ready," said Carmen.

"It is too short, your skirt," Maria said in Spanish. "What will they say?"

Carmen laughed. "It's what they all wear, except for you old ladies."

"Not to work! Not to school!"

"Yes, to work, to school! And Mama, you are going for an award for your English, for all you've learned, so please speak English!"

Maria squeezed into the pink high heels and held each foot out, one by one, so she could admire the beautiful slim arch of her own instep, like the feet of the American ladies on Fifth Avenue. Carmen laughed when she saw her mother take the first faltering steps, and Maria laughed too. How much she had already practiced in secret, and still it was so hard! She teetered on them back and forth from the kitchen to the bedroom, trying to feel steady, until Carmen finally sighed and said, "Mama, quick now or you'll be late!"

She didn't know if it was a good omen or a bad one, the two Indian women on the subway. They could have been sitting on the dusty ground at the market in San _____, selling corn or clay pots, with the bright-colored striped shawls and full skirts, the black hair pulled into two braids down each back, the deeply furrowed square faces set in those impassive expressions, seeing everything, seeing nothing. They were exactly as they must have been back home, but she was seeing them *here*, on the downtown IRT from the Bronx, surrounded by businessmen in suits, kids with big radio boxes, girls in skin-tight jeans and dark purple lipstick. Above them, advertisements for family planning and TWA. They were like stone-

age men sitting on the train in loincloths made from animal skins, so out of place, out of time. Yet timeless. Maria thought, they are timeless guardian spirits, here to accompany me to my honors. Did anyone else see them? As strange as they were,
120 nobody looked. Maria's heart pounded faster. The boys with the radios were standing right over them and never saw them. They were invisible to everyone but her: Maria was utterly convinced of it. The spirit world had come back to life, here on the number 4 train! It was a miracle!
125 "Mama, look, you see the grandmothers?" said Carmen.
"Of course I see them" Maria replied trying to hide the disappointment in her voice. So Carmen saw them too. They were not invisible. Carmen rolled her eyes and smirked derisively as she nodded in their direction, but before she could put her
130 derision into words, Maria became stern. "Have respect," she said. "They are the same as your father's people." Carmen's face sobered at once.

She panicked when they got to the big school by the river. "Like the United Nations," she said, seeing so much glass and
135 brick, an endless esplanade of concrete.
"It's only a college, Mama. People learn English here, too. And more, like nursing, electronics. This is where Anna's brother came for computers."
"Las Naciones Unidas," Maria repeated, and when the
140 guard stopped them to ask where they were going, she answered in Spanish: to the literacy awards ceremony.
"*English*, Mama!" whispered Carmen.
But the guard also spoke in Spanish: take the escalator to the third floor.
145 "See, he knows," Maria retorted.
"That's not the point," murmured Carmen, taking her mother by the hand.

Every inch of the enormous room was packed with people. She clung to Carmen and stood by the door paralyzed until
150 Cheryl, her teacher, pushed her way to them and greeted Maria with a kiss. Then she led Maria back through the press of people to the small group of award winners from other programs. Maria smiled shakily and nodded hello.
"They're all here now!" Cheryl called out. A photographer

155   rushed over and began to move the students closer together for a picture.

"Hey Bernie, wait for the Mayor!" someone shouted to him. He spun around, called out some words Maria did not understand, and without even turning back to them, he disappeared.
160   But they stayed there, huddled close, not knowing if they could move. The Chinese man kept smiling, the tall black man stayed slightly crouched, the Vietnamese woman squinted, confused, her glasses still hidden in her fist. Maria saw all the cameras along the sides of the crowd, and the lights, and the
165   people from television with video machines, and more lights. Her stomach began to jump up and down. Would she be on television, in the newspapers? Still smiling, holding his pose, the Chinese man next to her asked, "Are you nervous?"

"Oh yes," she said. She tried to remember the expression
170   Cheryl had taught them. "I have worms in my stomach," she said.

He was a much bigger man than she had imagined from seeing him on TV. His face was bright red as they ushered him into the room and quickly through the crowd, just as it was his turn to take the podium. He said hello to the other speakers
175   and called them by their first names. The crowd drew closer to the little stage, the people standing farthest in the back pushed in. Maria tried hard to listen to the Mayor's words. "Great occasion . . . pride of our city . . . ever since I created the program . . . people who have worked so hard . . . overcoming hardship
180   . . . come so far." Was that them? Was he talking about them already? Why were the people out there all starting to laugh? She strained to understand, but still caught only fragments of his words. "My mother used to say . . . and I said, Look, Mama . . ." He was talking about *his* mother now; he called her
185   Mama, just like Maria's kids called *her*. But everyone laughed so hard. At his mother? She forced herself to smile; up front, near the podium, everyone could see her. She should seem to pay attention and understand. Looking out into the crowd she felt dizzy. She tried to find Carmen among all the pretty young
190   women with big eyes and dark hair. There she was! Carmen's eyes met Maria's; Carmen waved. Maria beamed out at her. For a moment she felt like she belonged there, in this crowd. Everyone was smiling, everyone was so happy while the

Mayor of New York stood at the podium telling jokes. How
195   happy Maria felt too!

"Maria Perez grew up in the countryside of Guatemala,
the oldest daughter in a family of 19 children," read the Mayor
as Maria stood quaking by his side. She noticed he made a
slight wheezing noise when he breathed between words. She
200   saw the hairs in his nostrils, black and white and wiry. He
paused. "Nineteen children!" he exclaimed, looking at the audience. A small gasp was passed along through the crowd. Then
the Mayor looked back at the sheet of paper before him.
"Maria never had a chance to learn to read and write, and she
205   was already the mother of five children of her own when she
fled Guatemala in 1980 and made her way to New York for a
new start."
It was her own story, but Maria had a hard time following.
She had to stand next to him while he read it, and her feet had
210   started to hurt, crammed into the new shoes. She shifted her
weight from one foot to the other.
"At the age of 45, while working as a chambermaid and
sending her children through school, Maria herself started
school for the first time. In night courses she learned to read
215   and write in her native Spanish. Later, as she was pursuing her
G.E.D. in Spanish, she began studying English as a Second
Language. This meant Maria was going to school five nights a
week! Still she worked as many as 60 hours cleaning rooms at
the Plaza Hotel.
220   "Maria's ESL teacher, Cheryl Sands, says—and I quote—
'Maria works harder than any student I have ever had. She is
an inspiration to her classmates. Not only has she learned to
read and write in her new language, but she initiated an oral
history project in which she taped and transcribed interviews
225   with other students, who have told their stories from around
the world.' Maria was also one of the first in New York to apply
for amnesty under the 1986 Immigration Act. Meanwhile, she
has passed her enthusiasm for education to her children: her
son is now a junior in high school, her youngest daughter
230   attends the State University, and her oldest daughter, who we
are proud to have with us today, is in her second year of law
school on a scholarship."

Two older sons were dragged through the dirt, chickens squawking in mad confusion, feathers flying. She heard more gunshots in the distance, screams, chickens squawking She heard, she ran. Maria looked down at her bleeding feet. Wedged tightly into the pink high heels, they throbbed.

The Mayor turned toward her. "Maria, I think it's wonderful that you have taken the trouble to preserve the folklore of students from so many countries." He paused. Was she supposed to say something? Her heart stopped beating. What was folklore? What was preserved? She smiled up at him, hoping that was all she needed to do.

"Maria, tell us now, if you can, what was one of the stories you collected in your project?"

This was definitely a question, meant to be answered. Maria tried to smile again. She strained on tiptoes to reach the microphone, pinching her toes even more tightly in her shoes. "Okay," she said, setting off a high-pitched ringing from the microphone.

The Mayor said, "Stand back," and tugged at her collar. She quickly stepped away from the microphone.

"Okay," she said again, and this time there was no shrill sound. "One of my stories, from Guatemala. You want to hear?"

The Mayor put his arm around her shoulder and squeezed hard. Her first impulse was to wriggle away, but he held tight. "Isn't she wonderful?" he asked the audience. There was a low ripple of applause. "Yes, we want to hear!"

She turned and looked up at his face. Perspiration was shining on his forehead and she could see by the bright red bulge of his neck that his collar was too tight. "In my village in Guatemala," she began, "the mayor did not go along—get along—with the government so good."

"Hey, Maria," said the Mayor, "I know exactly how he felt!" The people in the audience laughed. Maria waited until they were quiet again.

"One day our mayor met with the people in the village. Like you meet people here. A big crowd in the square."

"The people liked him, your mayor?"

"Oh, yes," said Maria. "Very much. He was very good. He tried for more roads, more doctors, new farms. He cared very much about his people."

The Mayor shook his head up and down. "Of course," he said, and again the audience laughed.

275 Maria said, "The next day after the meeting, the meeting in the square with all the people, soldiers come and shoot him dead."

For a second there was total silence. Maria realized she had not used the past tense and felt a deep, horrible stab of shame
280 for herself, shame for her teacher. She was a disgrace! But she did not have more than a second of this horror before the whole audience began to laugh. What was happening? They couldn't be laughing at her bad verbs? They couldn't be laughing at her dead mayor! They laughed louder and louder and suddenly
285 flashbulbs were going off around her, the TV cameras swung in close, too close, and the Mayor was grabbing her by the shoulders again, holding her tight, posing for one camera after another as the audience burst into wild applause. But she hadn't even finished ! Why were they laughing?

290 "What timing, huh?" said the Mayor over the uproar. "What d'ya think, the Republicans put her here, or maybe the Board of Estimate?" Everyone laughed even louder and he still clung to her and cameras still moved in close, lights kept going off in her face and she could see nothing but the sharp white poof!
295 of light over and over again. She looked for Carmen and Cheryl, but the white poof! poof! poof! blinded her. She closed her eyes and listened to the uproar, now beginning to subside, and in her mind's eye saw chickens trying to fly, chickens fluttering around the yard littered with broken glass.

300 He squeezed her shoulders again and leaned into the microphone. "There are ways to get rid of mayors, and ways to get rid of mayors, huh Maria?"

The surge of laughter rose once more, reached a crescendo, and then began to subside again. "But wait," said
305 the Mayor. The cameramen stepped back a bit, poising themselves for something new.

"I want know just one more thing, Maria," said the Mayor, turning to face her directly again. The crowd quieted. He waited a few seconds more, then asked his question. "It says
310 here 19 children. What was it like growing up in a house with 19 children? How many *bathrooms* did you have?"

Her stomach dropped and twisted as the mayor put his hand firmly on the back of her neck and pushed her toward the

microphone again. It was absolutely quiet now in the huge
315   room. Everyone was waiting for her to speak. She cleared her
throat and made the microphone do the shrill hum. Startled,
she jumped back. Then there was silence. She took a big, trem-
bling breath.

"We had no bathrooms there, Mister Mayor," she said.
320   "Only the outdoors."

The clapping started immediately, then the flashbulbs
burning up in her face. The Mayor turned to her, put a hand on
each of her shoulders, bent lower and kissed her! Kissed her
on the cheek!

325   "Isn't she terrific?" he asked the audience, his hand on the
back of her neck again, drawing her closer to him. The audience clapped louder, faster. "Isn't she just the greatest?"

She tried to smile and open her eyes, but the lights were
still going off—poof! poof—and the noise was deafening.

330   "Mama, look, your eyes were closed *there*, too," chided
Jorge, sitting on the floor in front of the television set.

Maria had watched the camera move from the announcer
at the studio desk to her own stout form in bright pink, standing by the Mayor.

335   "In my village in Guatemala," she heard herself say, and the
camera showed her wrinkled face close up, eyes open now but
looking nowhere. Then the mayor's face filled the screen, his
forehead glistening, and then suddenly all the people in the
audience, looking ahead, enrapt, took his place. Then there
340   was her wrinkled face again, talking without a smile ". . . soldiers come and shoot him dead." Maria winced, hearing the
wrong tense of her verbs. The camera shifted from her face to
the Mayor. In the brief moment of shamed silence after she'd
uttered those words, the Mayor drew his finger like a knife
345   across his throat. And the audience began to laugh.

"Turn it off!" she yelled to Jorge. "Off! This minute!"

Late that night she sat alone in the unlighted room, soaking
her feet in Epsom salts. The glow of the television threw shadows across the wall, but the sound was off. The man called
350   Johnny was on the screen, talking. The people in the audience
and the men in the band and the movie stars sitting on the
couch all had their mouths wide open in what she knew were

screams of laughter while Johnny wagged his tongue. Maria
heard nothing except brakes squealing below on the street and
355 the lonely clanging of garbage cans in the alley.

She thought about her English class and remembered the
pretty woman, Ling, who often fell asleep in the middle of a
lesson. The other Chinese students all teased her. Everyone
knew that she sewed coats in a sweatshop all day. After the
360 night class she took the subway to the Staten Island Ferry,
and after the ferry crossing she had to take a bus home.
Her parents were old and sick and she did all their cooking
and cleaning late at night. She struggled to keep awake
in class; it seemed to take all her energy simply to smile and
365 listen. She said very little and the teacher never forced her,
but she fell further and further behind. They called her the
Quiet One.

One day just before the course came to an end the Quiet
One asked to speak. There was no reason, no provocation—
370 they'd been talking informally about their summer plans—but
Ling spoke with a sudden urgency. Her English was very slow.
Seeing what a terrible effort it was for her, the classmates all
tried to help when she searched for words.

"In my China village there was a teacher," Ling began. "Man
375 teacher." She paused. "All children love him. He teach mathe-
matic. He very—" She stopped and looked up toward the ceiling. Then she gestured with her fingers around her face.

"Handsome!" said Charlene, the oldest of the three Haitian
sisters in the class.

380 Ling smiled broadly. "Handsome! Yes, he very handsome.
Family very rich before. He have sister go to Hong Kong who
have many, many money."

"*Much* money," said Maria.

"Much, much money," repeated Ling thoughtfully. "Teacher
385 live in big house."

"In China? Near you?"

"Yes. Big house with much old picture." She stopped and
furrowed her forehead, as if to gather words inside of it.

"Art? Paint? Pictures like that?" asked Xavier.

390 Ling nodded eagerly. "Yes. In big house. Most big house in
village."

"But big house, money, rich like that, bad in China," said Fu
Wu. "Those year, Government bad to you. How they let him do?"

"In *my* country," said Carlos, "government bad to you if
395 you got *small* house, *no* money."

"Me too," said Maria.

"Me too," said Charlene.

The Chinese students laughed.

Ling shrugged and shook her head. "Don't know. He have
400 big house. Money gone, but keep big house. Then I am little
girl." She held her hand low to the floor.

"I *was* a little girl," Charlene said gently.

I *was*," said Ling. "Was, was." She giggled for a moment,
then seemed to spend some time in thought. "We love him. All
405 children love—all children did loved him. He giving tea in
house. He was—was—so handsome!" She giggled. All the
women in the class giggled. "He very nice. He learn music, he
go . . . he went to school far away."

"America?"

410 Ling shook her head. "Oh no, no. You know, another . . .
west."

"Europa!" exclaimed Maria proudly. "Espain!"

"No, no, another."

"France!" said Patricia, Charlene's sister. "He went to
415 school in France?"

"Yes, France," said Ling. Then she stopped again, this time
for a whole minute. The others waited patiently. No one said a
word. Finally she continued. "But big boys in more old school
not like him. He too handsome."

420 "Oooh!" sang out a chorus of women. "Too handsome!"

"The boys were jealous," said Carlos.

Ling seized the word. "Jealous! Jealous! They very jealous.
He handsome, he study France, he very nice to children, he give
tea and cake in big house, he show picture on wall." Her torrent
425 of words came to an end and she began to think again, visibly,
her brow furrowing. "Big school boys, they . . ." She stopped.

"Jealous!" sang out the others.

"Yes," she said, shaking her head "no." "But more. More
bad. Hate. They hate him."

430 "That's bad," said Patricia.

"Yes, very bad." Ling paused, looking at the floor. "And they
heat."

"Hate."

"No, they heat."

435   All the class looked puzzled. Heat? Heat? They turned to Cheryl.

     The teacher spoke for the first time. "Hit? Ling, do you mean hit? They hit him?" Cheryl slapped the air with her hand.

     Ling nodded, her face somehow serious and smiling at the
440 same time. "Hit many time. And also so." She scooted her feet back and forth along the floor.

     "Oooh," exclaimed Charlene, frowning. "They kicked him with the feet."

     "Yes," said Ling. "They kicked him with the feet and hit him
445 with the hands, many many time they hit, they kick."

     "Where this happened?" asked Xavier.

     "In the school. In classroom like . . ." She gestured to mean their room.

     "In the school?" asked Xavier. "But other people were they
450 there? They say stop, no?"

     "No. Little children in room. They cry, they . . ." She covered her eyes with her hand, then uncovered them. "Big boys kick and hit. No one stop. No one help."

     Everyone in class fell silent. Maria remembered: they could
455 not look at one another then. The could not look at their teacher.

     Ling continued. "They break him, very hurt much place." She stopped. They all fixed their stares on Ling, they could bear looking only at her. "Many place," she said. Her face had
460 not changed, it was still half smiling. But now there were drops coming from her eyes, a single tear down each side of her nose. Maria would never forget it. Ling's face did not move or wrinkle or frown. He body was absolutely still. Her shoulders did not quake. Nothing in the shape or motion of her eyes
465 or mouth changed. None of the things that Maria had always known happen when you cry happened when Ling shed tears. Just two drops rolled slowly down her two pale cheeks as she smiled.

     "He very hurt. He *was* very hurt. He blood many place.
470 Boys go away. Children cry. Teacher break and hurt. Later he in hospital. I go there visit him." She stopped, looking thoughtful. "I went there." One continuous line of wetness glistened down each cheek. "My mother, my father say don't go, but I see him. I say, 'You be better?' But he hurt. Doctors no did helped.
475 He alone. No doctor. No nurse. No medicine. No family." She

stopped. They all stared in silence for several moments.

Finally Carlos said, "Did he went home?"

Ling shook her head. "He go home but no walk." She stopped. Maria could not help watching those single lines of tears moving down the pale round face. "A year, more, no walk. Then go."

"Go where?"

"End."

Again there was a deep silence. Ling looked down, away from them, her head bent low.

"Oh, no," murmured Charlene. "He died."

Maria felt the catch in her throat, the sudden wetness of tears on her own two cheeks, and when she looked up she saw that all the other students, men and women both, were crying too.

Maria wiped her eyes. Suddenly all her limbs ached, her bones felt stiff and old. She took her feet from the basin and dried them with a towel. Then she turned off the television and went to bed.

[1992]

Uncommon Words or Meanings

a vanity ("fluffy towels on the bathroom *vanity*")—a low shelf or table with a mirror above it.

a game show ("The big mouth *game show* host")—a television program in which contestants compete in a game to win prizes.

Saginaw ("a boyfriend back in *Saginaw*")—a town in Michigan.

a hookup ("No *hookups* for a washer")—a connection to supply water or electricity.

a spread ("carefully smoothed out the quilted *spread*")—a bed-spread, the covering put over a bed during the day.

San _____ ("at the market in *San _____*")—a literary device suggesting that the author is thinking of a real town but is concealing its name.

the IRT ("the downtown *IRT*")—Interborough Rapid Transit, one of New York's three subway companies; the train is going south ("downtown") from the Bronx to Manhattan.

family planning ("advertisements for *family planning* and TWA")—birth control.

TWA ("advertisements for family planning and *TWA*")—Trans World Airlines.

to beam ("Maria *beamed* out at her")—to smile happily.

a G.E.D. ("pursuing her *G.E.D.* in Spanish")—General Equivalency Diploma, the equivalent of a high school diploma, earned by taking courses and passing examinations.

the 1986 Immigration Act ("amnesty under the *1986 Immigration Act*")—a U.S. law allowing any illegal immigrant who had entered the country before January 1, 1982 to apply for citizenship.

d'ya ("What *d'ya* think, the Republicans put her here . . . ?")—"do you."

the Republicans ("What d'ya think, *the Republicans* put her here . . . ?")—voters in one of the two major U.S. political parties; the vast majority of registered voters in New York City are Democrats.

the Board of Estimate ("or maybe the *Board of Estimate*")—at the time of the story, a small group, including the mayor, responsible for the New York City budget.

stout ("her own *stout* form")—tending to fatness.

enrapt ("people in the audience, looking ahead, *enrapt*")—paying complete attention.

Epsom salts ("soaking her feet in *Epsom salts*")—a white powder added to water to relieve pain.

Johnny ("The man called *Johnny* was on the screen, talking.")—Johnny Carson, for many years the highly popular host of a late-night television show.

a sweatshop ("sewed coats in a *sweatshop* all day")—a place where workers are employed at low wages for long hours under bad conditions.

the Staten Island Ferry ("took the subway to the *Staten Island Ferry*")—a boat providing regular public transportation between two boroughs of New York City in a thirty–minute crossing.

a provocation ("no reason, no *provocation*")—something that stirs one to action.

to furrow ("*furrowed* her forehead")—to wrinkle, make grooves in.

The Bass, the River, and Sheila Mant

"There was a summer in my life when the only creature that seemed lovelier to me than a largemouth bass was Sheila Mant."

The Bass, the River,
and Sheila Mant

W. D. Wetherell
(born 1948)

W. D. Wetherell is the author of seven books, including the novel *Chekov's Sister* (1990) and the essay collection *Upland Stream* (1992), which is subtitled "Notes on the Fishing Passion." He was born in Garden City, New York, not far from the setting of the title story in his collection *The Man Who Loved Levittown* (1985), which also includes "The Bass, the River, and Sheila Mant." Wetherell, who is a professor in the Master of Fine Arts program at Vermont College, lives with his family in rural New Hampshire. From his writing desk, a thousand yards to the west he can see the Connecticut River, which is the river of the bass and Sheila.

Sheila and the boy in the story, as well as their creator, Wetherell, are members of the baby-boom generation, the sons and daughters of the World War II veterans who returned home with money to spend and lost years to make up for. In the New York City area, those with professional skills bought homes in new communities like Garden City. Many blue-collar workers bought smaller, less expensive homes farther out on Long Island in Levittown, the prototypical planned community in the United States. The nearby Grumman Aircraft plant provided employment for many of those veterans, as it shifted to peacetime products such as aluminum canoes and lunar landers. The wives and children of the white-collar workers often spent the summer in a northern state, while the husbands remained at work in the hot, non-air-conditioned city. Sheila Mant was surely the daughter of such a middle-class family, rather than of wealthy parents, as today's readers might think, for it was normal for baby-boomers to expect to get everything.

While "The Bass, the River, and Sheila Mant" at first seems as undatable as any fishing story, it is carefully set in a specific time—the early 1960s. The clues are the aluminum canoe (which is shined up with a Brillo scouring pad), a transistor radio, and a Mitchell reel and Pfluger rod. This careful introduction of technological advances and brand names reaches its dramatic peak when a Corvette—the devastatingly sexy, quintessential sports car of the period—is used to deliver a stunning blow.

The Bass, the River, and Sheila Mant

There was a summer in my life when the only creature that seem lovelier to me than a largemouth bass was Sheila Mant. I was fourteen. The Mants had rented the cottage next to ours on the river; with their parties, their frantic games of softball, their constant comings and goings, they appeared to me denizens of a brilliant existence. "Too noisy by half," my mother quickly decided, but I would have given anything to be invited to one of their parties, and when my parents went to bed I would sneak through the woods to their hedge and stare enchanted at the candlelit swirl of white dresses and bright, paisley skirts.

Sheila was the middle daughter—at seventeen, all but out of reach. She would spend her days sunbathing on a float my Uncle Sierbert had moored in their cove, and before July was over I had learned all her moods. If she lay flat on the diving board with her hand trailing idly in the water, she was pensive, not to be disturbed. On her side, her head propped up by her arm, she was observant, considering those around her with a look that seemed queenly and severe. Sitting up, arms tucked around her long, suntanned legs, she was approachable, but barely, and it was only in those glorious moments when she stretched herself prior to entering the water that her various suitors found the courage to come near.

These were many. The Dartmouth heavyweight crew would scull by her house on their way upriver, and I think all eight of them must have been in love with her at various times during the summer; the coxswain would curse at them through his megaphone, but without effect—there was always a pause in their pace when they passed Sheila's float. I suppose to these jaded twenty-year-olds she seemed the incarnation of innocence and youth, while to me she appeared unutterably suave, the epitome of sophistication. I was on the swim team at school, and to win her attention would do endless laps between my house and the Vermont shore, hoping she would notice the beauty of my flutter kick, the power of my crawl. Finishing, I would boost myself up onto our dock and glance

casually over toward her, but she was never watching, and the miraculous day she was, I immediately climbed the diving board and did my best tuck and a half for her, and continued
40 diving until she had left and the sun went down and my longing was like a madness and I couldn't stop.

It was late August by the time I got up the nerve to ask her out. The tortured will-I's, won't-I's, the agonized indecision over what to say, the false starts toward her house and embar-
45 rassed retreats—the details of these have been seared from my memory, and the only part I remember clearly is emerging from the woods toward dusk while they were playing softball on their lawn, as bashful and frightened as a unicorn.

Sheila was stationed halfway between first and second,
50 well outside the infield. She didn't seem surprised to see me—as a matter of fact, she didn't seem to see me at all.

"If you're playing second base, you should move closer," I said.

She turned—I took the full brunt of her long red hair and
55 well-spaced freckles.

"I'm playing outfield," she said, "I don't like the responsibility of having a base."

"Yeah, I can understand that," I said, though I couldn't. "There's a band in Dixford tomorrow night at nine. Want to
60 go?"

One of her brothers sent the ball sailing over the left-fielder's head; she stood and watched it disappear toward the river.

"You have a car?" she said, without looking up.
65 I played my master stroke. "We'll go by canoe."

I spent all of the following day polishing it. I turned it upside down on our lawn and rubbed every inch with Brillo, hosing off the dirt, wiping it with chamois until it gleamed as bright as aluminum ever gleamed. About five, I slid it into the
70 water, arranging cushions near the bow to Sheila could lean on them if she was in one of her pensive moods, propping up my father's transistor radio by the middle thwart so we could have music when we came back. Automatically, without thinking about it, I mounted my Mitchell reel on my Pfluger spinning
75 rod and stuck it in the stern.

I say automatically, because I never went anywhere that summer without a fishing rod. When I wasn't swimming laps to impress Sheila, I was back in our driveway practicing casts, and when I wasn't practicing casts, I was tying the line to Tosca, our springer spaniel, to test the reel's drag, and when I wasn't doing any of those things, I was fishing the river for bass.

Too nervous to sit at home, I got in the canoe early and started paddling in a huge circle that would get me to Sheila's dock around eight. As automatically as I brought along my rod, I tied on a big Rapala plug, let it down into the water, let out some line and immediately forgot all about it.

It was already dark by the time I glided up to the Mants' dock. Even by day the river was quiet, most of the summer people preferring Sunapee or one of the other nearby lakes, and at night it was a solitude difficult to believe, a corridor of hidden life that ran between banks like a tunnel. Even the stars were part of it. They weren't as sharp anywhere else; they seemed to have chosen the river as a guide on their slow wheel toward morning, and in the course of the summer's fishing, I had learned all their names.

I was there ten minutes before Sheila appeared. I heard the slam of their screen door first, then saw her in the spotlight as she came slowly down the path. As beautiful as she was on the float, she was even lovelier now—her white dress went perfectly with her hair, and complimented her figure even more than her swimsuit.

It was her face that bothered me. It had on its delightful fullness a very dubious expression.

"Look," she said. "I can get Dad's car."

"It's faster this way," I lied. "Parking's tense up there. Hey, it's safe. I won't tip it or anything."

She let herself down reluctantly into the bow. I was glad she wasn't facing me. When her eyes were on me, I felt like diving in the river again from agony and joy.

I pried the canoe away from the dock and started paddling upstream. There was an extra paddle in the bow, but Sheila made no move to pick it up. She took her shoes off, and dangled her feet over the side.

Ten minutes went by.

"What kind of band?" she said.

"It's sort of like folk music. You'll like it."

"Eric Caswell's going to be there. He strokes number four."

"No kidding?" I said. I had no idea who she meant.

"What's that sound?" she said pointing toward shore.

"Bass. That splashing sound?"

"Over there."

"Yeah, bass. They come into the shallows at night to chase frogs and moths and things. Big largemouths. *Micropetrus salmonides*," I added, showing off.

"I think fishing's dumb," she said, making a face. "I mean, it's boring and all. Definitely dumb."

Now I have spent a great deal of time in the years since wondering why Sheila Mant should come down so hard on fishing. Was her father a fisherman? Her antipathy toward fishing nothing more than normal filial rebellion? Had she tried it once? A messy encounter with worms? It doesn't matter. What does, is that at that fragile moment in time I would have given anything not to appear dumb in Sheila's severe and unforgiving eyes.

She hadn't seen my equipment yet. What I *should* have done, of course, was push the canoe in closer to shore and carefully slide the rod into some branches where I could pick it up again in the morning. Failing that, I could have surreptitiously dumped the whole outfit overboard, written off the forty or so dollars as love's tribute. What I actually *did* do was gently lean forward, and slowly, every so slowly, push the rod back through my legs toward the stern where it would be less conspicuous.

It must have been just exactly what the bass was waiting for. Fish will trail a lure sometimes, trying to make up their mind whether or not to attack, and the slight pause in the plug's speed caused by my adjustment was tantalizing enough to overcome the bass's inhibitions. My rod, safely out of sight at last, bent double. The line, tightly coiled, peeled off the spool with the shrill, tearing zip of a high-speed drill.

Four things occurred to me at once. One, that it was a bass. Two, that it was a big bass. Three, that it was the biggest bass I had ever hooked. Four, that Sheila Mant must not know.

"What was that?" she said, turning half around.

"Uh, what was what?"

"That buzzing noise."

"Bats."

She shuddered, quickly drew her feet back into the canoe. Every instinct I had told me to pick up the rod and strike back at the bass, but there was no need to—it was already solidly

160 hooked. Downstream, an awesome distance downstream, it
jumped clear of the water, landing with a concussion heavy
enough to ripple the entire river. For a moment, I thought it
was gone, but then the rod was bending again, the tip dancing
into the water. Slowly, not making any motion that might alert
165 Sheila, I reached down to tighten the drag.

    While all this was going on, Sheila had begun talking and it
was a few minutes before I was able to catch up with her train
of thought.

    "I went to a party there. These fraternity men. Katherine
170 says I could get in there. If I wanted. I'm thinking more of UVM
or Bennington. Somewhere I can ski."

    The bass was slanting toward the rocks on the New Hamp-
shire side by the ruins of Donaldson's boathouse. It had to be
an old bass—a young one probably wouldn't have known the
175 rocks were there. I brought the canoe back out into the middle
of the river, hoping to head it of.

    "That's neat," I mumbled. "Skiing. Yeah, I can see that."

    "Eric said I have the figure to model, but I thought I should
get an education first. I mean, it might be a while before I get
180 started and all. I was thinking of getting my hair styled, more
swept back? I mean, Ann-Margret? Like hers, only shorter."

    She hesitated. "Are we going backwards?"

    We were. I had managed to keep the bass in the middle of
the river away from the rocks, but it had plenty of room there,
185 and for the first time a chance to exert its full strength. I
quickly computed the weight necessary to draw a fully loaded
canoe backwards—the thought of it made me feel faint.

    "It's just the current," I said hoarsely. "No sweat or any-
thing."

190   I dug in deeper with my paddle. Reassured, Sheila began
talking about something else, but all my attention was taken
up now with the fish. I could feel its desperation as the water
grew shallower. I could sense the extra strain on the line, the
frantic way it cut back and forth in the water. I could visualize
195 what it looked like—the gape of its mouth, the flared gills and
thick vertical tail. The bass couldn't have encountered many
forces in its long life that it wasn't capable of handling, and the
unrelenting tug at its mouth must have been a source of great
puzzlement and mounting panic.

200   Me, I had problems of my own. To get to Dixford, I had to

paddle up a sluggish stream that came into the river beneath a covered bridge. There was a shallow sandbar at the mouth of this stream—weeds on one side, rocks on the other. Without doubt, this is where I would lose the fish.

205   "I have to be careful with my complexion. I tan, but in segments. I can't figure out if it's even worth it. I wouldn't even do it probably. I saw Jackie Kennedy in Boston and she wasn't tan at all."

    Taking a deep breath, I paddled as hard as I could for the 210 middle, deepest part of the bar. I could have threaded the eye of a needle with the canoe, but the pull on the stern threw me off and I overcompensated—the canoe veered left and scraped bottom. I pushed the paddle down and shoved. A moment of hesitation . . . a moment more . . . The canoe shot clear into the 215 deeper water of the stream. I immediately looked down at the rod. It was bent in the same, tight arc—miraculously, the bass was still on.

    The moon was out now. It was low and full enough that its beam shone directly on Sheila there ahead of me in the canoe, 220 washing her in a creamy, luminous glow. I could see the lithe, easy shape of her figure. I could see the way her hair curled down off her shoulders, the proud, alert tilt of her head, and all these things were as a tug on my heart. Not just Sheila, but the aura she carried about her of parties and casual touchings and 225 grace. Behind me, I could feel the strain of the bass, steadier now, growing weaker, and this was another tug on my heart, not just the bass but the beat of the river and the slant of the stars and the smell of the night, until finally it seemed I would be torn apart between longings, split in half. Twenty yards 230 ahead of us was the road, and once I pulled the canoe up on shore, the bass would be gone, irretrievably gone. If instead I stood up, grabbed the rod and started pumping, I would have it—as tired as the bass was, there was no chance it could get away. I reached down for the rod, hesitated, looked up to 235 where Sheila was stretching herself lazily toward the sky, her small breasts rising beneath the soft fabric of her dress, and the tug was too much for me, and quicker than it takes to write down, I pulled a penknife from my pocket and cut the line in half.

240   With a sick, nauseous feeling in my stomach, I saw the rod unbend.

"My legs are sore," Sheila whined. "Are we there yet?"

Through a superhuman effort of self-control, I was able to beach the canoe and help Sheila off. The rest of the night is
245 much foggier. We walked to the fair—there was the smell of popcorn, the sound of guitars. I may have danced once or twice with her, but all I really remember is her coming over to me once the music was done to explain that she would be going home in Eric Caswell's Corvette.
250 "Okay," I mumbled.

For the first time that night she looked at me, really looked at me.

"You're a funny kid, you know that?"

Funny. Different. Dreamy. Odd. How many times was I to
255 hear that in the years to come, all spoken with the same quizzical, half-accusatory tone Sheila used then. Poor Sheila! Before the month was over, the spell she cast over me was gone, but the memory of that lost bass haunted me all summer and haunts me still. There would be other Sheila Mants in my life,
260 other fish, and though I came close once or twice, it was these secret, hidden tuggings in the night that claimed me, and I never made the same mistake again.

[1983]

Uncommon Words or Meanings

a largemouth bass ("the only creature that seemed lovelier to me than a *largemouth bass*")—a North American freshwater fish whose mouth is so large that it can swallow a frog or even a duckling.

too (noisy) by half ("'*Too noisy by half,*' my mother quickly decided.")—(idiom) excessively (noisy).

all but ("at seventeen, *all but* out of reach")—nearly, almost.

a float ("a *float* my Uncle Sierbert had moored")—a floating platform attached to a dock.

Dartmouth ("the *Dartmouth* heavyweight crew")—one of the eight prestigious Ivy League colleges, for men only at the time of the story. Dartmouth is in Hanover, New Hampshire, several miles south of this story's setting.

a crew ("heavyweight *crew*")—a team of eight rowers and a coxswain, who directs them.

the [Australian] crawl ("the beauty of my flutter kick, the power of my *crawl*")—a swimming stroke.

to sear ("have been *seared* from my memory")—to cause to wither or dry up.

the brunt ("I took the full *brunt* of her long red hair")—the main force or impact.

Brillo ("rubbed every inch with *Brillo*")—a brand name for a pad of steel wool with soap in it.

chamois ("wiping it with *chamois*")—soft leather made from the skin of a deer, sheep, or goat.

a thwart ("propping up my father's transistor radio by the middle *thwart*")—a wood or metal brace extending from one side of a canoe to the other.

a rod and reel ("I mounted my Mitchell *reel* on my Pfluger spinning *rod*")—a fishing pole (**rod**) with an attached spool (**reel**) for letting out or winding up the line.

a cast ("in our driveway practicing *casts*")—the action of throwing a baited hook or lure (defined below) with a fishing rod.

drag ("to test the reel's *drag*")—the slippage of the reel, without which the line would break if a fish suddenly pulled hard.

a plug ("I tied on a big Rapala *plug*")—a wooden or plastic cylinder that often resembles a bait fish.

tense ("Parking's *tense* up there.")—difficult.

to pry ("I *pried* the canoe away from the dock")—to move using a lever-like action.

to stroke ("he *strokes* number four")—to hold a position on a crew team.

to write (something) off ("*written off* forty or so dollars as love's tribute")—(idiom) to admit and accept that (something) is a loss or failure.

a lure ("Fish will trail a *lure*")—a shiny metal spoon-like object that flashes to attract a fish.

an inhibition ("enough to overcome the bass's *inhibitions*")—an inner check or restraint that prevents an action based on impulse or desire.

a concussion ("landing with a *concussion* heavy enough to . . .")—a violent shaking or shock.

a fraternity ("These *fraternity* men.")—a social club for a group of male students.

UVM; Bennington ("I'm thinking more of *UVM* or *Bennington*")—the University of Vermont at Montpelier; Bennington College.

Ann-Margret ("I mean, *Ann-Margret*? Like hers, only shorter.")—an actress who was a movie starlet in the 1960s.

no sweat ("*No sweat,* or anything.")—(slang) easily done or handled; no problem.

a gape ("the *gape* of its mouth")—a broad opening.

a covered bridge ("beneath a *covered bridge*")—a wooden bridge with walls and a roof to protect it from snow, found in New England.

Jackie Kennedy ("I saw *Jackie Kennedy* in Boston")—Jacqueline Kennedy Onassis, at the time of the story, the First Lady of the United States and a trendsetter in fashion.

to whine ("'My legs are sore,' Sheila *whined*.")—to speak in a self-pitying, complaining tone.

a Corvette ("going home in Eric Caswell's *Corvette*")—a two-seater Chevrolet sports car, introduced in 1953, known for its powerful engine and sexy styling.

a spell ("the *spell* she cast over me")—magic used to control someone's thoughts or actions.

to haunt ("that lost bass *haunted* me all summer")—to return to the mind repeatedly.

Fine Points

"A few years earlier, it might have been possible for me to find the necessary thrill simply in going out with white boys, the forbidden fruit of my mother's generation."

Fine Points

Andrea Lee
(born 1953)

Andrea Lee is one of the few black American authors who has presented the black middle class in fiction. A graduate of Harvard University, Lee is a staff writer for *The New Yorker* magazine, reporting on European topics from Milan, Italy, where she lives with her husband. Lee's first book, *Russian Journal* (1981), was based on her diary of the year that she and her husband spent in Moscow, where he had a graduate fellowship. The American couple's many contacts with Soviet young people gave them, as Lee said in 1981, "a view of life in Moscow and Leningrad that was very different from that of the diplomats and journalists we knew."

Lee's second book, the prize-winning *Sarah Phillips* (1984), is a collection of short stories originally published in *The New Yorker.* Together, the stories form an episodic novel and fictional autobiography. Like Andrea Lee, Sarah Phillips has grown up in comfortable circumstances in Philadelphia, attending private schools and enjoying social and academic success in the white world of her peers. In this privileged world, Sarah is able to distance herself from the more serious aspects of racial differences. She enjoys being seen as "exotic" because of her dark skin and she ignores the issues raised by the Civil Rights Movement of the 1960s, in which her parents have been active.

In "Fine Points," Sarah is in her third year at Radcliffe College, a distinguished institution of higher learning with close ties to Harvard University. (At the time of the story, 1973, Radcliffe admitted only women and Harvard College, the undergraduate division of the university, admitted only men; they have adjacent campuses in Cambridge, Massachusetts.) In the story, Lee uses real places: the "houses" (large dormitories with suites of rooms) where Harvard undergraduate men live; Harvard Yard, the lawn surrounded by the school's oldest buildings; Cambridge Common, a large city park between the Radcliffe and Harvard campuses; and the Café Pamplona, where members of the Harvard community still spend long hours talking over tiny cups of strong Italian coffee. Central Square, where Sarah's teacher Geoffrey Knacker lives, is a less expensive, less fashionable part of Cambridge.

The story is marked by irony, a contrast between the expected and the actual, the apparent and the real. The central dramatic irony is that Sarah (the narrator) and her roommate, who are intellectually gifted and socially privileged young women, want more than anything to be wicked women of the world. Why do you suppose they feel that way? What might they do to show their immorality? How good a chance do they have of realizing their desire on a college campus? What will the "fine points" of the title refer to?

One great thing about Margaret was that she wore exactly the same size clothing that I did, an excellent quality in a roommate; she had, however, completely different taste, with an inclination toward plunging necklines, crimson tights, and minidresses in big, bold Scandinavian prints. My own wardrobe ran to jeans and black turtlenecks, odd little somber-colored tunics that I felt made me look like a wood nymph, and short pleated skirts that seemed to me to convey a sexy *jeune fille* air worthy of Claudine at school. "You literary types are always trying to look understated," Margaret would say whenever she saw me dressed for seminar, for an *Advocate* meeting, or for a date. She was a chemistry major from Wellesley, Massachusetts, an avid lacrosse player with a terrific figure and a pair of unabashed blue eyes that revealed a forceful, stubborn nature—Margaret could keep an argument going for days. She adored fresh air and loathed reticence and ambiguity, and she had little patience with a roommate who, languid from lack of exercise, spent weeks reworking a four-word line of poetry.

"It's a question of fine points," I would retort loftily, though I had only a vague idea of what that might mean.

Margaret and I got along well for young women with such different souls. We spent a lot of time together in our cramped dormitory suite, squabbling comfortably over clothes and discussing romance—the one subject on which we were, to some extent, in agreement. The suite was on the fourth floor of Currier House; it consisted of two tiny rooms, a bathroom we'd decorated for a giggle with pinups of the bustiest *Playboy* Playmates we could find, and a kitchenette filled with moldy oranges stolen from the cafeteria. Our windows faced east, toward the corner of Garden and Linnaean streets—a lovely view, really, with the Observatory woods, the flat-bottomed, whale-shaped clouds that came sailing down from Maine, and the tall, somber Cambridge houses back of the trees.

In the winter of 1973, our junior year at Harvard, on afternoons when Margaret was back from the lab and I was sup-

posed to be at my desk reading Donne and Herbert for seminar
or writing poetry for Professor Hawks's versification class, we
would hang out in Margaret's room and drink oolong tea,
which Margaret brewed so black it became a kind of solvent.
Lounging on Margaret's bed, below a periodic table she'd
tacked up on the wall, we'd complain at length about our
boyfriends. These young men, a couple of blameless seniors
from Adams and Dunster Houses, were certainly ardent and
attentive, but they bored us because they seemed appropriate.
We yearned, in concert, to replace them with unsuitable men—
an array of Gothic-novel types who didn't seem at all hack-
neyed to Margaret and me. (Margaret, the scientist, had in fact
a positively Brontëesque conception of the ideal man.) We
envisioned liaisons with millionaires the age of our fathers,
with alcoholic journalists, with moody filmmakers addicted to
uppers; Margaret's particular thing was depraved European
nobility. A few years earlier it might have been possible for me
to find the necessary thrill simply in going out with white boys,
the forbidden fruit of my mother's generation; but in the arty
circles I frequented at Harvard, such pairings were just about
required, if one was to cut any dash at all.

What our fantasies boiled down to was that Margaret and
I, in the age-old female student tradition, ended up angling for
members of the faculty.

"It's just a question of days before Dr. Bellemere tumbles,"
said Margaret one afternoon. (She flirted shamelessly with her
adviser, but for some reason could not bring herself to call him
by his first name—Don.) "And *then*, what naughty delights!"

As a matter of fact, I was the one who first was offered the
chance to taste those delights. In February a genuine instructor—Geoffrey Knacker, who had taught my seminar on metaphysical poetry the previous semester, and who shared an
apartment in Central Square with Millicent Tunney, another
junior faculty member—asked me to meet him for a cup of coffee. Margaret sat cross-legged on my bed while I got dressed
for the date—we were to meet at six at the Café Pamplona—
and grew snappish when I refused the loan of a pair of red
tights. She told me that if I hid my light under a bushel, I
wouldn't even get him to kiss me. I didn't listen to her. I was
busy making myself look as beautiful and mysterious as I

could, and when I had slicked my hair back into a bun, rimmed
my eyes with dark pencil, and put on a severe gray dress with
a pair of black high heels I had bought in a thrift shop, even
80   Margaret had to applaud the result.

"If Hopalong calls, tell him I'm riding in the Tour de
France," I said. Hopalong Cassidy was the name we had privately given my boyfriend, who had what I thought was an
unnecessarily jaunty gait.

85   "You're a cold, hard thing," said Margaret in an approving
tone.

I owned a rather rubbed-looking sealskin jacket that had
belonged to my mother; when I had wrapped it around me,
waved goodbye to the girl who stood studying behind the bells
90   desk of the dormitory, and stepped outside into the February
twilight, I had an agreeable feeling of satisfaction about the
way I looked, and an agitated romantic feeling about the meeting to come. "Perhaps I'm in love," I thought, though in fact I
could barely remember what Geoffrey Knacker looked like.

95   It was ten minutes to six. I walked down Garden Street
toward Cambridge Common, listening to the unaccustomed
click of my high heels on the brick sidewalk, slippery with
melted snow and patches of dirty ice. In the darkness around
me, students riding bicycles or walking with book bags were
100   returning to dinner from classes in Harvard Yard. The sky over
the dark buildings and narrow streets was a deep lustrous
blue, streaked at the edges with pinkish light, and the air was
cold and damp. Near Follen Street a small battered Datsun
was trying unsuccessfully to park between a jacked-up Riviera
105   and a Volvo plastered with psychedelic stickers. The sound of
grinding gears made me think of the time during my sopho-
more year when a precursor of my boyfriend Hopalong had
gotten very stoned at the Dartmouth game and had pursued
me along Garden Street by backing up his car for a whole
110   block, all the while declaiming the words from the Temptations' song "My Girl." The incident had infuriated me at the
time, but now I thought of it as something gay and romantic,
the sort of thing that happened constantly to a woman des-
tined to exercise a fatal influence upon men.

115   My feeling of agitation increased as I approached the Common. The usual shouts and guffaws were coming from the war
monument in the middle, where Cambridge townies liked to

hang around smoking dope and drinking wine, but they seemed far away. I looked through the rows of leafless maples at the university towers and traffic lights clustering ahead of me, and felt an unreasonable, blissful happiness to be walking in high heels and a fur coat on a clear evening to a meeting with a man who was likely to mean trouble—the kind of trouble that mothers and magazine articles particularly warned against. I felt a bit like Anna Karenina, burning with a sinful glow; and as if someone beside me in the darkness had spoken a few passionate, muted words, it seemed to me that I was ravishingly beautiful. I began to pretend that someone *was* walking with me: a lover who didn't resemble my boyfriend, or even Geoffrey Knacker. This imaginary lover, in fact, didn't have much of any appearance at all, only a compelling simplicity of character that granted every dangerous wish I had ever had. As I walked through the Common, giving a wide berth to the monument, where two long-haired girls were giggling beside a guy who looked like Jimi Hendrix, I crooked my fingers very slightly inside the pocket of my fur jacket, as if I were holding hands with someone. And then I did something I never afterward admitted to anyone, not even Margaret: I recited a poem to my invisible companion—Donne's "The Flea."

By the time I got to the Pamplona, I had almost forgotten Geoffrey Knacker, who rose from his tiny table to greet me, with an air of being slightly startled by my appearance. He was a tall, thin man with a mournful, rather handsome face and gray half-moons of skin under his eyes; in the white-tiled, low-ceilinged interior of the Pamplona, surrounded by graduate students chatting over cappuccino, he appeared curiously yellowish and misanthropic, as if he'd lived most of his life in a remote tropical outpost. He helped me with my coat, and I ordered an ice cream. Then the two of us began to talk, rather constrainedly, about metaphysical poetry until Geoffrey began paying me heavy-handed compliments.

"I always felt that behind your reserved manner in class was a rare sensitivity of nature," he said, giving me a slow, gloomy smile, and I, who had been attracted by just that smile in the seminar, found myself filled not with rapture but with an inexplicable annoyance. It occurred to me that this meeting was just like a coffee date with any callow comp lit major, who would begin by throwing out portentous hints about his ideal

woman and end, ritually, by suggesting we drop mescaline and
160 swim nude in the Adams House pool. I tried to think of the
romantic fact that Geoffrey Knacker was an instructor, and
that both of us were flouting lovers in order to meet, but all I
could seem to feel was irritation at a flat, straw-colored mole
that Geoffrey had where his jaw met his neck, and at the way
165 that as he talked, he joined the tips of his fingers together and
pumped them in and out in a tiny bellowslike motion. We were
sitting at an inconspicuous table in a corner, but it seemed to
me, in my hypersensitive state, that all the other students in
the Pamplona could see the mole and the working fingertips,
170 and were laughing discreetly at them.

As I rattled my spoon in my ice-cream dish, some demon
prompted me to say, "But certainly you must have seen hundreds of exceptional students in all your years as a teacher.

"Hundreds?" repeated Geoffrey Knacker in an injured tone.
175 "Why, no, I finished my dissertation three years ago. I am only
thirty-one."

We didn't really have much to say to each other. It was
clear, in fact, that our original attraction had become puzzling
and abortive, and that this meeting was one of those muted
180 social disasters that can be devastating if one cares. I didn't
care much; nor, it seemed, did Geoffrey Knacker. We shook
hands and parted outside the Pamplona without even mentioning plans to get in touch. When he zipped up his jacket and,
with one last unhappy smile, trudged off in his L. L. Bean boots
185 toward Central Square, I clicked off back to Radcliffe in my
high heels, feeling positively elated. Geoffrey Knacker, I
decided, was a bore, but the *fact* of Geoffrey Knacker was
exciting. As I came into Harvard Square and threaded my way
through the slush and evening traffic on Massachusetts Avenue,
190 the romantic sensation I'd had while walking through the Common returned to me in full force. I seemed, agreeably, to be taking up the strands of an interrupted idyll, and in my right palm,
deep in the pocket of the fur jacket, was the pleasant tickling
feeling that denoted the grasp of my imaginary lover.

195 When I got back to the suite, Margaret was working on a
problem sheet for Chem 105, and her boyfriend—a young man
with such an earnest, childlike gaze that we'd nicknamed him
Christopher Robin—was seated cross-legged on her bed, using
a metal mesh contraption to sift seeds and stems out of an

200 ounce of grass he'd just bought. (One of Margaret's complaints about him was his methodical attitude toward sex and drugs.) "Oo-la-la—very thirties," said Christopher Robin, giving my outfit the old once-over, and then Margaret dragged me into the bathroom.

205 "Well, what happened?" she demanded, locking the door, turning on both faucets, and settling herself on the sink counter under the enormous bosom of one of the Playmates we'd pinned up. "He must have kissed you—or did you fall into bed together? You're absolutely beaming."

210 "Knacker was actually kind of a fizzle," I said, "But it was fun anyway."

"Idiot child," said Margaret. "Take off that coat—you've wasted it. I knew you should have worn red stockings."

When I tried to explain myself, she leaned back against the
215 bathroom mirror, closed her eyes, and giggled so that the frame of the mirror shook. "My artistic roommate," she said. "The woman of epiphanies. You're going to kill me with your fine points."

A few weeks later Margaret was dancing to a Stones tape
220 at a party in a converted airplane factory up near MIT when she ran into her adviser, Dr. Bellemere, whom she at last succeeded in calling Don. Bellemere, who was a post-doc a bit older than Geoffrey Knacker, and who fluttered hearts all through the chem labs with his leather vest and Buffalo Bill
225 mustache, had had a lot of the punch, which was a Techie grape-juice concoction laced with acid. He led Margaret out of the strobe lights into a dark corner of the loft, kissed her passionately, and told her he spent every lab session thinking about her legs. A triumph for Margaret—except that she inex-
230 plicably discovered a preference for Christopher Robin, and so the thing with Bellemere went no further, except for a bit of embarrassment in lab.

"But there was something really solid there—a kiss, not just daydreams," Margaret told me pointedly when we dis-
235 cussed it later. For a change, we were sitting among the scattered books and papers of my room, while I packed my book bag to go down and visit Hopalong at Adams House.

"I don't think the two situations were so different," I said. "I'm afraid, sweetheart, that whatever we try to do, in our two
240 different ways, we end up being just a couple of nice girls."

"Oh, I hope not!" said Margaret, flopping backward on the bed. "But anyway," she went on stubbornly after a minute, " a real kiss is better than an imaginary one.

And she thumped her booted feet on my bedspread for emphasis.

245

I wanted to contradict her, but then I remembered how bullheaded and tenacious Margaret could be in an argument, how tiresomely withholding of her oolong tea and the little English butter biscuits that her mother sent her, and that I loved. In the end I just raised my eyebrows with the air of one to whom has been granted higher knowledge, and kept my mouth shut.

250

[1984]

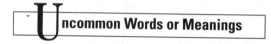

Uncommon Words or Meanings

fine ("It's a question of *fine* points.")—subtle or precise.

jeune fille ("a sexy *jeune fille* air worthy of Claudine")—(French) "young girl," suggesting youthful innocence.

Claudine ("worthy of *Claudine*")—the heroine of four novels by the early twentieth-century French writer Colette.

understated ("always trying to look *understated*")—deliberately simple.

the *Advocate* ("for an *Advocate* meeting")—the Harvard undergraduate literary magazine.

loftily ("I would retort *loftily*")—in a proud or superior manner.

busty ("the *bustiest Playboy* Playmates")—with large breasts, full-figured.

Donne, Herbert ("reading *Donne* and *Herbert* for seminar")—John Donne and George Herbert, seventeenth-century English metaphysical poets known for their elaborate images.

in concert ("We yearned, *in concert*")—in agreement, harmoniously.

a Gothic novel ("an array of *Gothic-novel* types")—a literary form characterized by horror, violence, and supernatural effects, often set in an isolated castle.

Brontëesque ("a positively *Brontëesque* conception of the ideal man")—in the style of the nineteenth-century English novelists who created dark, handsome, and masterful heroes in *Jane Eyre* (Charlotte Brontë) and *Wuthering Heights* (Emily Brontë).

a liaison ("envisioned *liaisons* with millionaires")—an illicit sexual relationship.

an upper ("moody filmmakers addicted to *uppers*")—(slang) a pharmaceutical drug that speeds up the metabolism and keeps a person awake.

to cut a dash ("were to *cut any dash* at all")—(British idiom) to be exciting and stylish in appearance and behavior.

to angle ("*angling* for members of the faculty")—to fish.

snappish ("grew *snappish* when I refused the loan")—bad-tempered, irritable.

to hide one's light under a bushel ("if I *hid my light under a bushel,* I wouldn't even get him to kiss me")—(idiom) to be modest about one's good qualities.

a thrift shop ("high heels I had bought in a *thrift shop*")—a store that sells second-hand clothing.

Hopalong Cassidy ("*Hopalong Cassidy* was the name we had privately given my boyfriend.")—the cowboy creation of actor William Boyd, first in films and comic books then in an enormously successful TV series of the 1950s, when Sarah was a child.

the bells desk ("behind the *bells desk* in the dormitory")—at the time of the story, the reception desk in a Radcliffe dormitory.

psychedelic ("a Volvo plastered with *psychedelic* stickers")—having vivid colors and distorted shapes that suggest drug-created hallucinations or distortions of perception.

stoned ("Hopalong had gotten very *stoned* at the Dartmouth game")—(slang) in an artificially (drug-) induced euphoric state.

Dartmouth ("at the *Dartmouth* game")—Dartmouth competes with Harvard and the other Ivy League colleges in sports.

the Temptations ("the *Temptations'* song 'My Girl'")—a black male quartet, popularizers of the "Motown sound" in the early 1960s.

a townie ("where Cambridge *townies* liked to hang around smoking dope")—(slang) a college-age person who lives in a college town but is not a college student.

dope ("hang around smoking *dope*")—(slang) here, marijuana or hashish, though the term can include other drugs.

Anna Karenina ("I felt a bit like *Anna Karenina*")—in Leo Tolstoy's nineteenth-century novel, a married woman who has an illicit love affair with a dashing younger man.

to give (something) a wide berth ("*giving a wide berth* to the monument")—(idiom) to stay as far away as possible from (something).

Jimi Hendrix ("a guy who looked like *Jimi Hendrix*")—a black guitarist and singer of the1960s who sported a wild Afro hairdo and psychedelic clothing.

"The Flea" ("I recited a poem to my invisible companion— Donne's *'The Flea'*")—a clever seduction poem by John Donne.

comp lit ("just like a coffee date with any callow *comp lit* major")—comparative literature.

to drop ("suggesting we *drop* mescaline")—(slang) to swallow a drug.

mescaline ("drop *mescaline*")—a drug that acts as a stimulant.

a dissertation ("finished my *dissertation* three years ago")—the last step in earning a doctoral degree, which is usually necessary for a full-time teaching appointment in a four-year college.

muted ("one of those *muted* social disasters")—quiet, softened.

L. L. Bean ("trudged off in his *L. L. Bean* boots")—a famous Maine sporting goods store.

Christopher Robin ("nicknamed him *Christopher Robin*")—the young boy in A. A. Milne's early twentieth-century Winnie-the-Pooh stories.

grass ("an ounce of *grass* that he'd just bought")—(slang) marijuana.

an epiphany ("The woman of *epiphanies*")—a moment of enlightenment when an underlying truth suddenly becomes clear.

the [Rolling] Stones ("dancing to a *Stones* tape")—the famous British rock-and-roll group that debuted in 1964.

a post-doc ("a *post-doc* a bit older than Geoffrey Knacker")—a person doing research at a university on a post-doctoral fellowship.

to flutter hearts ("*fluttered hearts* all through the chem labs")—to make hearts beat faster with romantic excitement.

Buffalo Bill ("a *Buffalo Bill* mustache")—William F. Cody, a nineteenth-century American frontier scout and showman who sported a wide, bushy mustache.

Techie ("a *Techie* grape-juice concoction")—(slang) created by a "Techie," a student at the Massachusetts Institute of Technology (MIT).

to lace ("a Techie grape-juice concoction *laced* with acid")—to add a small amount of a stronger substance to a drink.

acid ("laced with *acid*")—LSD, a drug that produces hallucinations.

There You Have Been, Where You Are Going

"'How long were
you in jail?' I ask
through everyone's
laughter.
Grandfather keeps
an even
expression."

Where You Have Been,
Where You Are Going

Mark Steven Hess
(born 1966)

Mark Steven Hess has lived nearly all his life on Colorado's vast High Plains, east of Denver. In high school, he was interested mostly in science until his senior year, when he wrote a short story that impressed his English teacher, who had just published a first novel. "I'd hate to suggest this to anyone," the teacher said, "but why don't you try writing?"

Hess took the advice, finding time to write during the summers. He also became a high school English teacher in Brush, Colorado, one hundred miles northeast of Denver. The school enrolls four hundred students, some of whom travel forty or more miles a day to attend classes. Sports are important in the school, so besides teaching, Hess coaches the Brush "Beetdiggers" teams in boys' and girls' track and girls' basketball. Hess offers this report on how the name came to be:

"School legend has it that the name 'Beetdiggers' was chosen in a contest in the 1940s. The prize for the winning student was to be a used car. Now, the basketball team's star player was a country kid who had no way to get home after practice and so was going to have to quit the team. What would you do in a case like that? At Brush High School, it was silently agreed that whatever name this player chose would win the contest. The rest is history."

"Where You Have Been, Where You Are Going"—Hess's first published story—was chosen for the 1989 volume of

The Best of the West: New Short Stories from the Wide Side of the Mississippi. "The story really came out my love for Colorado's High Plains," the author says. "When you stand on the open prairie, you get the sense that you're incredibly alone. Recently, irrigation has turned the High Plains into beautiful farmland, but there are still many places out here almost untouched by humans—miles and miles of prairie and sage that could just swallow you up."

Within that context of isolation, Hess dramatizes ways that connections are made between generations. He also reminds us that in the American West, as in other "uncharted" parts of the world, the "tall tale"—like those told by the grandfather in this story—became the way explorers described the wonders they had seen to open-mouthed audiences back home. Like the land that provides its setting, this story rises and falls between different time periods. (Extra space between paragraphs signals the shift from one time to another.) In the first time period ("today"), the narrator retraces the steps of a walk in his childhood. In the second time period (forty years earlier), he relives the day of that walk. In the third time period (forty-one years earlier), he remembers the time he met his grandfather and a story that the grandfather told. In the fourth time period (more than forty-one years earlier), the grandfather's story takes place. (This flashback technique—having a character remember a past event which the audience then sees—is familiar from movies.) As the title suggests, we must remember the past in order to understand the present and anticipate the future.

Where You Have Been, Where You are Going

I shut the door of my car. I can hardly hear the noise it makes. All sounds are sifted here, broken up by the prairie, digested and dispersed in fine pieces through the air. The color is brown—brown plains of brown dirt, brown weeds rolling off north, south, east, west with a brown road slashing across them. The sky contains no clouds. It is a solid blue sheet meeting brown prairie in one straight line as if someone had pasted two pieces of colored paper together.

I walk north across a ditch, and I thank God this is not my home.

This is my grandfather's home. He was born here. He spent his life here before he died seven miles away in a rest home in a town called Arickeree. There are five paved streets in that town, each lined with elm trees on both sides. It looks like an oasis as you approach it from the state highway—122 miles straight east of Denver by counting mile markers. When you get there, though, you can see that the trees are only a cover for more brown—brown-faced people with lines of brown underneath their fingernails from working in their brown yards.

I only saw my grandfather once. I was four years old. One day an old man appeared in our house. Dad said, "Son, this is your grandfather." The old man shook my hand and laughed. He slapped my back. He kneaded my shoulder. He wrestled me close to him and squeezed my knee until I squirmed and laughed and wrestled his big hand to get loose and finally he could say, "You're just about one of the girl-craziest persons I ever seen."

He stayed only for a week, and when he left I kept expecting to see him still in our house. I thought I'd see him just around the corner in the hallway, smoking cigarettes at night in his bedroom, or brushing thick lather onto his face as he whistled to himself in front of the bathroom mirror. I have never seen a man since who has whistled so often or so well.

I continue north now, keeping to the right tire rut—the same rut Dad and I followed to the old homestead I have only seen once before. The ruts lead up and down the swells of the prairie to the homestead. Each swell is like a tiny horizon, and there are places where the swells are so abrupt and so close together that I do not know what is ahead of me thirty yards away. When I walk I feel as if I am climbing ocean waves. I am surrounded by waves, and though the waves don't move, I still feel threatened. I walk on. I walk on because I know that soon I will rise up over a swell and there will be the windmill—there will be the lighthouse that tells me the homestead is not far away.

It is forty years before. Grandfather has just died. I am five years old. After the funeral Dad stops at a store with a green-and-white-striped awning. We go inside and there Dad buys me a pair of black cowboy boots. I wear the boots out of the store and run down the street to try them out. They are exactly the kind I want. "Yes," Dad says, satisfied, "those are very fine boots."

Dad says he wants to show me something. We get in the car and drive on dirt roads. On the way, Dad tells me of Indians and arrowheads and how he used to go hunting arrowheads after big rainstorms when the dust on the ground was newly melted away by the drops of rain. By the time Dad stops the car, my feet have begun to sweat in the leather boots. This can't be what he wants to show me because there is nothing here. I guess he has to pee. He gets out of the car and motions for me to follow. He takes my hand, and we walk north along tire ruts. "Just watch for the windmill," he says. "When you see the windmill we'll be there." We are going to see where my grandfather grew up, a place where there were real cowboys and real Indians.

My grandfather stretches his legs out in front of him. He is a big man. He takes up two spaces on the sofa just getting comfortable. He tells us a story about a windmill.

The windmill has stopped turning. They have had no way to get water for three days. They try greasing the windmill; they try replacing the gears. Nothing works. Two Indians pass by. Grandfather offers them a shotgun and a pint of whiskey if they will make it rain. They ask why doesn't he just try greasing the windmill. Grandpa throws two extra pints of whiskey into the deal. Finally they accept. The Indians dance all night, and the next day it rains—a thunderstorm. Lightning strikes the windmill, and the windmill begins to turn. It continues to rain for twelve days. No work gets done, and all the people around

Arickeree get scared because they have never seen so much rain. The sheriff comes from Arickeree and arrests Grandfather for negligence in giving rain dancers too much whiskey.

80   Dad has dropped my hand. He walks looking straight ahead and does not notice me. Now and then I have to skip to keep up. "Can't we drive?" I ask. "Ain't no vehicle could make the trip over this land," he says. He is talking like Grandfather. The new boots hurt my feet. "Is it far?" "Not far." "Are we
85 almost there?" "Look for the windmill," he says. "Dad . . ." I say. I pause. I make him see me. "My feet hurt." He looks solemn, slightly hurt, slightly pleading. "We'll try going slower," he says.
    He stops, points, and turns, indicating the horizon. "Right there," he says, "settlers used to come on covered wagons. It
90 wasn't easy out here. Sure there were Indians . . ."
    "Indians?"
    "Indians. And you had to watch out for them for too, but getting lost out here was just as dangerous. You might think it's hard getting lost in such an open place, but that's just the prob-
95 lem. There's nothing out here to look at to see if you're going in a straight line. And then there are these swells. You get down in between two swells and you can't see where you're going or where you've been. The only thing that can keep you going is hope and that next swell—hope that soon you'd come
100 over a swell and there would be a river you could follow, or maybe there would be the Rocky Mountains and you could head straight out to them."
    "There was Indians here?" I ask, walking again, forgetting now my discomfort.
105   "Indians? Sure."
    "Bad Indians?"
    "Well, some were bad, I guess. But most of them your Grandpa knew were good."
    "Grandpa knew Indians?"
110   "Sure. Don't you remember his stories? He knew as many Indians as you might ever want to know. He could name all the tribes, Sioux, Cheyenne, Papoose, Squaw, Hermoso. In fact . . . not far from here, just on the other side of your Grandpa's homestead, is an Indian grave."
115   "Can we see it?"

"Yes, I suppose a fellow could walk to it. No . . . it really isn't too far from here."

We walk faster.

There was the windmill, just above the horizon, pushing up higher and higher over the next swell with each step as if it were growing up out of the prairie. I remember now the way I yelled the first I saw it, how I ran ahead of Dad and laughed, feeling like a real cowboy in my black cowboy boots. This day, though, calls for silence.

I walk, hands in my pockets. I feel my pocketknife there, cold, familiar. The knife has no color anymore, though it was once shiny gold, and the end of the longest blade is chipped off square from using it as a screwdriver. Every family has an heirloom—a sort of talisman. This knife is ours. Somehow . . . when I touch it—when I fold my hand around it—I can feel Father's strong hands, and as I hold the knife now I do not want to let go.

I am certain that Dad must have been relieved, even satisfied that day with all my running and yelling as we approached the homestead. I am certain because I know what it is like to lose your father. I am certain because even now I want someone to fill this place with laughter. If I could have any wish right now, it would be that I could fill this place myself.

"How long were you in jail?" I ask through everyone's laughter. Grandfather keeps an even expression. "It was two weeks," he says, "two weeks and then the sheriff let me go." He talked while his fork rested on his plate. He talked with his fork poised in front of his mouth. He talked through mouthfuls of scalloped potatoes. He talked through bites of strawberry shortcake.

When Grandfather returned to the homestead he found the two Indians waiting for him. They had set up a teepee and had waited there two weeks for Grandfather for the sole purpose of learning from Grandfather how to operate the shotgun he had given them. There was never a time when it had rained for twelve days before on the prairie. It was as if the ground didn't know what to do with all that water, so for a while the water just stayed there, and the prairie was dotted all over with small lakes. Grandfather wasn't going to let an opportunity like this

slip away, so he grabbed his shotgun and his bird dog Scooter
155 and took the Indians out to see if they might be able to hunt a
few of the ducks that flew in off the lakes.

Grandfather was a bit worried that Scooter might not quite
know what to do with a duck. Scooter had never seen a duck
before, nor a lake for that matter. But right away they saw
160 some ducks and one, two, Grandfather gets off two shots and
two ducks fall to the ground. Scooter brought the ducks back,
not even hesitating, and neither duck had so much as one
tooth mark on its body. Meanwhile the Indians were shooting
wildly with their shotgun and coming closer to killing them-
165 selves than any duck. One would shoot and the kick of the old
shotgun would knock him all the way to the ground. Before
that one had time to swear, the other one would grab the shotgun and fire. Then both Indians tried holding the shotgun at
the same time, but both barrels shot off and knocked both the
170 Indians to the ground. Pretty soon, the Indians got more than
fed up with this, and finally they asked Grandfather to come
along with them; they'd show him the real way to hunt ducks.

When they arrived at the next lake, the Indians walked up
close without any noise and crouched down low into their own
175 shadows. Now Grandfather can't figure out how the hell the
Indians are going to catch a duck this way, but soon the Indians start making sort of low and throaty duck noises with their
palms cupped over their mouths. Sure enough, within five minutes four or five ducks swim up close to the edge where the
180 Indians crouch. Suddenly one of the Indians springs into the
water and grabs a duck by the neck, twisting its head nearly
off before the duck has time to quack even once in surprise.

An hour of crouching, springing, and twisting passes before
the Indians relax. The result is a pile of a dozen ducks with bro-
185 ken necks lying on the ground beside the Indians. Grandfather
was so happy at this that he forgot himself for a moment and
shot a duck sitting on top of the water. He completely forgot
about Scooter and his ignorance about duck hunting and water.
Before Grandfather could do anything, though, Scooter was off
190 and running on top of the water just like Jesus Christ. Scooter
was there and back even before Grandfather had time tell him
he would drown, and just as always the hound laid the bird in
Grandfather's hand without a solitary tooth mark. From then
on the Indians never did get closer than a careful arm's length

195   to Scooter in fear that whatever demon that made the dog run on the water might suddenly let loose and jump inside one of them. Grandfather's brain was swiveling faster than a weather cock in a tornado, but he never let the Indians see he was affected. Later, though, when Grandpa got the chance to fill up

200   a pipe and sit down to think, he worked it all out in his head. After then, he wasn't troubled anymore because it was all just a matter of finding a logical explanation. And it didn't take Grandpa too long to realize that the reason Scooter could walk right on top of the water like that was because Grandpa never

205   did teach the dog how to swim, and the dog was too dumb to figure out for himself that trying to run on top of water was likely to result in drowning.

    It is getting darker. The prairie is silver; the prairie is grey. We stand by the windmill. It is just an old windmill, nothing else.

210   There are no lightning marks, no buffalo hides tacked to it. I don't know why we have to stay here so long. Perhaps dad sees more to this place than I do. Maybe he can still see what used to be here, the sod house, the turning windmill, my grandfather at the window, his face, his hands. I look at the windmill. I want to

215   ask where the lightning struck it. I want to ask how it brings up water. I want to ask how long it will be until we can go to the Indian grave. But Dad does not notice me, so I turn sideways and try to make myself thinner. I don't want to get in the way.

    Grandfather is wearing black cowboy boots that he and I

220   polished the night before. He is boarding the bus that will take him back to Colorado. He shakes my hand. He tells me I have a strong hand. He slaps my back, kneads my shoulder, and then gets on the bus—black boots clunking up the steps.

    Dad says we will have to hurry to make it to the Indian

225   grave before dark. He starts east, each stride a mountain. I nearly have to run to keep up. At first I am eager, but it doesn't take too long for me to remember my boots. "My feet hurt," I say. Dad keeps striding. "It is only a little farther," he says. "But they really hurt," I say, letting a whine slip into my tone.

230   "Watch the horizon," he says, "that next swell, maybe there will be that grave on the other side."

    It does not work. I feel the blister anyway.

Dad is striding—flying—and I keep falling away, my arm getting longer, his hand holding tighter to mine until he is
235 almost dragging me with him. Tears come now. My feet drag and stumble over the hard mounds of dirt. No wagon full of settlers can stop the tears; no promise of an Indian grave can keep me silent. I let the tears force my mouth to open, and I cry.

I reach to feel the pocketknife. For an instant my hand
240 does not find it, and I imagine the knife already lost—already buried in the dust somewhere on the prairie. For an instant my body, neck, and head shrivel together, my trachea constricts and I cannot breathe; for an instant I want to let my body fall, fold together, and collapse on the prairie. But then I find it. I
245 hold the knife tight in my hand and do not let go. It is my turn now to stand at the windmill and remember. Jesus . . . they were handsome men.

We are almost back to the car again. Dad carries me on his shoulders, my cowboy boots bouncing off his chest. Dad is
250 striding still, now happily, now jokingly telling me stories of rattlesnakes, cowboys and cattle drives, and how Grandma used to make lye soap. I try not to be happy. I try not to smile, but it is no use. My tears are already dry.
Before we get into the car, Dad crouches low in front of me.
255 In his hand is a pocketknife. He wants me to take it. In my hand the knife seems much larger. "I got that knife on my tenth birthday," he says. "Your grandfather gave it to me." I put the knife in my pocket, feeling on the outside to make sure it is safe there. We get in the car. I feel older now, grown up because I
260 have my own knife. I look at my father and somehow he too is older.
"Dad," I say, "I really wanted to see that Indian grave."
"Yes," he says, "yes . . . so did I."

I turn and walk east, away from the windmill. I watch the
265 next swell of prairie in front of me. I walk until I am on top of the swell, and then I stop. You can see both ways here. I stay there only a moment; then I continue east knowing that over the next swell will be the Indian grave.

[1988]

Uncommon Words or Meanings

a rest home ("died seven miles away in a *rest home*")—a residence for older people who need housekeeping services (meals, sheets and towels, laundry) but not extensive medical treatment.

to knead ("He *kneaded* my shoulder.")—to massage firmly.

lather ("brushing thick *lather* onto his face")—a soapy foam used to soften a man's beard before he shaves.

girl-craziest ("one of the *girl-craziest* persons")—romantically excited by girls; when said to a four-year-old boy, this is a form of good-natured teasing.

a swell ("The ruts lead up and down the *swells* of the prairie")—(1) a gradual rise in ground level; (2) a long wave that moves without breaking; in the story, the prairie is described in terms of the ocean.

a homestead ("the old *homestead*")—in the nineteenth-century United States, land granted by a state government to any settler who would build a home, dig a well for water, and clear and farm the land.

an arrowhead ("Indians and *arrowheads*")—a piece of stone, one or two inches in length, chipped to make a pointed tip for an arrow.

to pee ("he has to *pee*")—(informal) to urinate.

Papoose, Squaw, Hermoso ("he could name all the tribes, Sioux, Cheyenne, *Papoose, Squaw, Hermoso*")—American Indian words for "baby" (*papoose*) and "woman" (*squaw*) and the Spanish word for "beautiful" (*hermoso*); only "Sioux" and "Cheyenne" are real tribal names.

even ("keeps an *even* expression")—unchanging.

a teepee ("had set up a *teepee*")—a cone-shaped tent made of buffalo hide.

a bird dog (his *bird dog* Scooter")—a dog used to hunt game birds.

Where You Have Been, Where You Are Going 243

a kick ("the *kick* of the old shotgun")—the jerk backwards of a gun when it is fired.

fed up ("the Indians got more than *fed up* with all this")—annoyed, out of patience.

walking on water ("*running on top of the water* just like Jesus Christ")—the miracle of Jesus walking on the waters of the Sea of Galilee is described in Matthew 14:25.

to swivel ("*swiveling* around faster than a weather cock")—to turn or spin quickly on a single point.

a weather cock ("faster than a *weather cock*")—a thin plate of wood or metal that turns to indicate the direction of the wind, often in the shape of a male chicken (a "cock").

sod ("the *sod* house")—a grass-covered piece of earth held together by roots; in the U.S., used for home-building by early white settlers on the Great Plains, where there were very few trees.

lye ("how Grandma used to make *lye* soap")—a strong chemical substance (sodium hydroxide), obtained by passing water through wood ashes; American pioneer women combined lye with animal fat to make soap for washing clothes.

Christmas Snow

"First, standing in the doorway but still outside, he stripped three gloves from each hand and tossed them ahead of him into the shed."

Christmas Snow

Donald Hall
(born 1928)

Since his undergraduate days at Harvard, Donald Hall, the Poet Laureate of the state of New Hampshire, has been a prolific writer, publishing poetry, prose, short stories, and children's stories at the rate of four books a year. Hall's interest in writing began at the age of seven, he has said, when he was home for several weeks with a childhood illness. Bored with fifteen-minute serials on the radio, he turned to a school storybook. "Thus I became fluent with reading for the first time," Hall recounts, "and discovered the bliss of abandonment to print, to word and story. From the love of reading [came] the desire to write, a lifelong commitment to making things that might (if I were diligent, talented, and lucky) resemble the books I loved reading."*

Grace in expressing his ideas and a generous enthusiasm for the work of others are two of Hall's distinguishing characteristics. In *Remembering Poets* (1977; revised and republished as *Their Ancient Glittering Eyes,* 1992), Hall combined mature literary criticism with anecdotes of his youthful meetings with four of the twentieth century's major poets: Dylan Thomas, Robert Frost, T. S. Eliot, and Ezra Pound. His collected short stories, published as *The Ideal Bakery* (1987), is dedicated to his fellow poets Raymond Carver (represented in volume 1 of this text) and Tess Gallagher. In *Life Work* (1993), Hall speaks of the importance of work in his life and that of his forebearers, including the people who appear in "Christmas Snow." His earlier

* From Donald Hall, "The Books Not Read, the Lines Not Written: A Poet Confronts His Mortality." *The New York Times Book Review,* August 1, 1993.

autobiographical memoir *String Too Short To Be Saved* (1961) tells of the same New Hampshire family.

In "Christmas Snow," a middle-aged narrator, Donnie, remembers "the snows of Christmas in New Hampshire" in 1938, the year of his tenth birthday. The story is framed, like a picture, by events from the evening of December 23 to the evening of December 24; other events, both recent and distant, are presented within the frame. During the day, three generations of family members talk of their experience with heavy snow in other years. By the time Donnie has been sent to bed, long past his usual bedtime, his knowledge of the world has, in the words of the poet Yeats, been changed utterly.

When *The Ideal Bakery* appeared in 1987, novelist and short-story writer John Casey called the book "brilliant" and "a flare of beauty and pity." Singling out "Christmas Snow" for special praise, the reviewer confessed that rereading the story before writing his review, he "was startled to tears all over again the second time through." How could a story cause a man to cry both the first and second times he reads it? And how could it take him by surprise the second time? What will change Donnie's view of the world? To find out for yourself, read on.

Christmas Snow

The real snows I remember are the snows of Christmas in New Hampshire. I was ten years old, and there was a night when I woke up to the sound of grown-ups talking. Slowly, I realized that it wasn't that at all; the mounds of my grandfather and
5 grandmother lay still in their bed under many quilts in the cold room. It was rain falling and rubbing against the bushes outside my windows. I sat up in bed, pulling the covers around me, and held the green shade out from the frosty pane. There were flakes of snow mixed into the rain—large, slow flakes fluttering down
10 like wet leaves. I watched as long as I could, until the back of my neck hurt with the cold, while the flakes grew thicker and the snow took over the rain. When I looked up into the dark sky, just before lying back in my warm feather bed, the whole air was made of fine light shapes. I was happy in my own world of snow,
15 as if I were living inside one of those glass paperweights that snow when you shake them, and I went back to sleep easily. In the morning, I looked out the window as soon as I woke. There were no more leaves, no more weeds turned brown by the frost, no sheds, no road, and no chicken coops. The sky was a dense
20 mass of snowflakes, the ground covered in soft white curves.

It was the morning of Christmas Eve, 1938. The day before, we had driven north from Connecticut, and I had been disappointed to find that there was no snow on my grandfather's farm. On the trip up, I had not noticed the lack of snow
25 because I was too busy looking for hurricane damage. (September 1938 was the time of the great New England hurricane.) Maples and oaks and elms were down everywhere. Huge roots stood up like dirt cliffs next to the road. On distant hillsides, whole stands of trees lay pointing in the same direc-
30 tion, like combed hair. Men were cutting the timber with double handsaws, their breaths blue-white in the cold. Ponds were already filling with logs—stored timber that would corduroy the surface of New Hampshire lakes for years. Here and there I saw a roof gone from a barn, or a tree leaning into a house.
35 We knew from letters that my grandfather's farmhouse was all right. I was excited to be going there, sitting in the front seat between my mother and father, with the heater blasting at my knees. Every summer we drove the same route and I spent two weeks following my grandfather as he did chores, listening

40   to his talk. The familiar road took shape again: Sunapee, Georges Mills, New London; then there was the shortcut along the bumpy Cilleyville Road. We drove past the West Andover depot, past Henry's store and the big rock, and climbed the lit- tle hill by the Blasington's, and there, down the slope to the
45   right, we saw the lights of the farmhouse. In a porch window I could see my small Christmas tree, with its own string of lights. It stood in the window next to the large one, where I could see it when we drove over the hill.

    We stopped in the driveway and the kitchen door loosened
50   a wedge of yellow light. My grandfather stood in his milking clothes, tall and bald and smiling broadly. He lifted me up, grunting at how big I was getting. Over his shoulder, which smelled happily of barn and tie-up, I saw my grandmother in her best dress, waiting her turn and looking pleased.
55   As we stood outside in the cold, I looked around for the signs of the hurricane. In the light from the kitchen window I could just see a stake with a rope tied to it that angled up into the tall maple by the shed. Then I remembered that my grand- mother had written my mother about that tree. It had blown
60   over, roots out of the ground, and Washington Woodward, a cousin of ours who lived on Ragged Mountain, was fixing it. The great tree was upright now.

    My grandfather saw me looking at it. "Looks like it's going to work, don't it? Of course you can't tell until spring, and the
65   leaves. A lot of the root must have gone." He shook his head. "Wash is a wonder," he said. "He winched that tree back upright in two days with a pulley on that oak." He pointed to a tree on the hill in back of the house. "I thought he was going to pull that oak clear out of the ground. Then he took that rock-
70   moving machine of his" (I remembered that Wash had con- structed a wooden tripod about fifteen feet high for moving rocks. I never understood how it worked, though I heard him explain it a hundred times. He moved rocks for fun mostly; it was his hobby.) "and moved that boulder down from the pas-
75   ture and set it there to keep the roots flat. It only took him five days in all, and I think he saved the tree."

    It was when we moved back to the group around the car that I realized, with sudden disappointment, that there was no snow on the ground.
80   I turned from the window the next morning and looked over at my grandparents' bed. My grandmother was there, but

the place beside her was empty. The clock on the bureau, among snapshots and perfume bottles, said six o'clock. I heard my grandfather carrying wood into the living room. Logs
85 crashed into the big, square stove. In a moment I heard another sound I had been listening for—a massive animal roar from the same stove. He had poured a tin can of kerosene on the old embers and the new logs. Then I heard him fix the kitchen stove and pause by the door to put on coats and
90 scarves and a cap—his boots were in the shed,—and then the door shut between the kitchen and the shed, and he had gone to milk the cows.

It was warm inside my bed. My grandmother stood up beside her bed, her gray hair down to her waist. "Good morn-
95 ing," she said. "You awake? We've had some snow. You go back to sleep while I make the doughnuts." That brought me out of bed quickly. I dressed next to the stove in the dark living room. The sides of the stove glowed red, and I kept my distance. The cold of the room almost visibly receded into the farther cor-
100 ners, there to dwindle into something the size of a pea.

My grandmother was fixing her hair in the warm kitchen, braiding it and winding it up on her head. She looked like my grandmother again. "Doughnuts won't be ready for a long time. Fat's got to heat. Why don't you have a slice of bread and go
105 see Gramp in the tie-up?"

I put peanut butter on the bread and bundled up with galoshes and a wool cap that I could pull over my ears. I stepped outside into the swirl of flakes, white against the gray of the early morning. It was my first snow of the year, and it set
110 my heart pounding with pleasure. But even if it had snowed in Connecticut earlier, this would have been my first real snow. When it snowed in Connecticut, the snowplows heaped most of it in the gutters and the cars chewed the rest with chains and blackened it with oil. Here the snow turned the farm into a
115 planet of its own, an undiscovered moon.

I walked past our Studebaker, which was humped already with two inches of snow. I reached down for a handful, to see if it would pack, but it was dry as cotton. The flakes, when I looked up into the endless flaking barrel of the sky, were fine
120 and constant. It was going to snow all day. I climbed the hill to the barn without lifting my galoshes quite clear of the snow

and left two long trenches behind me. I raised the iron latch and went into the tie-up, shaking my head and shoulders like a dog, making a little snowstorm inside.

125 My grandfather laughed. "It's really coming down," he said. "It'll be a white Christmas, you can be sure of that."

"I love it," I said.

"Can you make a snowman today?"

"It's dry snow," I said. "It won't pack."

130 "When it melts a little, you can roll away the top of it—I mean, tomorrow or the next day. I remember making a big one with my brother Fred when I was nine—no, eight. Fred wasn't much bigger than a hoptoad then. I called him Hoptoad when I wanted to make him mad, and my, you never saw such a red

135 face. Well, we spent the whole day Saturday making this great creature. Borrowed a scarf and an old hat—it was a woman's hat, but we didn't mind—and a carrot from the cellar for the nose, and two little potatoes for the eyes. It was a fine thing, no doubt about it, and we showed your Aunt Lottie, who said

140 it was the best one she ever saw. Then my father came out of the forge—putting things away for the Sabbath, you know, shutting things away—and he saw what we'd been up to and came over and stood in front of it. I can see him now, so tall, with his big brown beard. We were proud of that snowman,

145 and I guess we were waiting for praise. 'Very good, boys,' he said." Here my grandfather's voice turned deep and impressive. "'That's a fine snowman. It's too bad you put him in front of the shed. You can take him down now.'" My grandfather laughed. "Of course, we felt bad, but we felt silly, too. The back

150 of that snowman was almost touching the carriage we drove to church in. We were tired with making it, and I guess we were tired when we came in for supper! I suppose that was the last snowman I ever made."

I loved him to tell his stories. His voice filled the white-

155 washed, cobwebby tie-up. I loved his imitations, and the glimpses of an old time. In this story I thought my great-grand-father sounded cruel; there must have some *other* way to get to church. But I didn't really care. I never really got upset by my grandfather's stories, no matter what happened in them. All

160 the characters were fabulous, and none more so than his strong blacksmith father, who had fought at Vicksburg.

My grandfather was milking now, not heavily dressed against the cold but most of the time wedged between the bodies of two huge holsteins, which must have given off a good bit of heat. The alternate streams of milk went swush-swush from his fists into the pail, first making a tinny sound and then softening and becoming more liquid as the pail filled. When he wasn't speaking, he leaned his head on the rib cage of a cow, the visor of his cap turned around to the back like a baseball catcher's. When he spoke, he tilted his head back and turned toward me. He sat on an old easy chair with the legs cut off, while I had taken down a three-legged stool from a peg on the wall. We talked about the hurricane a bit, and he made jokes about "Harry Cane" and "Si Clone." Whenever the pail was full, he would take it to the milk room and strain it into the big milk can, which the truck would pick up late in the day. We went from cow to cow, from Sally to Spot to Betty to Alice Weaver. And then we were done. While the last milk strained into the big can, I helped my grandfather clean out the tie-up, hoeing the cowflops through the floor onto the manure heap under the barn. Then he fitted tops on the milk cans and craned them onto his wheelbarrow. I unlatched the door and we went into the snow.

The trenches that I had scraped with my galoshes were filled in. The boulder that Washington Woodward had rolled over the roots of the maple wore a thick white cap; it looked like an enormous snowball. The air was a chaff of white motes, the tiny dry flakes. (I remembered last summer in the barn, sneezing with the fine dust while my grandfather pitched hay.) The iron wheel of the wheelbarrow made a narrow cut in the snow and spun a long delicate arc of snow forward. Our four boots made a new trail. Crossing the road to the platform on the other side, we hardly knew where the road began and the ditch ended. We were all alone with no trace of anything else in the world. We came back to the kitchen for breakfast, slapping our hands and stamping our feet, exhilarated with cold and with the first snow of winter.

I smelled the doughnuts when we opened the door from the shed to the kitchen. My father was standing in the kitchen, wearing a light sweater over an open-neck shirt, smoking his before-breakfast cigarette. On the stove, the fat was bubbling, and I could see the circles of dough floating and turning brown. When she saw me, my grandmother tossed a few more doughnuts into the fat, and I watched them greedily as they floated among the bubbles. In a moment, my mother came downstairs, and we all ate doughnuts and drank milk and coffee.

"Is it going to snow all day?" my father asked my grandfather.

"It looks so," said my grandfather.

"I hope the girls can get through," said my grandmother. She always worried about things. My mother's schoolteacher sisters were expected that night.

"They will, Katie," said my grandfather.

"They have chains, I suppose," said my father.

"Oh, yes," said my grandfather, "and they're good drivers."

"Who else is coming?" I asked.

"Uncle Luther," said my grandfather, "and Wash. Wash will have to find his way down Ragged."

That morning after breakfast, my Aunt Caroline arrived, and before noon my Aunt Nan. Each of them talked with me for a while, and then each of them was absorbed by the kitchen and preparations for tomorrow's dinner. I kept looking at the presents under both trees—a pile for the grown-ups under the branches of the big tree, and almost as many under mine. After lunch, Nan drove up to "Sabine," Uncle Luther's small house a quarter mile north, and brought him back. He was my grandmother's older brother, a clergyman who had retired from his city parish and was preaching at the little South Danbury church that we went to in New Hampshire. My grandfather disappeared for a while—nobody would tell me where he was—and a little later my grandmother was plucking feathers from a hen named Old Rusty that had stopped laying eggs. Then my grandfather dressed up in a brown suit, because it was Christmas Eve, and read a novel by Kathleen Norris. My father read magazines or paced up and down with a cigarette. I must have seemed restless, because after a while my father plucked one of my presents from under my tree and told me to open it. It was a Hardy Boys mystery. I sat in the living room with my father and grandfather and read a Christmas book.

By four-thirty, it was a perfectly dark, and the snow kept coming. When I looked out in the sitting-room window, past the light the windows cast into the front yard, I saw darkness with shadows of snow upon it. Inside the cup of light, the snow floated like feathers. It piled high on the little round stones on each side of the path from the driveway. Farther on in the darkness I could see the dark toadstool of the birdbath weighted down under an enormous puff of whiteness. I went to the kitchen window to look at our car, but there was only a car-shaped drift of snow, with indentations for the windows.

It was time for milking again. My grandfather bundled up with extra socks and sweaters and scarves, and long boots over his suit trousers, and my grandmother pinned his coat around his neck with a huge safety pin. She always fretted about his health. She had also been fretting for an hour over Washington Woodward. (Wash had been sort of an older brother to her when she was a little girl; his family had been poor and had farmed him out to the Keneston cousins.) My grandfather stepped out the shed door and sank into the snow. He started to take big steps toward the barn when suddenly he stopped and we heard him shout, "Katie, Donnie, look!" Peering out the shed window, we could just see my grandfather in the reflected light from the kitchen. He was pointing past that light, and while we watched, a figure moved into it, pacing slowly with a shuffling sort of gait. Then the figure said, "Wesley!" and started talking, and we knew it was Wash.

It would have been hard to tell what it was if it hadn't talked. Wash looked as if he was wearing six coats, and the outermost was the pelt of a deer. He shot one every winter and dried its pelt on the side of his hut; I think the pelts served to keep out the wind, for one thing. His face was almost covered with horizontal strips of brown cloth, covered with snow now, leaving just a slit for the eyes. The same sort of strips, arranged vertically, fastened his cap to his head and tied under his chin.

When he shuffled up to the shed door, my grandmother opened it. "Snowshoes," she said. "I knew that's how you'd do it, maybe." She laughed—with relief I suppose, and also at Wash's appearance. Wash was talking—he was always talking— but I didn't notice what he said. I was too busy watching him take off his snowshoeing clothes. First, standing in the doorway but still outside, he stripped three gloves from each hand and tossed them ahead of him into the shed. It was even cold for us to stand watching him in the open door, but Wash had to take off his snowshoes before he could come inside. His thick cold fingers fumbled among leather thongs. Finally, he stood out of them, and stepped inside. As we closed the shed door, I saw my grandfather trudge up the blue hill toward the barn.

A single naked light bulb burned at the roof of the shed. Wash stamped his feet and found his gloves and put them on a table. All the time, his voice went on and on. "About there, McKenzie's old place, my left shoe got loose. I had to stop there by the big rock and fix it. It took me a while, because I didn't have a good place to put my foot. Well, I was standing there pretty quiet, getting my breath, when a red fox came sniffing along. . . ."

Now he began taking off the layers of his clothing. He unknotted the brown bands around his face, and they turned into long socks. "How do you like these, Katie?" he interrupted himself. "You gave them to me last Christmas, and I hain't worn them yet." He went on with his story. When all the socks were peeled off, they revealed his beard. Beards were rare in 1938. I saw a few in New Hampshire, usually on old men. Washington shaved his beard every spring and grew it again in the fall, so I knew two Washington Woodwards—the summer one and the winter one. The beard was brown-gray, and it served him most of the winter instead of a scarf. It was quite full already and wagged as he talked. His eyes crinkled in the space left between the two masses of his beard and his hair. Wash never cut his hair in winter, either—also for the sake of warmth. He thought we should use the hair God gave us before we went to adding other things.

He unwound himself now, taking off the pelt of the deer, which was frozen and stiff, and then a series of coats and jackets. Then there was a pair of overalls, then I saw that he had wrapped burlap bags around his shins and thighs, underneath the legs of the overalls, and tied them in place with bits of string. It took him a long time to undo the knots, but he refused to cut them away with a knife; that would have been a waste. Then he was down to his boots, his underneath overalls, his old much-mended shirt, and a frail brown cardigan over it. He took off his boots, and we walked through the kitchen and into the living room.

Everyone welcomed Wash, and we heard him tell about his four-hour walk down Ragged on snowshoes, about the red fox and the car he saw abandoned. "Come to think of it," my father said, "I haven't heard any traffic going past."

Wash interrupted his own monologue. "Nothing can get
325   through just now. It's a bad storm. I suppose Benjamin's plow
broke down again. Leastways we're all here for the night."

"Snowbound," said Uncle Luther.

"Got the wood in?" Washington asked my grandfather.

Aunt Nan recited:

330   Shut in from all the world without,
        We sat the clean-winged hearth about,
        Content to let the north-wind roar
        In baffled rage at pane and door,
        While the red logs before us beat
335   The frost-line back with tropic heat . . .

She giggled when she was through.

Aunt Caroline said, "I remember when we had to learn that."

"Miss Headley," my mother said. She turned to me. "Do you
have that in school? It's John Greenleaf Whittier, 'Snow-
340   bound.'"

"Are we really snowbound?" I said. I liked the idea of it. I
felt cozy and protected, walled in by the snow. I wanted it to
keep on snowing all winter, so that I wouldn't have to back to
Connecticut and school.

345   "If we have to get out, we'll get out," my father said quickly.

In a moment, my grandfather came in from milking, his
cheeks red from the cold. My grandmother and her daughters
went out to the kitchen, and the men added leaves to the dining-room table. We sat down to eat, and Uncle Luther said
350   grace. On the table, the dishes were piled high with boiled
potatoes and carrots and string beans, boiled beef, and white
bread. Everyone passed plates to and fro and talked all at
once. My two aunts vied over me, teasing and praising.

"How was the hurricane up your way?" I heard my father
355   say to Wash. He had to interrupt Wash to say it, but it was the
only way you could ever ask Wash a question.

As I'm sure my father expected, it got Wash started. "I was
coming back from chasing some bees—I found a hive, all right,
but I needed a ladder—and I saw the sky looking mighty peculiar
360   down South Pasture way, and . . ." He told every motion he made
and named every tree that fell on his land and the land of his
neighbors. When he spoke about it, the hurricane took on a sort
of malevolent personality, like someone cruel without reason.

The rest of the table talked hurricane, too. My grandfather
365   told about a rowboat that somehow moved half a mile from

its pond. My aunts talked about their towns, my father of
how the tidal wave had wrecked his brother's island off the
Connecticut coast. I told about walking home from school
with a model airplane in my hand and how a gust of wind took
370 it out of my hand and whirled it away and I never found it. (I
didn't say that my father bought me another one the next day.)
I had the sudden vision of all of us—the whole family, from
Connecticut to New Hampshire—caught in the same storm.
Suppose a huge wind had picked us up in its fists? . . . We
375 might have met over Massachusetts.

After supper, we moved to the living room. In our family,
the grown-ups had their presents on Christmas Eve and the
children had Christmas morning all to themselves. (In 1938 I
was the only child there was.) I was excited. The fire in the
380 open stove burned hot, the draft ajar at the bottom and the flue
open in the chimney. We heard the wind blowing outside in the
darkness and saw white flakes of snow hurtle against the
black windowpanes. We were warm.

I distributed the presents, reading the names on the tags
385 and trying to keep them flowing evenly. Drifts of wrapping
paper rose beside each chair, and on laps there were new Zane
Grey books, toilet water, brown socks and work shirts, bars of
soap, and bracelets and neckties. Sentences of package opening ("Now *what* could *this* be?") gave way to sentences of
390 appreciation ("I certainly can use some handkerchiefs, Caroline!"). The bright packages were combed from the branches
of the big tree, and the floor was bare underneath. My eyes
kept moving toward a pile under and around the small tree.

"Do you remember the oranges, Katie?" said Uncle Luther.
395 My grandmother nodded. "Didn't they taste good!" she
said. She giggled. "I can't think they taste like that anymore."

My grandfather said, "Christmas and town meeting, that's
when we had them. The man came to town meeting and sold
them there, too." He was talking to me. "They didn't have
400 oranges much in those days," he said. "They were a great treat
for the children at Christmas."

"Oranges and popcorn balls," said my grandmother.

"And clothes," said Uncle Luther. "Mittens and warm clothes."

My grandfather went out into the kitchen, and we heard him
405 open the door. When we came back, he said, "It's snowing and
blowing still. I reckon it's a blizzard, all right. It's starting to drift."

"It won't be like '88," Uncle Luther. "It's too early in the year."

"What month was the blizzard of '88?" said my father.

Uncle Luther, my grandfather, and my grandmother all started to talk at once. Then my grandparents laughed and deferred to Uncle Luther. "March 11 to 14," he said. "I guess Nannie, would have remembered, all right." My great-aunt Nannie, who had died earlier that year, was a sister of Uncle Luther and my grandmother.

"Why?" said my father.

"She was teaching school, a little school back of Grafton, in the hills. She used to tell this story every time it started to snow, and we teased her for saying it so much. It snowed so hard and drifted so deep Nannie wouldn't let her scholars go home. All of them, and Nannie, too, had to spend the night. They ran out of wood for the stove, and she wouldn't let anyone go outside to get some more wood—she was afraid he'd get lost in the snow and the dark—so they broke up three desks, the old-fashioned kind they used to have in those old schoolhouses. She said those boys really loved to break up those desks and see them burn. In the morning, some of the farmers came and got them out."

For a moment, everyone was quiet—I suppose, thinking of Nannie. Then my father—my young father, who is dead now—spoke up: "My father likes to tell about the blizzard of '88, too. They have a club down in Connecticut that meets once a year and swaps stories about it. He was a boy on the farm out in Hamden, and they drove the sleigh all the way into New Haven the next day. The whole country was nothing but snow. They never knew whether they were on a road or not. They went right across Lake Whitney, on top of fences and all. It took them eight hours to go four miles."

"We just used to call it the big snow," said my grandmother. "Papa was down in Danbury for town meeting. Everybody was gone away from home overnight, because it was town meeting everyplace. Then in the morning he came back on a wild engine."

I looked at my grandfather.

"An engine that's loose—that's not pulling anything," he explained.

"It stopped to let him off right down there," my grandmother continued. She pointed through the parlor, toward the front door and across the road and past the chickens and sheep, to the railroad track a hundred yards away. "In back of the sheep barn. Just for him. We were excited about him riding the wild engine."

"My father had been to town meeting, too," said my grandfather. "He tried to walk home along the flats and the meadow, but he had to turn back. When it was done, my brothers and I walked to town on the tops of stone walls. You couldn't see the stones, but you could tell from how the snow lay." Suddenly I could see the three young men, my grandfather in the lead, single-filing through the snow, bundled up and their arms outstretched, balancing like tightrope walkers.

Washington spoke, and made it obvious that he had been listening. He had broken his monologue to hear. "I remember that snow," he said.

I settled down for the interminable story. It was late and I was sleepy. I knew that soon the grown-ups would notice me and pack me off to bed.

"I remember it because it was the worst day of my life," said Wash.

"What?" said my father. He only spoke in surprise. No one expected anything from Wash but harangues of process—how I moved the rock, how I shot the bear, how I snowshoed down Ragged.

"It was my father," said Wash. "He hated me." (Then I remembered, dimly, hearing that Wash's father was a cruel man. The world of cruel fathers was as far from me as the world of stepmothers who fed poisoned apples to stepdaughters.) "He hated me from the day I was born."

"He wasn't a good man, Wash," said my grandmother. She always understated everything, but this time I saw her eyes flick over at me, and I realized she was afraid for me. Then I looked around the room and saw all eyes except Washington's were glancing at me.

"That Christmas, '87," Washington said, "the Kenestons' folks" (he meant my grandmother's family) "gave me skates. I'd never had any before. And they were the good, new, steel kind, not the old iron ones where you had to have an iron plate fixed to your shoe. There were screws on these, and you just clamped them to your shoes. I was fifteen years old."

"I remember," said Uncle Luther. "They were my skates, and then I broke my kneecap and I couldn't skate anymore. I can almost remember the name."

"Peck & Snider," said Wash. "They were Peck & Snider

skates. I skated whenever I didn't have chores. That March tenth I skated for maybe I thought the last time that year, and I hung them on a nail over my bed in the loft when I got home. I was skating late, by the moon, after chores. My legs were good then. In the morning, I slept late—I was tired—and my father took my skates away because I was late for chores. That was the day it started to snow."

"What a terrible thing to do," said my grandfather.

"He took them out to the pond where I skated," said Wash, "and he made me watch. He cut a hole in the ice with his hatchet. It was snowing already. I begged him not to, but he dropped those Peck & Snider skates into the water, right down out of sight into Eagle Pond."

Uncle Luther shook his head. No one said anything. My father looked at the floor.

Washington was staring straight ahead, fifteen years old again and full of hatred. I could see his mouth moving inside the gray-brown beard. "We stayed inside for four days. Couldn't open a door for the snow. I always hated the snow. I had to keep looking at him."

After a minute when no one spoke, Aunt Caroline turned to me and made silly guesses about the presents under my tree. I recognized diversionary tactics. Other voices took up several conversations around the room. Then my mother leapt upon me, saying it was *two hours* past my bedtime, and in five minutes I was warming my feather bed, hearing the grown-up voices dim and far away like wind, like the wind and snow outside my window.

[1987]

Uncommon Words or Meanings

a hurricane ("too busy looking for *hurricane* damage")—a storm with violent winds of more than seventy–five miles an hour; it may be combined with a **cyclone,** a strong wind rotating around a calm central area. The grandfather in this story jokes about "Harry Cane" and "Si Clone."

to corduroy ("logs . . . that would *corduroy* the surface of . . . lakes for years.")—create a surface with parallel ridges, like those in the cotton fabric called corduroy.

chains ("chewed the rest with *chains*")—links of heavy metal put around automobile tires to keep them from spinning on snow or ice.

to pack ("to see if it would *pack*")—to become a firm mass when pressed together.

a hoptoad ("Fred wasn't much bigger than a *hoptoad*")—a small amphibious animal, similar to a frog.

Vicksburg ("fought at *Vicksburg*")—a city in Mississippi, the site of a decisive Northern victory in April 1863 in the American Civil War.

Kathleen Norris ("a novel by *Kathleen Norris*")—a popular American writer of the day, the author of more than eighty romantic novels and many short stories.

the Hardy Boys ("a *Hardy Boys* mystery")—a popular series of adventure books for boys.

a toadstool ("the dark *toadstool* of the birdbath")—a poisonous mushroom.

to farm out ("his family had . . . *farmed* him *out* to the Keneston cousins")—to let (something) be used temporarily in exchange for payment; here, send a child to live with relatives because his own family couldn't afford to feed and clothe him.

a plow ("I suppose Benjamin's *plow* broke down again.")—a snowplow, a machine for moving large quantities of snow to clear a road.

leastways ("*Leastways*, we're all here for the night.")—(informal) anyway, in any case.

John Greenleaf Whittier ("It's *John Greenleaf Whittier*, 'Snowbound'")—a nineteenth-century American poet whose poem "Snowbound," first published in 1866, was a standard of elementary school English classes for close to one hundred years.

grace ("Uncle Luther said *grace*.")—a short prayer of thanks said before eating.

Zane Grey ("new *Zane Grey* books")—the author of many popular Westerns, including *Riders of the Purple Sage.*

a scholar ("Nannie wouldn't let her *scholars* go home")—(through the nineteenth century) a child being taught in a school.

a town meeting ("Christmas and *town meeting*")—In New England, a meeting of the qualified voters of a town to discuss and act on public business.

a stone wall ("walked back to town on the tops of *stone walls*")— a low wall (perhaps three feet high and a foot wide), made by laying stones one on top of another, common in New England.

Text Credits

Art Credit